Part One

Convert to C

Convert
to
C and C++

WITHDRAWN

B.J.Holmes B.Sc,M.Sc,MBCS,Cert.Ed.

Principal Lecturer in the
School of Computing and Mathematical Sciences,
Oxford Polytechnic, Headington, Oxford, OX3 0BP

DP PUBLICATIONS LTD
Aldine Place, 142/144 Uxbridge Road,
Shepherds Bush Green, London W12 8AW

1992

£9.95

Disclaimer

The programs presented in this book have been included for their instructional value. They have been computer-tested with considerable care and are not guaranteed for any particular purpose. The author does not offer any warranties or representations, nor does he accept any liabilities with respect to the programs.

A CIP catalogue record for this book is available from the British Library

First Edition 1992

ISBN 1 873981 20 1

© 1992 B.J.Holmes

Typeset and illustrated by B.J.Holmes

Printed by The Guernsey Press Company Ltd, Braye Road, Vale, Guernsey, Channel Islands.

Contents

Preface

Prerequisite knowledge

This book is written for those already conversant with the fundamentals of programming in a high-level language, wanting to extend their knowledge of programming to include C and C++. The author has assumed that the reader has an understanding of the following programming concepts.

Identifiers, data types, constants, variables, assignment, arithmetic and Boolean operators, control structures for selection and repetition, program structures including procedures, functions and parameters.

Data structures such as sequential text files and array structures.

Compilation, linking and running programs.

The purpose and use of an operating system.

This level of knowledge can be gained by anyone who has taken a beginners course in programming, or has learned to program a computer at home for their own amusement.

This text should also prove valuable for those who only have a knowledge of programming at an assembly level and yet want to convert to C and C++.

Audience

The text is intended to be used by people from very diverse backgrounds and disciplines who have the common aim of learning about C and C++. For example, the book should prove useful to college students who are required to study C and C++ as a second programming language, or to programmers in industry who need to re-train in C and C++.

Format

In converting to C and C++, the emphasis throughout the book is on the use of carefully chosen examples that highlight the features of the language being studied. Explanation about the language follows from, and is put into context with, the example programs.

The development of the language statements and the programs are taken in manageable steps, to enable the reader to build a firm foundation of knowledge. The type of programming examples used are simple enough to give the reader confidence at each stage of learning the language.

A section on programming questions is found at the end of each chapter. These questions serve to test the reader's understanding of the topics, and reinforce the material of the chapter. The reader is advised to complete the answers to the questions before progressing to the next chapter. The answers to all the questions are given in the appendix.

With the concise presentation of the material in this book, it is possible to convert to C and C++ in the shortest possible time.

Studying the languages can be more effective if a computer is used for running the demonstration programs and writing, compiling and running the test programs to the questions. Although the author has used TopSpeed C and C++ compilers from Jensen and Partners International (JPI), running on a PC compatible microcomputer, it should be possible to compile all the C programs using only a C++ compiler.

Advantages

The major strengths and weaknesses of both languages can be compared and contrasted.

Since ANSI C is a subset of C++ the reader is encouraged, through the order of presentation, to learn about C before embarking on C++.

The transition from ANSI C to C++ is taken in three easy stages, covering enhancements to procedural programming, techniques for data abstraction, and object-oriented programming.

The reader who can already program in an older, non ANSI, version of C can use the text as a refresher course in ANSI C, and quickly progress to learning C++.

Those who want a quick guide to C++ can turn to part two, knowing that revision material on ANSI C is also available in part one, should it be needed.

Brief history

The C language was designed and implemented as far back as 1972, by Dennis Ritchie of Bell Laboratories. However, it was as recent as 1990 that the first ANSI standard for the language was completed. C is noted for its translation into efficient machine-code, portability of source-code, power and flexibility of language statements and the use of a standard library.

C++ is essentially a superset of ANSI C. The modification of C to C++, in 1983, is attributed to Bjarne Stroustrup of AT & T Bell Laboratories Computing Science Research Centre. The extensions to the language are threefold. Firstly C++ offers many features that make the language an improvement over C as a procedural language. Secondly C++ incorporates features that allow for the techniques of data abstraction to be used. Thirdly, as a natural progression from the second extension, C++ can be used as a language for object-oriented programming.

Although C++ can be regarded as a superset of the C language, there are still a few incompatibilities between C++ and ANSI C. However, work started in 1990 on the production of an ANSI C++ standard, and any incompatibilities are expected to be resolved when the standard is completed.

The language described in part one conforms to ANSI C, therefore, any certified ANSI C compiler is suitable for use with the demonstration programs and answers. Since there is no standard for C++ at the time of writing, the language described in part two is based on version 2.1, described in *The Annotated C++ Reference Manual* by Margaret Ellis and Bjarne Stroustrup, and implemented using JPI TopSpeed C++.

Lecturers' Supplement

A disc containing all the demonstration programs and answers is available free of charge to lecturers adopting the book as a course text.

BJH - Oxford, July 1992

1.
The Organisation
of a C Program

This chapter explains the organisation of a C program. It introduces the use of the ANSI standard library and the structure of a program using functions. The declaration of data and access to data within functions is also examined.

Contents

1.1 A simple program

The first program in this chapter may appear extremely trivial to the experienced programmer. The reason for introducing the program is not for its functionality but to demonstrate some of the fundamental features of the C language.

```
#include <stdio.h>
/* program to input a character from a keyboard
and display the character on the screen of a monitor */

main()
{
     /* declare data type and variable name of character */
     int symbol;

     /* input character from keyboard */
     symbol = getchar();
     /* display character on screen */
     putchar(symbol);
}
```

The program is written using a text editor and the source file created is stored, by convention, with a filename extension of .c, for example *simple.c*. A thorough examination of each line of this program will provide an initial insight into the organisation of a C program and the meaning of several language statements.

1.2 Preprocessor directives

Prior to the compilation of a C program, a C preprocessor is automatically invoked by the system. During preprocesing, the C program source text is modified according to the preprocessing directives that are embedded in the program. Every line in a C program that begins with the # character will contain a directive to the preprocessor. There are six categories of preprocessor directive of which #include is just one category.

The #include directive makes it possible to include any previously written ASCII format file in the source file. The directive **#include <stdio.h>** causes the contents of <stdio.h> to be included in the program. Notice that header files are always given the suffix .h, by convention.

The header file stdio.h includes sets of *function declarations*, for example:

```
int fgetc(FILE *_st);
int fputc(int _c, FILE *_st);
```

macro definitions, for example:

```
#define getchar() fgetc(stdin)
#define putchar(c) fputc((c), stdout)
```

and *type definitions*, for example:

typedef struct _iobuf { . . . } FILE;

to permit the use of statements in a program that allow for input and output. For example **getchar** and **putchar** appear in the program, and are defined in the **stdio.h** file. Since the C language does not specifically define statements for input and output, the compiler would fail to resolve the identifiers getchar and putchar without the contents of the stdio.h file being included in the source program.

If a source file contains a call to a function declared in a header file, or uses one of the types or macros defined in the header file, then the header must be included at the beginning of the source file.

The header file does not contain any pre-compiled routines, these are stored in the standard library and will be linked into the program after the compilation phase.

1.3 Standard library

The ANSI C standard library is divided into fifteen parts, with each part described by a header. The following list is a summary of the names of the headers and their applicability. Notice that **<stdio.h>** is the header for one part of the library that includes the routines to permit input and output.

<assert.h>	diagnostics
<ctype.h>	character handling
<errno.h>	errors
<float.h>	characteristics of floating types
<limits.h>	sizes of integral types
<locale.h>	localisation
<math.h>	mathematics
<setjmp.h>	non-local jumps
<signal.h>	signal handling
<stdarg.h>	variable arguments
<stddef.h>	common definitions
<stdio.h>	input/output
<stdlib.h>	general utilities
<string.h>	string handling
<time.h>	date and time

The details of the functions, types and macros that are defined by each header file are given in the library reference manual supplied with the C compiler being used.

1.4 Comments

Continuing through the program to the lines:

**/* program to input a character from a keyboard
and display the character on the screen of a monitor */**

All text contained between the opening delimiter character-pair /* and the closing delimiter character-pair */

is treated as a comment. Comments can be listed on the same line as language statements, or be listed on one or more lines. Comments cannot be nested one within another. The compiler ignores comments and replaces each comment by a single space character.

Warning ! If you forget to terminate a comment with the closing delimiter */, the compiler will ignore the lines in the program up to the next occurrence of a closing delimiter.

1.5 Main function

The line following the comment is **main**().

A C program is organised into functions, and main() represents the function where program execution must begin, and as the name suggests is the main or controlling function. The empty parenthesis () after the name main indicates that this is a parameterless function. However, as will be seen later, a main function can contain command line parameters.

The declarations and language statements contained within a function are delimited by the opening brace { and the closing brace }. The purpose of these braces is similar to the reserved words *begin* and *end* in other high-level languages. However, in such languages as Pascal and Modula-2 the compound statements formed between *begin* and *end* only contain language statements, whereas in C, the compound statement formed between { } can contain declarations and statements and is referred to as a block. Notice that the declarations and executable statements within the function are separated by semi-colons. However, there is no semi-colon after the function parameter list, main(), or delimiting braces.

1.6 Variable declaration

The first variable declaration in the program is given as **int symbol**; where **int** represents an *integer* data type and **symbol** is a *variable name*.

The names of variables and functions are known as identifiers, and in common with other high-level languages there are rules for the composition of identifiers. In ANSI C there is no maximum limit to the number of characters in an identifier. Identifiers are composed from letters, digits and underscores, and an identifier must begin with either a letter or an underscore.

C is case-sensitive, therefore the same letter of the alphabet as an upper case character and as a lower case character are regarded as different characters.

The following list of ANSI C keywords cannot be used as identifiers. Keywords must appear exactly as shown with all letters in lower-case.

auto	double	int	struct
break	else	long	switch
case	enum	register	typedef
char	extern	return	union
const	float	short	unsigned
continue	for	signed	void
default	goto	sizeof	volatile
do	if	static	while

The names of functions, types and macros defined in a header are also reserved and should not be used as identifiers.

The comment written above the declaration of the variable symbol, as an integer, will probably cause the reader some initial confusion. The comment reads:

/* declare data type and variable name of character */

yet the declaration of symbol is clearly an integer type and not a character type. For those readers who were brought up on a strictly typed language the bad news is that C treats characters as integers! However, C also contains a type char (character), but more of this later in the text. The integer value of a particular character depends upon the character set in use. ASCII characters are numbered 0 through 127, with character 'A' = 65, 'a' = 97, etc. A table of ASCII characters and their corresponding codes is given in figure 1.1.

1.7 Library functions

The next statement to consider from the program is **symbol = getchar()**; As the comment line indicates the function getchar will enable a character to be input from a keyboard. The character is stored as an integer corresponding to the ASCII code for the character (see figure 1.1).

A library reference manual is normally supplied with a C compiler. Each library function is described in detail in this manual, with at least one page being devoted to each function. A function is normally described under the following headings.

> *The name of the function.*
> *The name of the header file associated with the function.*
> *A see also list of related or alternate functions.*
> *A comment on the portability of the statement, for example ANSI standard, UNIX/DOS/OS2, etc.*
> *Multi-thread (pseudo-concurrent) capabilities of the function.*
> *A summary of the function.*
> *A return value of the function and how to detect errors from it.*
> *An example of how to use the function.*

An extract from the Jensen & Partners TopSpeed C Library Reference manual contains a description for the function getchar. This is given in figure 1.2.

In this extract the name of the function **int getchar(void)** gives the user information about the type of the return value **int** (integer) and the number and types of parameters. The word **void** implies there are no parameters in the getchar function. Since getchar returns a value that is of type integer, the assignment symbol = getchar(); has values of the same integer type on either side of the = (assignment) operator.

Finally the last statement of the program **putchar(symbol)**; will display on a screen the character, whose corresponding ASCII integer code, is stored in the variable symbol. The library entry for putchar is described in the Jensen & Partners Library Reference manual as depicted in figure 1.3.

Notice that the function putchar is described as returning an **int** (integer) value and must use a parameter, **int ch**, of type integer. However, the function has been used in the same manner as a procedure would be used in other block-structured languages. Confused?

code	character	code	character	code	character
000	NUL	043	+	086	V
001	SOH	044	,	087	W
002	STX	045	-	088	X
003	ETX	046	.	089	Y
004	EOT	047	/	090	Z
005	ENQ	048	0	091	[
006	ACK	049	1	092	\
007	BEL	050	2	093	]
008	BS	051	3	094	^
009	HT	052	4	095	_
010	LF	053	5	096	`
011	VT	054	6	097	a
012	FF	055	7	098	b
013	CR	056	8	099	c
014	SO	057	9	100	d
015	SI	058	:	101	e
016	DLE	059	;	102	f
017	DC1	060	<	103	g
018	DC2	061	=	104	h
019	DC3	062	>	105	i
020	DC4	063	?	106	j
021	NAK	064	@	107	k
022	SYN	065	A	108	l
023	ETB	066	B	109	m
024	AN	067	C	110	n
025	EM	068	D	111	o
026	SUB	069	E	112	p
027	ESC	070	F	113	q
028	FS	071	G	114	r
029	GS	072	H	115	s
030	RS	073	I	116	t
031	US	074	J	117	u
032	space	075	K	118	v
033	!	076	L	119	w
034	"	077	M	120	x
035	#	078	N	121	y
036	$	079	O	122	z
037	%	080	P	123	{
038	&	081	Q	124		
039	'	082	R	125	}
040	(	083	S	126	~
041	)	084	T	127	del
042	*	085	U		

Figure 1.1 Table of ASCII codes

---

int getchar (void);   A

Header file	stdio.h
See also	fputc, fputchar, getc, fgetc, fgetchar
Portability	ANSI
Multi-thread	Access to the stream is not controlled by semaphore. Use Lock if another thread may be accessing the specified stream.

The routine get c reads a character from stdin. the routine getchar is equivalent to getc (stdin). See getc.

Note: The routine getchar is equivalent to fgetchar, but is a macro instead of a function.

Return value

The macro returns the character read as an integer value. A return value of EOF may indicate an error or end of file condition. To determine which is the case, use ferror or feof.

Example   ...

Figure 1.2 Description of Library Function getchar

C does not differentiate between procedures and functions.

C uses only functions. Depending upon the function, it can be used either on its own (as a procedure call), or used in an assignment (as a function call).

The value that the putchar function returns is the ASCII code for the character that is being displayed on the screen. The function can, therefore, be used on its own to display a character, or in an assignment statement if the value of the ASCII code is required.

1.8 Functions

A C program normally consists of at least one function, the main function. However, the program given in the first section of this chapter can be re-coded to illustrate the use of more than one function within a program. In the program that follows a function has been introduced to display the character on the screen. This may appear somewhat of an overuse of functions, since it is merely a function within a function. The program illustrates how to define a function within a program and how to call the function so that it can be executed.

9

---

int putchar (int ch);   A

Header file	stdio.h
See also	getc, fputchar, fgetchar, fgetc, putc.
Portability	ANSI
Multi-thread	Access to the stream is not controlled by semaphore in multi-thread program.

The routine putchar puts a character ch on stdout. the routine is equivalent to putc (ch, stdout). See putc.

Note: putchar is identical to fputchar but is a macro, not a function.

Return value
The macro returns the character written as an integer value. A return value of EOF may indicate an error or end of file condition. To determine which is the case, use ferror or feof.

Example ...

Figure 1.3 Description of the Library Function putchar

```
#include <stdio.h>
/* program to demonstrate the use of a function that does not
contain parameters or return a value */

int symbol;

void display(void)
{
     putchar(symbol);
}

main()
{
     symbol = getchar();
     display();
}
```

Observations to make about this program are as follows.

A general form of function definition is:

```
return-type function-name ( formal-parameters )
{
        declarations
        statements
}
```

In this example both the return-type and formal-parameters for the function **display**, do not exist, and are replaced by the keyword **void**.

There are no declarations present in the function and the only statement is a call to the library function putchar.

The function is called from the main function by using the name of the function followed by empty parenthesis display(), indicating there are no arguments to pass to the function.

Warning! Failure to include parenthesis in a function call causes the compiler to ignore the call.

The declaration of the variabie symbol in the first program (section 1.1) was local to the function main. To enable symbol to be accessed by the function display, it has been necessary to declare it externally before the declaration of the two functions. The variable symbol has in effect become a *global* variable. An external variable can be accessed from the point it is declared to the end of the program.

If the declaration of the function display is to made after the function main, then the compiler will need a forward reference to the identifier display. This can be achieved by specifying the first line of the function before the function main.

```
#include <stdio.h>
/* program to demonstrate the use of a forward reference to a function */

int symbol;
void display(void);

main()
{
        symbol = getchar();
        display();
}

void display(void)
{
        putchar(symbol);
}
```

Programs should never be built on global variables alone. The program can be modified so that the variable symbol remains local to the function main, yet can be passed across as an argument to the function display.

In C, all arguments are passed by value. When a function is called, each actual parameter (argument) is evaluated and its value is assigned to the corresponding formal parameter. This means that a local copy of the value passed is used by the function and not the original.

```
#include <stdio.h>
/* program to demonstrate the use of a function that requires
a parameter, but does not return a value */

void display(int character)
{
        putchar(character);
}

main()
{
        int symbol;

        symbol = getchar();
        display(symbol);
}
```

A function may be given a type. The type is the type assigned to a value associated with a **return** statement in the body of the function. If a function is written without a type being assigned, the function is assumed to have a default type of int (integer), unless the type is described as being **void**.

The final program in this section shows how the function display can be modified to return the ASCII value of the symbol. The variable value, assigned to function display is then increased by 1, and the character having this new ASCII code is then displayed.

```
#include <stdio.h>
/* program to demonstrate the use of a function that requires a parameter, and returns a value */

int display(int character)
{
        return putchar(character);
}

main()
{
        int symbol, value;

        symbol = getchar();
        value = display(symbol);
        /* increase the value of the ASCII code obtained by 1 */
        value = value + 1;
        /* display the character having the ASCII code assigned to value */
        display(value);
}
```

In this last example the **return** statement has been used to return a value to the function, and terminate the function.

Notice that the function type has been declared as **int** and not **void** as in previous examples.

1.9 Storage classes

There are four storage classes that can be assigned to variables - **auto, static, extern** and **register**.

Auto variables are declared inside a function after the opening brace and are allocated storage space whenever a function is called. In the last example both symbol and value are, by default, auto variables. When an auto variable is allocated storage space it contains garbage, unless specifically initialised. An auto variable only has a meaningful value for the life of a function. The next time a function is called the values of the auto variables cannot be determined unless they are re-initialised. Auto variables have the same meaning as *local* variables in other languages.

Static variables are allocated storage for the life of the program and not just the life of a function. In the following example the variable *character* has been descibed as being static. Although this value is initialised to 65 (the ASCII code for the character 'A'), in the function AnotherOne, repetitive calls to the procedure causes the previous value of character to be stored, and not re-initialsed to 65. The program will display the characters ABC.

```
#include <stdio.h>
/* program to demonstrate the use of static storage */

AnotherOne(void)
{
        static int character = 65;

        putchar(character);
        character = character + 1;
}

main()
{
        AnotherOne();
        AnotherOne();
        AnotherOne();
}
```

If the variable character was not declared as being static, then upon every call to the function AnotherOne, the value of character would be re-initialied to 65, and the output from the program would be AAA.

In the first program of section 1.8, the variable symbol was defined outside or externally to the functions display and main. In other languages the variable would be regarded as being *global*. Not only can the variable be accessed by both functions, but the variable is also static, by default, since its value is preserved for the life of the program, and not just the life of the functions.

A variable can also be accessed from another source file, by declaring the variable as extern. This implies that the variable has already been allocated storage in another source file, and is not allocated any additional storage. In the example that follows, two source files, *first.c* and *second.c*, contain function *main* and function *ChangeChar* respectively. A variable *character* is declared and initialised in the file *first.c*, and the *character* is declared as being external in the file *second.c*. Both files are separately compiled then linked together to form one executable program. Separate compilation is covered later in the text.

13

Source file *first.c*

```
#include <stdio.h>
int character = 65;

main()
{
        putchar(character);
        ChangeChar();
        putchar(character);
}
```

Source file *second.c*

```
extern int character;        /* extern implies that character has already been allocated storage space
                             in another file */

ChangeChar()
{
        character = character + 1;
}
```

The output from the program is AB.

Warning! When declarations of the same variable appear in different files, the compiler cannot check that the declarations are consistent. It is not usually advisable to make variables global in this way.

When the same variables are frequently used, it might improve execution speed if the variables are stored in the cpu registers, by declaring them as register storage class. A variable declared as register storage class has the same properties as auto storage class.

Function declarations, like variable declarations, may include a storage class. The only options available are extern and static. The extern storage class indicates that a function may be called from other files. The static storage class indicates that a function may be called only within the file in which it is defined. If no class is specified then the function is assumed to be external, as was depicted in the last example where ChangeChar, stored in second.c, was called from the function main, stored in first.c,

1.10 Scope

From the examples given in this chapter it should be clear to the reader that the body of a function is declared between open and closed braces { } known as a compound statement. When the compound statement contains declarations it is known as a **block**.

Variables declared between corresponding braces are by default automatic. Storage is allocated to the variable when the block is entered and deallocated when the block is exited.

A variable can either have **block scope** (the variable is visible from its point of declaration to the end of the closing block) or **file scope** (the variable is visible from its point of declaration to the end of the enclosing file).

A variable declared at the beginning of a function is only accessible by that function.

The scope of an external variable is from the point it is declared to the end of the source file. It can be accessed from other source files by using the extern storage class.

When a declaration inside a block names an identifier that is already visible, the new declaration temporarily hides the old declaration, and the identifier takes on a new meaning. At the end of the block the identifier regains its old meaning.

In the following example the variable symbol has been initialised to the ASCII code for the character Z, and should be visible throughout the function main. However, a new block has been defined within main, with symbol being assigned the ASCII code for the character A. According to the scope rules, the new declaration in the inner block hides the old declaration of symbol, so the letter A will be displayed. At the end of the inner block the old declaration of symbol is assumed and the character Z will be displayed.

```
#include < stdio.h>
/* program to demonstrate scope rules */

int symbol = 90; /* static storage duration with file scope */
main()
{
        {
                int symbol = 65; /* auto storage duration with block scope */
                putchar(symbol); /* output the character A */
        }
        putchar(symbol); /* output the character Z */
}
```

1.11 Summary

Having discussed the format of several C programs it is now possible to conclude this chapter by presenting the organisation of a C program.

A C program consists of one or more source files. Each source file will contain C code and may contain preprocessor directives. Each source file can be compiled separately, and linked together to produce an executable program. Only programs using single source files will be used in the introductory part of the book.

A source file may contain the following components.

- preprocessor directives

- declarations of external (global) variables

- definitions of functions other than main

- definition of the main function

C places no restriction on the order of these elements in a program, however, it is important to remember:

- A preprocessor directive doesn't take effect until the line at which it appears. By putting preprocessor directives at the beginning of a program implies they have effect over the whole program.

- The declaration of a variable must precede all uses of the variable.

- A function should be defined or declared before it is called.

Variables can be defined as being:

- Auto or register if declared within a function.

- Static if declared within a function, and static by default, if declared externally to a function.

- External if the same variable exists over different source files.

A function is external by default, however, it may be explicity declared as being external or static when it may only be called within the file in which it is defined.

1.12 Questions   *answers begin on page 244*

1. Identify and describe the errors in the following program.

```
alpha, beta int;
main
/* program to input a characters from the keyboard
{
        alpha = GetChar()
        beta = getchar
        /* output the characters in reverse order */
        putchar(beta); putchar(alpha)
}
```

2.(a) In the description of the library functions getchar and putchar, given in the chapter, why are they described as macros and not functions?

Hint. You should be able to deduce the answer from the partial listing of the stdio.h header file.

(b) How would you declare function main, as described in this chapter, using C notation?

3. Find the legal variables names, and state why the remaining identifiers are illegal.

alpha	size_of
register	parameter
REGISTER	standard_8
fgetc	lotus 123
character	'hello'

4. Which of the following statements are true or false?

(a) Character 'a' is less than character 'A'.
(b) Character '!' is not a case sensitive character.
(c) #include can be placed anywhere in a C program.
(d) The main function can be placed anywhere in a C program.
(e) The use of braces { } is identical to *begin .. end* in other high-level languages.
(f) The C preprocessor is invoked after compilation and linking has taken place.

5.(a) What is the value of alpha after the function grab has been executed?

```
void grab(int character)
{
        character = getchar();
}

main()
{
        int alpha;

        grab(alpha);
}
```

(b) Discuss the errors in the following program.

```
#include <stdio.h>
int omega

main()
{
        epsilon(delta);
}

int epsilon(omega)
{
        return putchar()
}
```

6. Determine the output from the following program.

```
#include <stdio.h>
int alpha = 122;

main()
{
        int alpha = 97;
        {
                int alpha = 98;
                {
```

```
                    int alpha = 99;
                    putchar(alpha);
            }
          putchar(alpha);
        }
      putchar(alpha);
}
```

7. What are the values of x when the following program is executed?

```
#include <stdio.h>
int x = 68;

display(void)
{
      static  int character = 100;
             int x;

      x = putchar(character);
      character = character + 10;
}

main()
{
      display();
      display();
      display();
}
```

8. Which of the statements are true or false? Give reasons for you answer.

(a) A variable declared as having register storage class can also be treated as an external variable?
(b) An external variable has storage allocated for every declaration of the variable in every source file that it is found?
(c) All variables in a block have an auto storage class?
(d) All variables are assumed to be static unless otherwise specified?
(e) A function may take on any of the four storage classes that are applicable to variables?

2.

Data Types and Input/Output

This chapter introduces the reader to the basic data types in C, and explains how data can be input via a keyboard and information can be output to the screen of a monitor.

Contents

2.1 Integer

Integers can be described as:

short int
int
long int

where each description can be qualified as being unsigned.

The physical storage of an integer is normally over several bytes of computer memory. If an integer normally occupies two bytes of memory, an integer described as being short may occupy one byte of memory, and an integer described as being long may occupy four bytes of memory.

In the representation of an integer, the most significant bit is normally used to denote the sign of the integer. A bit set at zero implies the number is positive. Negative integers are represented in a two's complement form, hence forcing the sign-bit to one to indicate that the number is negative. When an integer is described as being unsigned, the sign bit is used in the representation of the magnitude of the number, thus providing a higher maximum value for the integer. The minimum value for the integer then becomes zero.

All integers, by default, are assumed to be signed.

The range of integer values that can be stored in the memory of a computer is machine dependent. The standard library contains a header file <limits.h> that contains the maximum and minimum values for each integer type for the computer system being used. The Jensen & Partners TopSpeed C compiler is designed for PC compatible computers and the contents of the <limits.h> header file reflects the fact that the smallest addressable memory cell will be 8 bits. A partial listing from the <limits.h> file follows.

```
#define SCHAR_MAX 127
#define SCHAR_MIN (-128)
#define UCHAR_MAX 255

#define SHRT_MAX 32767
#define SHRT_MIN (-32767-1)
#define USHRT_MAX 65535U

#define INT_MAX 32767
#define INT_MIN (-32767-1)
#define UINT_MAX 0xFFFFU

#define LONG_MAX 2147483647L
#define LONG_MIN (-2147483647L-1)
#define ULONG_MAX 4294967295UL
.
.
```

Notice from this listing that in TopSpeed C the range for short int (SHRT_MIN, SHRT_MAX) and the range for int (INT_MIN, INT_MAX) are identical, although in other implementations their ranges could be different.

In the previous chapter it was stated that characters are treated as integers. Although a character can be explicitly defined as type **char**, the value stored is the ASCII code of the character, which is an integer in the range 0 .. 127. ANSI C does not specify whether char is signed or unsigned. However, in TopSpeed C char has been taken to be signed by default.

From the partial listing of the <limits.h> header file the reader should note that signed char has a maximum value (SCHAR_MAX) of 127 and a minimum value (SCHAR_MIN) of -128. An unsigned char (UCHAR_MAX) would have a maximum value of 255. From these values you may assume that a character occupies one byte of storage.

2.2 Floating-point

Real numbers can be described as:

> **float**
> **double**
> **long double**

where float represents a single-precision floating-point number, double represents a double-precision floating-point number and long double represents an extended-precision floating-point number.

The physical representation of a real number takes place over several bytes or words of computer memory. The representation of the number is expressed in two parts, a mantissa and an exponent. The mantissa represents the real number as a decimal fraction, and the exponent signifies the number of places the decimal point was shifted in order to form the fractional mantissa.

The more storage space that is allocated to the mantissa, results in the real number being represented to a greater precision. When more storage space is allocated to the exponent the range of real numbers that can be stored will increase.

The range and precision for numbers described in this manner is given in the header file <float.h> A partial listing of the Jensen & Partners TopSpeed C header file <float.h> follows.

```
#define FLT_DIG 6 /* number of decimal digits of precision */
#define FLT_GUARD 0
#define FLT_MANT_DIG 24 /* number of bits in mantissa */
#define FLT_MAX_10_EXP 38 /* maximum decimal exponent */
#define FLT_MAX_EXP 128 /* maximum binary exponent */
#define FLT_MIN_10_EXP -37 /* minimum decimal exponent */
#define FLT_MIN_EXP -125 /* minimum binary exponent */
#define FLT_NORMALIZE 0
#define FLT_RADIX 2 /* exponent radix */
#define FLT_ROUNDS 1 /* addition rounding chops */
#define FLT_EPSILON 1.192092896e-07 /* smallest such that 1.0+FLT_EPSILON != 1.0 */
#define FLT_MAX 3.402823466e+38 /* maximum value */
#define FLT_MIN 1.175494351e-38 /* minimum positive value */

#define DBL_DIG 15 /* number of decimal digits of precision */
#define DBL_MANT_DIG 53 /* number of bits in mantissa */
```

```
#define DBL_MAX_10_EXP 308 /* maximum decimal exponent */
#define DBL_MAX_EXP 1024 /* maximum binary exponent */
#define DBL_MIN_10_EXP -307 /* minimum decimal exponent */
#define DBL_MIN_EXP -1021 /* minimum binary exponent */
#define DBL_RADIX 2 /* exponent radix */
#define DBL_ROUNDS 1 /* addition rounding */
#define DBL_EPSILON 2.2204460492503131e-016 /* 1.0+DBL_EPSILON != 1.0 */
#define DBL_MAX 1.7976931348623151e+308 /* maximum value */
#define DBL_MIN 2.2250738585072014e-308 /* minimum positive value */

#define LDBL_DIG 19 /* number of decimal digits of precision */
#define LDBL_EPSILON 5.4210108624275221706e-20 /* smallest 1.0+LDBL_EPSILON != 1.0 */
#define LDBL_MANT_DIG 64 /* number of bits in mantissa */
#define LDBL_MAX 1.189731495357231765e+4932L /* maximum value */
#define LDBL_MAX_10_EXP 4932 /* maximum decimal exponent */
#define LDBL_MAX_EXP 16384 /* maximum binary exponent */
#define LDBL_MIN 3.3621031431120935063e-4932L /* minimum positive value */
#define LDBL_MIN_10_EXP (-4931) /* minimum deimal exponent */
#define LDBL_MIN_EXP (-16381) /* minimum binary exponent */
#define LDBL_RADIX 2 /* exponent radix */
#define LDBL_ROUNDS DBL_ROUNDS /* addition rounding */
```

2.3 Type conversion

The arithmetic operators in C can be divided into three categories:

unary operators

> **+ unary plus**
> **- unary minus**

binary multiplicative operators

> *** multiplication**
> **/ division**
> **% remainder**

and *binary additive* operators

> **+ addition**
> **- subtraction**

The normal precedence rules, that are found in other high-level languages, apply to these operators. Unary operators have a higher order of precedence than multiplicative operators and multiplicative operators a higher order of precedence over additive operators.

Expressions are evaluated by taking the operators with a higher priority before those of a lower priority.

Where operators are of the same priority the expression is evaluated from left to right.

Expressions in parenthesis will be evaluated before non-parenthesised expressions. Parenthesis, although not an operator, can be considered as having an order of precedence after unary operators.

The unary operators only require one operand, whereas the binary operators require two operands.

With the exception of the % remainder operator, which must have integer operands, all other operators can have integer or floating point operands or a mixture of both.

In a division if both the operands are integer then the result will have the fractional remainder truncated.

When using either a division operator with two integer operands or a remainder operator, if one operand is a negative integer then the result is implementation dependent. For example, the value of -5 / 2 is -2 in TopSpeed C, however, it could be -3 in other implementations. Similarly, -5 % 2 is -1 and 5 % -2 is +1 in TopSpeed C (the sign of i % j is the same sign as the left operand). In other implementations the sign of i % j, when either i or j are negative, depends upon the implementation.

When operands are of different types, one or more of the operands must be converted before the operation can be performed. The operands are converted to the type that can safely accommodate both values. For example, an operation involving an integer type and a long integer type would cause the integer type to be promoted to the long integer type; an operation involving a float type and a double type would cause the float type to be promoted to a double type. Notice in the second example that float is promoted to double and not long double, since double can be used to store both operands without incurring any extra overhead of memory. Type conversion can be implicit, in which case it is performed automatically when the following cases occur.

- The operands in an expression do not have the appropriate types.

- The type of the expression on the right-hand side of an assignment does not match the type of the variable on the left-hand side. In this case the value on the right-hand side of the assignment is converted to the type of the variable on the left-hand side.

- The type of an actual parameter in a function call does not match the type of the corresponding formal parameter.

- The type of the expression in a return statement does not match the function's return type.

Type conversion may also be explicit through the use of a *cast* operation. A cast expression has the form *(type name) expression* where the *type name* in parenthesis indicates the type to which the expression should be converted. For example,

float alpha, int beta;

/* (float)beta is used to convert beta in the expression to a number of type float, this does not imply that beta has changed its type from int to float, only the value of beta has been converted to type float in the expression */

alpha = (float)beta;

2.4 Constants

Integer constants can be represented in base 10 decimal, base 8 octal or base 16 hexadecimal.

Decimal integer constants contain the digits 0 .. 9 and must NOT begin with 0 (zero), for example 237, 18567, -789.

Octal integer constants contain the digits 0 .. 7 and MUST begin with 0 (zero), for example 017, 05643, 0234.

Hexadecimal integer constants contain the digits 0 .. 9 and the letters a .. f, or A .. F, and MUST begin with 0x, for example: 0x12FF, 0x56ABC, 0x89A345.

Integer constants can be defined as being long, if the letter L or l appears after the number, for example 12345678L.

Integer constants can be defined as being unsigned if the letter U or u appears after the number, for example 43456U.

Since integer constants can be both unsigned and long, both suffixes may appear after the number, for example 67543679UL.

A floating constant can be represented in either decimal notation or in exponential (scientific) notation using the letter E or e to denote the exponent, for example 1234.56, 0.78654E+02.

Floating constants are, by default, stored in double precision. If either single precision or long double precision is required then either the letters f or l or (F or L) should appear after the number, for example 6.784f, 67812.87L, 0.456321E+05L.

Character constants are enclosed between single apostrophes, for example 'A', 'a', '5'.

String constants are enclosed between double quotes, for example "abracadabra", and the compiler marks the end of the string with a null character (ASCII code 0).

Constants can be used in the following statements.

* Expressions, for example: y = 2 * x + 3.5; where 2 and 3.5 are integer and floating constants respectively.

* Assignment of a constant value, for example: **const** char letter = 'a'; where a program can access the value of the constant *letter* but not change it.

* In macro definitions:

    #define pi 3.14159
    #define magic "abracadabra"

In this last example macro definitions have been used to define the floating constant pi and the string constant magic. Any occurrence in a program of the identifier pi and magic will automatically be replaced by the preprocessor before compilation begins, with the value 3.14159 or abracadabra, respectively.

The reader may remember from the last chapter that #define appeared in the <stdio.h> header file. The example given was:

```
#define getchar() fgetc(stdin)
#define putchar(c) fputc((c), stdout)
```

where the preprocessor replaced getchar() by fgetc(stdin) and putchar(c) by fputc((c), stdout). This is why, in the description of getchar() and putchar(c) in the library reference manual, they are described as macros and not functions. If the macro replacement is to take effect globally then the #define directive should be placed near the beginning of a program. The format of the simple macro definition is:

#define   identifier   replacement list

A separate macro definition MUST be used for every constant that is required.

Warning ! When using #define do not terminate the replacement list with a semi- colon, and do not use the assignment = symbol to assign an identifier to a literal.

There are advantages of using **const** compared with #define.

- A set of read-only values of any type may be defined in a program.

- Any attempt to change a const value in a program will be flagged as an error by the compiler.

- Values defined as const are subject to the same scope rules as variables.

Although #define can also be used to specify constants in a program, it is quite a different approach to using const. The #define preprocessor directive offers the following advantages over const.

- #define is not subject to the same scope rules as variables, and

- it allows constants to be used in any constant expression.

2.5 Pointers

The variables that have been introduced so far in the text have been associated with integer, float or char types. It is understood that a declaration of the form:

int largest = INT_MAX;

implies that the identifier largest contains, or stores, the value of INT_MAX which happens to be 32767 on a 16-bit computer. Pictorially largest might be seen as a box containing the value 32767, as shown in figure 2.1.

This box represents an area of computer memory used for storing the integer largest. The address of this area of memory is denoted by &largest, where & is the *address operator*.

Address
= &largest

largest
= 32767

**Figure 2.1 An illustration of an area of memory used to store
an integer, largest, where the address of this location is &largest.**

A pointer is an identifier that does not store data of type integer, float or char, but stores an address of where to find the data in memory. The address literally points to where the data is stored. The declaration:

int *IntPointer;

implies that the variable IntPointer contains an address of a variable of type integer. The asterisk * in front of IntPointer instructs the compiler that IntPointer is a pointer and not a variable of type integer.

Although the value of a pointer variable may change during the execution of a program, the variable must always point to data of the same type. In this example data of type integer.

The statement IntPointer = &largest; assigns the address of largest to IntPointer, causing IntPointer to point at the variable largest, as depicted in figure 2.2.

An *indirection operator* * allows the programmer to identify the value of the integer that is being pointed at by IntPointer, therefore, the result of this assignment implies that *IntPointer = largest.

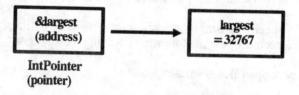

&dargest
(address)

largest
= 32767

IntPointer
(pointer)

IntPointer = &largest /* an address in computer memory */

IntPointer = largest / value contained in memory at the address &largest */

**Figure 2.2 Relationship between the Address Operator & and the indirection operator *,
the figure shows two boxes, both are locations in computer memory, the first box contains
the address of the second box &largest, the second box contains a value largest.**

In the previous chapter it was stated that all arguments in an actual parameter list are passed by value (by content), implying that a local copy of the value passed, is used by the function and not the original.

In other high-level languages an argument can be passed by variable (by reference), implying that the value of the argument can be changed by the procedure and its new value accessed outside of the procedure. This is possible in C if the formal parameters in a function are declared as pointers, and the actual parameters (arguments) used in the function call are treated as addresses of the variable and not the variable itself.

For example, a function used to separate the whole part of a real number from its decimal fraction may be coded as:

```
void split(float LocalNumb, int *WholeNumber, float *FractionalPart)
{
        *WholeNumber = LocalNumb;
        *FractionalPart = LocalNumb - (int) LocalNumb;
}
```

and called by **split(number, &whole, &fraction);** where *number, whole* and *fraction* are declared in the main function as **float number; int whole; float fraction;**

Figure 2.3 illustrates that number is passed to the function split as a local copy, and that any changes to LocalNumb in the function split do not alter number in the main function. The addresses &whole and &fraction are passed to the pointers WholeNumber and FractionalPart. Any reference to *WholeNumber and *FractionalPart in the function split must change the contents of whole and fraction in the main function.

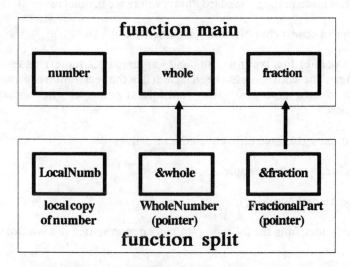

Figure 2.3 Passing parameters by content and by reference

In the previous section the concept of a character string was introduced. A string is stored as successive characters in the computer's memory, with the last character of the string being the string terminator (a null character). The beginning of the string is represented as a pointer to the first character of the string. For example:

```
char *magic;
magic = "abracadabra";
```

then magic is assigned as a pointer to the first character of "abracadabra", as depicted in figure 2.4.

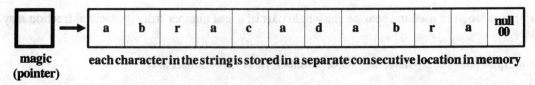

**magic
(pointer)**   each character in the string is stored in a separate consecutive location in memory

**Figure 2.4. An illustration of the storage of a string in C. The variable name of the string is a pointer
to the first character of the string. The end of the string is terminated by a null character (00).**

There will be further coverage of pointers later in the book. For now the reader has been given enough
information to gain a better understanding of the format of the two functions, printf and scanf.

2.6 Printf

The function printf is found in the standard library header file <stdio.h>. The purpose of this function is to
display in a formatted form, numbers and characters on a standard output device, which is normally the
screen of a monitor.

The declaration of printf is given in the C standard library reference manual as:

> **int printf(const char *format [,argument] ...);**

where char *format is a pointer to a control string and [,argument] ... represents zero or more arguments
each separated by a comma. The word const has been included in the declaration of format to indicate that the
function printf does not change the control string that format points to. The function printf returns the
number of characters printed.

A control string may contain up to three different character sequences.

(i) A string of ordinary characters, for example:

> **printf("input a real number ");**

(ii) Escape sequence characters, from the following set, can be represented in a control string:

\a	alert (bell)
\b	backspace
\f	form feed
\n	new line
\r	carriage return
\t	horizontal tab
\v	vertical tab
\\	backslash
\?	question mark
\'	single quote
\"	double quote
\ddd	where ddd is an octal number in the range 0 .. 377 and represents the ASCII code for the character
\xdd	where dd is a hexadecimal number in the range 0 .. FF and represents the ASCII code for the character

(note the value of ddd and dd in the last two escape sequences will depend upon the character set being used)

For example printf("WARNING\a"); would display the string *WARNING* and give an audible warning (bell), and printf("input dimensions of room\n\n"); would display the string *input dimensions of room* followed by two new line characters.

(iii) Format specifications corresponding to the list of arguments passed to printf after the control string. This will take the form *%width [.precision] type* where type is one of the following:

d, i	decimal integer
o	unsigned octal
x, X	unsigned hexadecimal
u	unsigned decimal integer
c	single character
s	string
f	floating-point number
e, E	floating-point number in exponential format
g, G	floating-point number in either fixed decimal or exponential format, whichever is more compact

The types d,o,x, X or u may be preceded by the letter l to indicate they are long integers.

The types e, E, f, g or G may be preceded by the letter L to indicate they are long double.

Width is a number that represents the minimum size of the field for displaying a number. The number is right-justified unless a negative width is used, in which case the number is displayed left justified. If the value to be printed is larger than the width specified, then the width is automatically expanded to accommodate the number. Regardless of the value of the width the displayed number will never be truncated. Thus no field width may be specified and a number will still be displayed.

The precision after the decimal point indicates the number of decimal places to display a number of type float, double or long double.

The following program illustrates some of the different ways in which printf can be used to display numbers and strings.

```
#include <stdio.h>

const   int                 A = 32;
const   unsigned long int   B = 123456789UL;
const   long int            C = 0x56A7C;
        unsigned int        D = 0347;
        float               E = 67.123;
        double              F = 0.987654321E+20L;
        char                letter = 'Z';
const   char                *string = "Popocatapetl";
```

```
main()
{
        printf("value of    A\t %-10d\n", A);
        printf("            B\t %-15lu\n", B);
        printf("            C\t %10X\n", C);
        printf("            D\t %o\n", D);
        printf("            E\t %10.4f\n", E);
        printf("            F\t %20.12G\n\n", F);
        printf("            letter\t %c\n", letter);
        printf("            string\t %s\n", string);
}
```

The results from running this program are as follows. The letter b indicates blank spaces in the output of numerical values.

```
value of    A       32
            B       123456789
            C         bbbbbb6A7C
            D       347
            E       bbb67.1230
            F       bbbbbb9.87654321E+19

            letter  Z
            string  Popocatapetl
```

2.7 Scanf

The function scanf is found in the standard library header file <stdio.h>. The purpose of the function is to read characters from a standard input device, normally a keyboard, and store the converted data in the locations given by the arguments.

The format of the scanf function described in the standard library reference manual is:

$$\text{int scanf(const char *format, [arguments] ...);}$$

where const char *format represents a control string, and arguments represent one or more *addresses* for storing the data that is read.

A simplified version of the control string has the following structure *%[width] type* where width is the maximum number of characters to be scanned for the current argument. When this value is omitted scanf will read the characters being input, up to the first space, horizontal or vertical tab, form-feed or new-line character.

Type refers to the following:

    d   signed decimal integer
    i   signed integer where the base is determined by the format of the number input:
                prefix 0 expects octal integer;

30

prefix 0x expects hexadecimal integer;
otherwise decimal integer

u unsigned decimal integer
o unsigned octal integer
x unsigned hexadecimal integer using the digits 0 to 9 and either abcdef or ABCDEF
e, f, g signed floating point value
l is used to prefix the types d, o, u and x as long int;
L is used to prefix the types e, f and g as long double.

Examples of the use of scanf are given in the following program.

```
#include <stdio.h>

        int        alpha;
        float      beta;
        double     gamma;
        int        delta;
long    int        epsilon;

main()
{
        printf("input integer value for alpha ");
        scanf("%d", &alpha);
        printf("input float value (10 digits) for beta ");
        scanf("%10f", &beta);
        printf("input double value (15 digits) for gamma ");
        scanf("%le", &gamma);
        printf("input octal unsigned integer ");
        scanf("%o", &delta);
        printf("input hexadecimal unsigned integer ");
        scanf("%lx", &epsilon);

        printf("\n\n");
        printf("alpha = %-5d\n", alpha);
        printf("beta = %10.4f\n", beta);
        printf("gamma = %15.4e\n", gamma);
        printf("delta = %-10o\n", delta);
        printf("epsilon = %lX\n", epsilon);
}
```

The output from this program follows, the letter b has been used to indicate a space.

input integer value for alpha 31678
input float value (10 digits) for beta 1.23456789
input double value (15 digits) for gamma 9.876543210E-15
input octal unsigned integer 0347
input hexadecimal unsigned integer 0xAC3F

alpha = 31678

```
        beta = bbbb1.2346
        gamma = bbbbb9.8765e-15
        delta = 347
        epsilon = AC3F
```

These examples illustrate scanf with one argument, however, the control string can contain any number of formats for any number of arguments. Consider the following example:

#include <stdio.h>

```
unsigned     int          octal;
unsigned     long int     hex;
             float        number;
main()
{
        scanf("%o%lx%f", &octal, &hex, &number);
        printf("\n\toctal %o\n", octal);
        printf("\thex %lX\n", hex);
        printf("\tnumber %f\n", number);
}
```

When this program is run the following information appears on the screen of the terminal. The letter b indicates a blank space.

```
        0567b0x5BDF
        1.23456

        octalb567
        hexbbbbb5BDF
        numberbb1.234560
```

Notice from the output that the input data does not appear on one line. The scanf function regards white-space characters (space, horizontal and vertical tabs, form-feed and new-line characters) as field delimiters. Therefore, since a space separates the octal number from the hexadecimal number, the field for the octal number will contain 0567 and the field for the hexadecimal number will contain 0x5BDF. A new-line character separates the hexadecimal number from the floating-point number, therefore, the field for the floating-point number will contain 1.23456.

The function scanf returns the number of fields converted and assigned.

Finally the reader may question why the input of single characters or strings has not been catered for in this section. The use of scanf to input strings will be covered later in the book, the input and output of characters has already been covered in the functions getchar and putchar.

2.8 Example programs

This first program illustrates the use of the printf function to display the ranges for the data types introduced in this chapter. Since all the ranges are given in the header files <limits.h> and <float.h> it is possible to include these files at the beginning of the program and print the constants defined in them.

```c
/* program to illustrate the ranges for the data types: char, int, long int, float, double */
#include <stdio.h>
#include <limits.h>
#include <float.h>
main()
{
        char          char_min, char_max, char_unsigned_max;
        int           int_min, int_max, int_unsigned_max;
        long int      long_int_min, long_int_max, long_int_unsigned;
        float         float_small, float_max;
        double        double_small, double_max;

        /* range of characters */
        char_min = SCHAR_MIN;
        char_max = SCHAR_MAX;
        char_unsigned_max = UCHAR_MAX;
        printf("char min: %d\n",char_min);
        printf("char max: %d\n",char_max);
        printf("char unsigned max: %u\n\n", char_unsigned_max);

        /* range of integers */
        int_min = INT_MIN;
        int_max = INT_MAX;
        int_unsigned_max = UINT_MAX;
        printf("int min: %d\n",int_min);
        printf("int max: %d\n",int_max);
        printf("int unsigned max: %u\n",int_unsigned_max);

        /* range of long integers */
        long_int_min = LONG_MIN;
        long_int_max = LONG_MAX;
        long_int_unsigned = ULONG_MAX;
        printf("long int min: %ld\n",long_int_min);
        printf("long int max: %ld\n",long_int_max);
        printf("long int unsigned max: %lu\n\n",long_int_unsigned);

        /* range of float */
        float_small = FLT_MIN;
        float_max = FLT_MAX;
        printf("float smallest: %15.9e\n",float_small);
        printf("float max: %15.9e\n\n",float_max);

        /* range of double */
        double_small = DBL_MIN;
        double_max = DBL_MAX;
        printf("double smallest: %25.16e\n",double_small);
        printf("double max: %25.16e\n\n",double_max);
}
```

The second program illustrates two ways of defining constants in a program. The first is to qualify a type by using const and the second is to use #define. The program displays the Morse code for SOS. Both dot and dash have been defined as constants using const, whereas the format string in the printf statement has been defined as a constant using #define.

```
/* program to display the Morse code for SOS */
#include <stdio.h>
#define PrintFormat "%c%c%c%c%c%c%c%c%c\n"
main()
{
        const char    dot = '.';
        const char    dash = '-';

        printf("Morse code for SOS is ");
        printf(PrintFormat, dot,dot,dot,dash,dash,dash,dot,dot,dot);
}
```

The purpose of the third program is to calculate the number of tins of emulsion required, to paint the interior walls of a rectangular room. The window area and door area are already known, and must be subtracted from the total wall area. The amount of wall surface area that one tin of emulsion covers is also known. The number of tins of paint required is clearly the surface area of the walls divided by the surface area one tin of paint covers. If this figure is computed to be a fraction, then the figure must be rounded up to the next whole tin of paint. For this reason a correction factor of 0.99 has been introduced into the calculation *tins = (WallArea / EmulsionCover) + CorrectionFactor* where tins is an integer value.

```
/* program to calculate the number of tins of paint required to emulsion the walls of a room */
#include <stdio.h>
#define EmulsionCover 25.0
#define WindowArea 3.0
#define DoorArea 1.5
#define CorrectionFactor 0.99
main()
{
        float    length, width, height;
        float    WallArea;
        int      tins;

        printf("input dimensions of room\n\n");
        printf("length ");
        scanf("%f", &length);
        printf("width ");
        scanf("%f", &width);
        printf("height ");
        scanf("%f", &height);
        WallArea = 2 * height * (length + width) - (WindowArea + DoorArea);
        tins = (WallArea / EmulsionCover) + CorrectionFactor;
        printf("area of walls %8.2f\n\n", WallArea);
        printf("number of tins of emulsion %d\n", tins);
}
```

The fourth program in this section is designed to illustrate the use of a function. The number of 0.5m lengths that can be cut from one length of picture moulding needs to be calculated. From the moulding that remains after the cutting has taken place, the number of 0.2m lengths that can be cut is calculated. Finally the number of 0.5m, 0.2m and the amount of waste moulding is displayed.

```
/*program to input a length of picture moulding and report on the maximum number of 0.5 sections, 0.2m
sections and waste */
#include <stdio.h>

float waste(float length, float size)
/* function to calculate the amount of waste moulding having cut a number of pieces of a set size */
{
        int pieces;

        pieces = length / size;
        printf("number of lengths of size %4.2f", size);
        printf(" is %d\n", pieces);
        return length - pieces * size;
}

main()
{
        float   moulding, remainder;

        printf("input the length of the moulding ");
        scanf("%f", &moulding);
        remainder = waste(moulding, 0.5);
        remainder = waste(remainder, 0.2);
        printf("length of moulding wasted %5.3f\n", remainder);

}
```

The final program in this section serves the purpose of introducing a function where the parameters return values to the rest of the program.

```
/* program to input a real number and split the number into a whole number and fractional part */
#include <stdio.h>

void split(float LocalNumb, int *WholeNumber, float *FractionalPart)
/*      this function uses a pointer to the whole number and a pointer to the fraction, and NOT the local
        values of whole and fraction */
{
        *WholeNumber = LocalNumb;
        *FractionalPart = LocalNumb - (int) LocalNumb;
}

main()
{
        float number; int whole; float fraction;
```

35

```
        printf("input a real number ");
        scanf("%f", &number);
        split(number, &whole, &fraction);
        printf("whole part of number is %d\n", whole);
        printf("fractional part of number is %f\n", fraction);
}
```

2.9 Summary

● The basic data types in the C language are char (character), int (integer), float (floating-point real), double (double precision floating-point real) and long double (extended-precision floating-point real).

● Characters and integers may be qualified as being unsigned, signed (by default), short or long in storage space.

● Arithmetic operators are (highest to lowest precedence) unary + or -, * multiplication, / division, %remainder, and + addition and - subtraction.

● The operators in an expression can be of mixed type.

● Type conversion occurs automatically when:

> operands in an expression have mixed types;
> type on right-hand side does not match type on left-hand side;
> actual and formal parameters do not have same type;
> function type does not match return type.

● Type conversion can be explicit through the use of a cast operation.

● Constants can be integer (decimal, octal or hexadecimal), character or string.

● Constants can appear as literals in expressions, qualified by the use of const or defined by a preprocessor macro definition.

● A pointer is an address type having an address operator & and an indirection operator *.

● The * operator is used to declare a pointer and also gain access to the value being pointed at. The & operator provides the address of the value being pointed at.

● Parameters in a function may be passed by reference, if the actual parameters are addresses and the formal parameters are pointers.

● Information can be displayed on a standard output device using the printf function.

● Data can be read from a standard input device by using the scanf function.

2.10 Questions *answers begin on page 246*

1. Using the header files <limits.h> and <float.h> answer the following questions.

(a) What is the maximum value of an unsigned long integer?
(b) What is the maximum value of an unsigned character?
(c) In a floating-point number what is the maximum decimal exponent, and the smallest difference that can be stored?
(d) What is the largest double number that can be stored?
(e) How many decimal digits of precision are there in a long double number?

2. What is the resultant type when the following expressions are evaluated? Notice that only the type of each operand is given.

(a) float * int   (b) int / int   (c) int * double

(d) What is the resultant type of the parameter in the segment of code?
```
void function(float) { }

function(int);
```

(e) What is the resultant return type in the segment of code?
```
double function(int)
{
        return int
}
```

3. Discuss the errors in the following program segments.

(a)
```
#include <stdio.h>;
#define pi = 3.14159;
const vat = 0.175;
```

(b) printf("length of room %c\n, length);

(c)
```
{       int *alpha;
        scanf("%f", alpha);
}
```

(d)
```
{       char *string;
        scanf("%s", &string);
}
```

4. A person buys three newspapers, the Courier, Globe and Mercury. Write a program to input the cost in pence of each newspaper, calculate the total cost and average cost, and display the results of these two computations.

5. Write a program to input the length, width and depths at the deepest and shallowest ends of a rectangular swimming pool. Calculate and display the volume of water required to fill the pool.

6. Write a program to input a decimal number and display the equivalent number in octal and hexadecimal.

7. Write a function to calculate the diameter, circumference and area of a circle, when supplied with the radius. Use this function in a program to input a radius and display the various measurements of the circle.

8. Write a program to input an amount of money as a whole number, and display the minimum number of fifty, twenty, ten and five pound notes, and one pound coins, that make up this amount.

3.
Control Statements

Within this chapter the statements that permit selection and repetition will be introduced. The reader should already be familiar with if .. else .. , while and for statements, since these are found in the majority of high-level languages. In addition to these statements C offers a switch statement that is similar to case, and a do .. while statement that is similar to repeat .. until. The chapter concludes with a miscellany of C statements that should be new to most readers.

Contents

3.1 Conditions

Program language statements for either selection or repetition have one thing in common. Each statement normally contains a condition. This is either a condition on which a selected path in a program will be taken, or a condition for continuing to repeat statements within a loop structure. Conditions in many high-level languages equate to either false or true. However, in C false and true are NOT keywords, and conditions equate to 0 (zero) for false and a non-zero value, usually 1, for true.

The set of relational operators and equality operators for comparing integers and floating-point numbers follow.

relational operators
    <   less than
    >   greater than
    <=   less than or equal to
    >=   greater than or equal to

equality operators
    ==   equal to
    !=   not equal to

The precedence of the relational operators is less than for arithmetic operators. For example a+b > c+d implies (a+b) > (c+d). However, the precedence of the equality operators is lower than the relational operators. For example a > b == c > d is equivalent to (a > b) == (c > d).

Both the relational and equality operators are left associative. This implies that the operators are grouped from left to right. For example the expression a > b > c implies (a > b) > c, which means that if (a > b) is false (0) or true (1, say) then this result is compared with c. Thus 0 > c or 1 > c is either false (0) or true (1, say).

The reader might like to determine the values of the following conditions.

A == 6	where A is 6
B > 15	where B is 13
X < Y	where X is 15 and Y is 8
H >= I+J	where H is 5, I is 3 and J is 2
A+B > C+D	where A is 6, B is 13, C is 5 and D is 4
i < j < k	where i is 2, j is 3 and k is 4
i < j == j < k	where i is 5, j is 3 and k is 2

The answers to these questions are 1, 0, 0, 1, 1, 1, 1 assuming that 0 represents false and 1 represents true.

Conditions can be combined using the logical operators:

    &&   logical and
    || logical or

Both these operators are binary since they require two operands. The precedence of these operators is lower than the relational and equality operators. For example a > b && c < d implies (a > b) && (c < d). These operators are also left associative. A further logical operator is ! logical not, which is a unary operator since it only requires one operand. Logical not has the same precedence as unary + and -, and is right associative.

The truth tables for logical and, logical or and logical not follow.

a	b	a && b	a || b	!a
0	0	0	0	1
0	1	0	1	
1	0	0	1	0
1	1	1	1	

The reader might like to determine the values of the following conditions.

(A > 3 && B < 5)	where A is 4 and B is 5
(A == 4 || B <= 6)	where A is 4 and B is 7
(X == Y && Y >= Z)	where X is 3, Y is 4 and Z is 5
(X != Y || A >= B)	where X is 3, Y is 3, A is 5 and B is 5

The answers to these questions are 0, 1, 0, 1

In the third condition it might appear obvious that when X is compared to Y (X == Y) and the answer is 0, there is little point in continuing the evaluation when the operator is && since any value logically anded with 0 must be 0. This is known as short-circuit evaluation. Both && and \|\| perform short-circuit evaluation of their operands. That is, these operators evaluate first the left operand, and if the value of the operand can be deduced from the value of the left operand alone then there is no need to evaluate the right operand, otherwise the right operand is also evaluated.

3.2 Enumeration

In order to clarify the coding in a computer program it sometimes helps if integer values such as 0 and 1, are replaced by meaningful names. For example in the evaluation of a condition, the constants false and true convey a greater meaning than 0 and 1. An enumeration is a collection of integer values that have been given names by the programmer. For example

$$\text{enum \{false, true\} SalesExecutive;}$$

defines a variable SalesExecutive that can be assigned the values false or true. All enumerated constants start with the integer value 0, unless otherwise specified by the programmer, and successive constants have successive integer values. In this example false = 0 and true = 1.

An alternative approach is to define a data type as having a range of enumerated constants. For example

$$\text{typedef enum \{false, true\} boolean;}$$

describes a data type boolean having values false and true corresponding, by default, to the values 0 and 1. Variables can then be designated the data type boolean, for example:

$$\text{boolean SalesExecutive;}$$

and initialised to SalesExecutive = false.

The programmer can change the default values of the enumerated objects by assigning new integer values at the time of the enumeration declaration. For example:

typedef enum {storm = 1, rain = 2, change = 3, fair = 4, dry = 5} BarometerReading;

If a variable, say MenuCode, is of type BarometerReading then MenuCode can have values of 1, 2, 3, 4 or 5 that correspond to the enumerated constants in the enumeration. When no value is specified for an enumeration constant, its value is one greater than the value of the previous constant. Therefore, the previous enumeration could be written as:

typedef enum {storm = 1, rain, change, fair, dry} BarometerReading;

and retain the same meaning.

3.3 If .. else

In common with most high-level languages, C has an if .. else statement to allow a choice of program path to be taken depending upon the outcome of a particular condition. The format of the if .. else statement is:

if (expression) statement else statement

where else statement can be omitted and the expression contained within parenthesis MUST equate to either 0 or a positive non-zero value. Normally the expression is a condition that equates to 0 (false) or 1 (true). If the expression equates to 0 (false) then either the statement following else is executed or if else is omitted the next statement after the if statement is executed. Consider the following examples:

```
if (reply == yes) SalesExecutive = true;
printf("input mileage ");
        .
        .
```

In this segment of code if the expression (reply == yes) equates to 1 (true) the assignment SalesExecutive = true will be executed and the next statement after the if statement, printf("input mileage "); will then be executed. However, if the expression (reply == yes) equates to 0 (false) the computer will branch to the next statement after the if statement, printf("input mileage").

```
if (SalesExecutive && EngineSize > 1500)
        expenses = mileage * HigherRate;
else
        expenses = mileage * NormalRate;
printf("weekly travelling expenses due %6.2f\n", expenses);
        .
        .
```

In this segment of code if the expression (SalesExecutive && EngineSize > 1500) equates to non-zero (true) the statement expenses = mileage * HigherRate will be executed, otherwise if the value of the expression equates to zero (false) the statement expenses = mileage * NormalRate will be executed. In either case after the execution of the relevant statement the computer will branch to the printf statement that follows the if .. else statement.

Warning! In converting from say Pascal or Modula-2 to C a common mistake is in the use of parenthesis around the expression of an if .. else statement. Notice in the last example that the complete expression is parenthesised and NOT the individual conditions. Individual conditions can also be parenthesised.

In the last example only one statement was executed whether the expression evaluated to zero or non-zero. What if more than one statement is to be executed? The answer is to treat the group of statements as a compound statement by introducing braces { }, for example:

```
if (alpha = = beta && gamma = = delta)
{
        A = B;
        C = D;
}
else
{
        A = D;
        C = B;
}
```

If .. else statements can be nested to any depth, however, you should pay particular attention to the use of indentation and the grouping of else statements. In the following example, to which if statement does the single else statement belong?

```
if (alpha = = 3)
    if (beta = = 4)
            printf("alpha 3 beta 4\n");
else
        printf("alpha beta not valid");
```

The indentation suggests that the else belongs to if (alpha = = 3), however, as you might expect this is wrong. The rule in C regarding which else belongs to which if is simple. An else clause belongs to the nearest if statement that has not already been paired with an else. This example can be rewritten taking into account the correct indentation.

```
if (alpha = = 3)
        if (beta = = 4)
                printf("alpha 3 beta 4\n");
        else
                printf("alpha beta not valid");
```

If the else clause did belong to if (alpha = = 3) then braces would be introduced into the coding thus:

```
if (alpha = = 3)
{
        if (beta = = 4)
                printf("alpha 3 beta 4\n");
}
else
        printf("alpha beta not valid");
```

3.4 Switch

In the following example an integer variable MenuCode can take on the legal values 1, 2, 3 or 4. Each value corresponds to a choice of whether to add, subtract, multiply or divide two integers alpha and beta. In the segment of code several if .. else statements have been used to represent the selection based upon the value of the variable MenuCode.

```
if      (MenuCode == 1)
        answer = alpha + beta;
else if (MenuCode == 2)
        answer = alpha - beta;
else if (MenuCode == 3)
        answer = alpha * beta;
else if (MenuCode == 4)
        if (beta != 0)
                answer = alpha / beta;
        else
                printf("Warning! attempt to divide by zero\n");
else
        printf("Warning! incorrect menu code\n");
```

This coding can be simplified by the use of a switch statement as follows.

```
switch (MenuCode)
{
        case 1 : answer = alpha + beta; break;
        case 2 : answer = alpha - beta; break;
        case 3 : answer = alpha * beta; break;
        case 4 : if (beta != 0)
                        answer = alpha / beta;
                else
                        printf("Warning! attempt to divide by zero\n");
                break;
        default: printf("Warning! incorrect menu code\n");
}
```

Upon inspection of this code the reader may recognise the format to be similar to case statements found in other high-level languages, however, the syntax of the statement is clumsy compared with its counterparts in other languages.

The following points should be observed when using the switch statement.

The keyword switch must be followed by an expression, enclosed within parenthesis, that evaluates to an integer. Characters and enumerated constants are stored as integer values, and may be used in a switch statement.

Each case label must contain only one integer or character expression that is a constant. If several labels refer to the same statement, then each label must be preceded by the word case. For example:

```
switch (mm)
{
        case Apr: case Jun: case Sep: case Nov: days = 30; break;
        .
        .
}
```

The last statement, of each group of statements, must be break. A break statement used in a switch statement causes the computer to branch out of the enclosing switch statement. The reason for using break is to prevent the computer from executing the next set of statements or all the statements to the end of the switch statement.

In the example a default label has been used to trap an illegal value for the MenuCode. If the default label is omitted and none of the case labels match MenuCode the computer would execute the next statement after the end of the switch statement.

Notice that the body of a switch statement is treated as a compound statement.

3.5 While and do .. while

In common with other high-level languages C contains a while loop in which the body of the loop can be executed zero or more times.

The format of the while loop is:

while (expression) statement

where expression must evaluate to either zero or non-zero, and statement represents the body of the loop. The body of the loop can be a single statement or a compound statement. Since the property of a while loop allows for zero or more iterations, the test to exit from the loop must take place before the body of the loop has been entered. Only when the expression equates to zero (false) will the loop be exited. The computer then branches to the next executable statement after the end of the body of the loop.

A while loop contains three parts.

        (i) initialisation of the control variable;
        (ii) evaluation of an expression containing the control variable;
        (iii) changing the value of the control variable.

For example,

```
counter = 1; /* initialisation of counter */
while (counter < 4) /* evaluate expression containing counter */
{
        printf("%4d", counter);
        counter = counter +1; /* increase counter by 1 */
}
printf("\n");
.
.
```

This segment of code would display the values 1 2 3, corresponding to the values of counter. When counter was increased to 4 the expression (counter < 4) would equate to zero (false) and the computer would branch to the next statement printf("\n"); after the end of the body of the loop.

At this point in the chapter it is worth digressing to the topic of incrementing and decrementing values, in particular in the context of control variables found in loops.

An lvalue (pronounced el-value) and representing l(eft)value refers to an area of storage in computer memory. In practice lvalues are normally the names of simple variables, since these represent storage locations in computer memory.

In the previous example counter is an lvalue.

The C language contains increment and decrement operators, written as ++ and -- respectively, and are used to increase or decrease an lvalue. In other languages these might be functions INC and DEC. However, unlike other languages, these operators can be described as prefix or postfix operators depending upon whether they come before the lvalue or after the lvalue.

Prefix operators change an lvalue before the value is used, whereas postfix operators change an lvalue after the value is used. When the following program is run the values for counter displayed on the screen are 2 1 2 9 9, for the reasons given in the comments.

```
/* program to demonstrate prefix and postfix operators */
#include <stdio.h>

main()
{
        int counter;

        counter = 1;
        printf("%4d", ++counter); /* counter increased to 2 before use */

        counter = 1;
        printf("%4d", counter++); /* value of counter is 1 and increased after printf to 2*/
        printf("%4d", counter); /* value of counter is 2 after last increase */

        counter = 10;
        --counter;/* counter = counter -1 */
        printf("%4d", counter);

        counter = 10;
        counter--; /* counter decreased to 9 after use */
        printf("%4d", counter); /* value of counter is 9 after last decrease */
}
```

Returning to while loops, the previous example used to demonstrate a while loop can be re-coded in one of two ways to demonstrate the use of increment operators.

Using a prefix operator the code becomes:

```
counter = 1;
while (counter < 4)
{
        printf("%4d", counter);
        ++counter;
}
printf("\n");
```

.
.
.

alternatively using a postfix operator the code is modified to:

```
counter = 1;
while (counter < 4)
        printf("%4d", counter++);
printf("\n");
```

.
.
.

both segments of code produce the same result.

There is also a do .. while loop in which the body of the loop is executed at least once. This type of loop is represented in other languages usually by a repeat .. until structure.

The format of do .. while is:

do statement while (expression)

where statement is the body of the loop and expression evaluates to either zero or a non-zero value. The body of the loop is always executed once, the expression is then evaluated, and if it is equal to zero (false) the loop is terminated and the computer passes to the next statement after the expression.

An example of a do .. while statement is :

```
int counter = 1;

do
{
        printf("%4d", counter);
        counter++;
}
while (counter < 4);
```

3.6 For

Once again the reader should be familiar with the concept of a for statement since they are to be found in many high-level languages.

The format of for in C is:

```
          for ( expression_1 ; expression_2 ; expression_3 ) statement
```

and can be regarded as a shorthand version of the following while loop.

```
     expression_1; /* initialisation of a loop control variable */
     while (expression_2) /* evaluate expression containing loop control variable */
     {
          statement;
          expression_3 /* change value of the loop control variable */
     }
```

The example of the while loop in the previous section can be recoded as a for loop.

```
     for (counter = 1; counter < 4; counter++)
          printf("%4d", counter);
```

In other high-level languages it is common practice to state the range of values over which the loop control variable is applicable, however, in C only the initial value is given, followed by the condition under which loop execution continues, and the incremental or step value of the loop control variable.

3.7 Example programs

This section contains a series of programs to demonstrate the features of the language that have been explained in this chapter.

Company executives are paid a weekly travelling allowance for the use of their cars. Sales executives with cars whose engines are larger than 1500 cc receive a higher mileage rate of 25p per mile and the remaining executives irrespective of the size of their car's engine are paid at the normal rate of 20p per mile. The program has three inputs, whether you are a sales executive, the size of your car's engine and the weekly mileage. The travelling expenses are calculated and displayed. This program demonstrates the use of enumerated types and if .. else statements.

```
/* program to calculate weekly travelling expenses */
#include <stdio.h>

#define NormalRate 0.2
#define HigherRate 0.25
#define yes 'y'

typedef enum {false, true} boolean;

main()
{
     int mileage, EngineSize;
     int reply;
     float expenses;
     boolean SalesExecutive = false;
```

```
        printf("are you a sales executive answer y(es) or n(o) ");
        reply = getchar();
        if (reply = = yes) SalesExecutive = true;

        printf("input mileage ");
        scanf("%d", &mileage);
        printf("input size of engine in cc ");
        scanf("%d", &EngineSize);

        if (SalesExecutive && EngineSize > 1500)
                expenses = mileage * HigherRate ;
        else
                expenses = mileage * NormalRate;

        printf("weekly travelling expenses due £%6.2f\n", expenses);
}
```

A barometer for measuring atmospheric pressure, equates different pressures to different climatic conditions displayed on the dial as storm, rain, change, fair and dry. The program invites the user to input a code for a descriptive barometer reading and informs the user the type of protective clothing to wear according to the following rules.

For storm wear overcoat and hat; for rain wear raincoat and take umbrella, for change behave as for fair if it rained yesterday and for rain if it did not; for fair wear light over-jacket and take umbrella and for dry wear light over-jacket.

This program demonstrates the use of enumerated types, the switch and if statements.

```
/* program to inform what to wear in different climatic conditions */
#include <stdio.h>

#define yes 'y'

typedef enum {storm =1, rain=2, change=3, fair=4, dry=5} BarometerReading;

/* function to display a menu and return the user's choice */
BarometerReading menu(void)
{
        BarometerReading MenuCode;

        printf("input barometer code\n\n");
        printf("1\tstorm\n");
        printf("2\train\n");
        printf("3\tchange\n");
        printf("4\tfair\n");
        printf("5\tdry\n\n");
        scanf("%d", &MenuCode);
        return MenuCode;
}
```

```
main()
{
        int reply;

        switch (menu())
        {
                case storm:   printf("wear overcoat and hat");
                              break;
                case rain:    printf("wear raincoat and take umbrella");
                              break;
                case change:  printf("did it rain yesterday y(es) or n(o) ");
                              getchar(); /* flush input buffer */
                              reply = getchar();
                              if (reply == yes)
                                      printf("wear over-jacket and take umbrella");
                              else
                                      printf("wear raincoat and take umbrella");
                              break;
                case fair:    printf("wear over-jacket and take umbrella");
                              break;
                case dry:     printf("wear over-jacket");
        }
}
```

The third program allows a user to input a date in the form day month year (dd mm yy) and will validate the date. The program illustrates the use of enumerated constants as case labels in a switch statement and the if statement.

```
/* program to validate a date in the range 1901 .. 1999 */
#include <stdio.h>

typedef enum {false, true} boolean;
enum   {Jan=1, Feb=2, Mar=3, Apr=4, May=5, Jun=6,
        Jul=7, Aug=8, Sep=9, Oct=10, Nov=11, Dec=12};

/* function to validate a date */
boolean ValidDate(int dd, int mm, int yy)
{
        int days;

        switch (mm)
        {
                case Jan: case Mar: case May: case Jul: case Aug: case Oct: case Dec:   days = 31; break;
                case Apr: case Jun: case Sep: case Nov:                                 days = 30; break;
                case Feb:                                                               if (yy % 4 == 0)
                                                                                                days = 29;
                                                                                        else
                                                                                                days = 28;
                                                                                        break;
```

50

```
            default:                                       return false;
        }
        if (dd > days)
                return false;
        else
                return true;
}

main()
{
        int dd, mm, yy;

        printf("input a date in the format dd mm yy ");
        scanf("%d%d%d", &dd, &mm, &yy);
        if (ValidDate(dd,mm,yy))
                printf("date is valid\n");
        else
                printf("error in date\a\n");
}
```

The next program allows a user to input a sentence and will analyse the number of words in the sentence. The program demonstrates the use of the while loop.

```
/* program to input a sentence and display the number of words it contains */
#include <stdio.h>

#define yes 'y'
#define QuestionMark '?'
#define ExclamationMark '!'
#define FullStop '.'
#define comma ','
#define SemiColon ';'
#define colon ':'
#define space ' '
#define LF 10
#define CR 13

/* function to return the number of words in a sentence */
int WordCount(void)
{
        int words = 0;
        int character;

        printf("\n[input a sentence]\n\n");
        character = getchar();
        /* test for terminator */
        while (character != FullStop &&
                character != QuestionMark &&
                character != ExclamationMark)
```

```
        {
                /* test for separator */
                if      (character = = comma ||
                        character = = SemiColon ||
                        character = = colon ||
                        character = = space ||
                        character = = LF)
                {

                        + +words;
                        character = getchar();
                        /* ignore further separators */
                        while   (character = = space ||
                                character = = CR ||
                                character = = LF)
                        {

                                character = getchar();
                        }
                }
                else

                        character = getchar();
        }
        return + +words;
}

main()
{
        int answer;

        do
        {
                printf("\nnumber of words in sentence is %d\n", WordCount());
                getchar(); /* flush return from buffer */
                printf("\nmore sentences y(es) or n(o)? ");
                answer = getchar();
                getchar(); /* flush return from buffer */
        }
        while (answer = = yes);
}
```

A collection of wooden building bricks each have a different pattern printed on the surface of the brick. If the bricks are placed in a row then the combination of patterns that can be produced is the factorial value of the number of bricks. Thus two bricks will give two different line patterns, three bricks will give six different line patterns, four bricks will give twenty- four different line patterns, etc. This program invites the user to input the number of bricks and displays the number of line patterns. It is assumed that no one brick has the same pattern.

The program demonstrates the use of for and while loops.

/* program to calculate combinations of patterns */

```
#include <stdio.h>

/* function to calculate numbers of combinations of patterns */
double patterns(int bricks)
{
        double combinations = 1.0;
        int BrickCounter;

        for (BrickCounter = 2; BrickCounter <= bricks; ++BrickCounter)
                combinations = combinations * BrickCounter;
        return combinations;
}

main()
{
        int NumberOfBricks;
        int bricks;

        printf("input number of different patterned bricks ");
        scanf("%d", &NumberOfBricks);
        while (NumberOfBricks > 1)
        {
                printf("\nbricks\tpatterns\n\n");
                for (bricks = 2; bricks <= NumberOfBricks; ++bricks)
                        printf("%6d\t%-30.25G\n", bricks, patterns(bricks));
                printf("\ninput number of different patterned bricks ");
                scanf("%d", &NumberOfBricks);
        }
}
```

3.8 Miscellany

The C language contains a variety of extra features that sometimes facilitate coding a program. Use some of these features sparingly, since they can contribute towards the production of very compact programs that can be difficult to read. Such code may, in the future, be difficult to maintain by a different person.

break statement

A break statement, first discussed in section 3.4, can be used in conjunction with an if statement anywhere in a loop to terminate the loop.

continue statement

A continue statement causes the computer to branch to the end of the last statement in a loop, but not outside the loop. If used in conjunction with an if statement, statements inside the loop can be by-passed if a particular condition happens to be true. Continue is different to break in so much as the computer remains in the loop, whereas with break the computer was taken outside the loop or selection statement.

for statement

The for statement described in section 3.6 can spawn various formats.

If expression_1 is omitted, then the initialisation of the loop control variable can take place outside the beginning of the loop.

```
counter = 1;
for (; counter < 4; ++counter)
        printf("%4d", counter);
```

If expression_2 is omitted then the loop does not terminate unless it contains a break statement.

```
for (counter = 1; ; ++counter)
{
        printf("%4d", counter);
        if (counter = 3) break;
}
```

If expression_3 is omitted then the loop control variable must be incremented/decremented within the body of the loop.

```
for (counter = 1; counter < 4; )
        printf("%4d", counter++);
```

By omitting all three expressions it is possible to set up an infinite loop!

```
for ( ; ; )
        printf("forever and ever ... ");
```

Notice that despite the expressions being omitted in for loops the semi-colon ; separators must be present.

In the use of for loops only one variable has been initialised or incremented, this was the value of the loop control variable. Using a comma operator it is possible to initialise and increment/decrement other variables in addition to the loop control variable. Either expression_1 and/or expression_3 in a for statement can be composed from single expressions that are separated from each other by commas.

Consider the following program in which the positions of each of the letters in the alphabet is displayed. Comma operators in the for statement have been used to initialise the value of the index and letter, and increment both the value of the index and the letter.

```
/* program to display the position of each letter of the alphabet */
#include <stdio.h>

main()
{
        char letter;
        int index;

        for ( index = 0, letter = 'A';     index < 26;   ++index, ++letter)
                printf("%d\t%c\n", index+1, letter);
```

}

Since some or all of the expressions that control the loop variable in a for statement can be omitted, and other expressions can be included that have no relationship with the loop variable it should be clear that there is no restriction placed on the three expressions that control the behaviour of the loop, and indeed these expressions need not involve the same variable.

Use both the comma operator and omitting expressions in a for statement, with great care! Indeed the for statement in C is very versatile, indeed more versatile than in other high-level languages. You might produce very short, tight code, but can it be easily read and modified by someone else?

conditional operator ?:

The conditional operator requires three operands in the format:

expression_1 ? expression_2 : expression_3

The conditional expression is evaluated as follows: expression_1 is evaluated to either zero (false) or non-zero (true). If the value of expression_1 is zero then the entire conditional expression takes the value of expression_3. However, if the value of expression_1 is non-zero (true), then the entire conditional expression takes on the value of expression_2.

For example in the following program the results displayed on the screen are 5 and 11. Do you understand why? If not refer back to the previous paragraph.

```
#include <stdio.h>
main()
{
        int alpha = 5, beta = 6, gamma;

        gamma = alpha < beta ? alpha : alpha+beta;
        printf("%4d", gamma);
        gamma = alpha > beta ? alpha : alpha+beta;
        printf("%4d\n", gamma);
}
```

The precedence of the conditional operator ?: is less than the other operators, with the exception of assignment, that have been discussed in this book.

Once again a word of warning. Don't overuse conditional statements. The syntax of these statements is not particularly obvious which makes them difficult to read and interpret.

compound assignment

Normally when performing arithmetic it is quite usual to write statements such as a = a + b, etc. However, C has a shorthand notation for this type of assignment, a+=b, where += is known as a compound assignment operator. The advantage of such an operator is that a is only evaluated once, compared with twice in the expression a = a + b. Clearly the compound statement contributes nothing towards the ease of reading and interpreting a program, only to the speed of execution of the statement. Similar compound statements exist for the other binary additive and multiplicative operators, -=, *=, /=, %=.

goto statement

The author does not wish to get entangled in the age-old debate about goto statements. They of course allow for unconditional branching and should be avoided whenever possible. The break, continue and return statements all permit a restricted form of unconditional branching and it should not usually be necessary to use goto. However, the statement is part of the language and a brief mention is all it will receive. The format of a goto statement is: goto label; where the label is an identifier. A label must be followed by a statement and any statement can have more than one label. In the example that follows the label is end and it is followed by the statement prinf("unconditional branch");

```
{
    .
    .
    .
    goto end;
    .
end:    printf("unconditional branch");
    .
}
```

null statement

If the label in the last example had been at the end of the compound statement it would still require to be followed by a statement. The null statement is represented by a semi-colon ; and is used whenever a statement is required to complete the syntax, as in end : ;

A null statement can be used in the body of a loop if the body is required to be kept empty, for example:

```
        while ((character = getchar()) == space)
        ;       /* this is the body of the loop and contains a null statement */
```

This loop will keep receiving input from a keyboard as long as the character is a space, or in other words, ignore all space characters.

Warning! Be very careful where you place null statements with regard to if, while and for statements.

3.9 Summary

● Conditions can be constructed using the relational operators <, >, <=, >= the equality operators == and !=, and combined using the logical operators &&, ||, and !

● Conditions evaluate to either zero (false) or non-zero (true).

● It is possible to specify new data types and define the constants that make up the data of that type. These are known as enumerated types and are useful in defining a boolean type with constants false and true, corresponding to the values 0 and 1 respectively.

● The default integer values associated with enumerated constants can be re-assigned different integer values.

- Statements that allow for selection are if .. else, switch and the conditional operator ?: .

- Statements that allow for repetition are while, do .. while and for.

- Integer and character storage locations are known as lvalues. These can be incremented or decremented by the prefix and postfix operators + + and --.

- Unconditional branching is possible through the use of break, continue and goto.

- Assignment statements can be expressed in a shorthand form using the compound assignments +=, -=, *=, /= and %=.

- Null statements can be used with labels or as empty loop bodies.

3.10 Questions *answers begin on page 248*

1. A student studying Computer Science at a college is examined by coursework and written examination. Both components of the assessment carry a maximum of 50 marks. The following rules are used by the examiners in order to pass or fail students.

A student must score a total of 40% or more in order to pass.

A total mark of 39% is moderated to 40%.

Each component must be passed with a minimum mark of 20. If a student scores 40% or more but does not achieve the minimum mark in either component he is given a technical fail of 39% (this mark is not moderated to 40%).

Grades are awarded on marks that fall into the following categories.

100 - 70 inclusive	A
69 - 60 inclusive	B+
59 - 50 inclusive	B
49 - 40 inclusive	C
39 - 0 inclusive	F

Write a program to input the marks for both components, output the final mark and grade after any moderations.

2. Write a program to input two real numbers and give the user the choice of adding, subtracting, multiplying or dividing these numbers. Perform the appropriate calculation and display the result. Your program should trap any attempt to divide by zero.

3. Write segments of code in one program to display:

    (i)   the odd integers in the range 1 to 29;
    (ii)   the squares of even integers in the range 2 to 20;

    (iii)   the sum of the squares of the odd integers between 1 and 13;

    (iv)   the alphabet in both upper and lower case;

    (v)   the first sixteen terms of the Fibonacci series (1 1 2 3 5 8 . . .).

4. Write a program to find the maximum, minimum and arithmetic mean of a list of positive integers that are input at the keyboard. The number of integers is not known in advance, and the list of integers is terminated by a negative value.

5. Write a program to input a sentence, count the number of words, frequency of each vowel and the number of consonants. Display the results of your analysis.

6. Write a program to convert numbers represented in Roman numerals to decimal numbers. For example MDCLXIV = 1664. The following table indicates the size of each Roman numeral.

Roman	Arabic
M	1000
D	500
C	100
L	50
X	10
V	5
I	1

7. Write a program to convert positive integer numbers in the range 1 - 999 into words.

8. Comment upon the following segments of code.

(i)   counter = 1;

```
counter = 1;
while (counter < 4) ;
        printf("%4d",counter++);
```

(ii)   if (counter > 1000) ;

```
if (counter > 1000) ;
        printf("Warning! counter exceeds range");
```

(iii)   counter = 0;

```
counter = 0;
while (++counter < 4) ;
        printf("%4d",counter);
```

(iv)   for (counter = 1 ; counter < 4 ; ++counter) ;

```
for (counter = 1 ; counter < 4 ; ++counter) ;
        printf("%4d",counter);
```

4.

Arrays

In common with most high-level languages C incorporates array data structures.
This chapter explores the mechanics of array structures, access through subscripts
and pointers, static and dynamic allocation of memory for arrays, and finally
record structures.

4.1 One-dimensional arrays

In common with most high-level languages C supports arrays. A typical pictorial representation of an array is given in figure 4.1. This illustrates integers stored in consecutive cells of an array named table, where the contents of each cell is accessible through the name of the array and the subscript or index of the cell. Notice that in C the subscript of the first cell is zero. Thus the contents of table[0] is 16, table[1] is 21, etc.

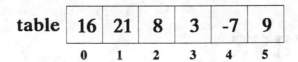

Figure 4.1 An illustration of a one-dimensional array

The contents of an array must always be of the same data type, and therefore the declaration of an array is given as the data type for the elements in the array followed by the maximum number of cells in the array. The declaration for the array depicted in figure 4.1 would be:

int table[6];

Warning! Since the lowest subscript in an array is zero, always declare one cell extra to the value of the highest subscript, when declaring the size of an array. Failure to do this will result in unpredictable results when the program is executed.

Always initialise the contents of an array. Never assume that the system has initialised the contents to zero or any other value.

An array can be initialised after the declaration, for example, the array table can be assigned the values depicted in figure 4.1 as follows.

int table[6] = {16, 21, 8, 3, -7, 9};

However, if the initialisation values are fewer than cells in the array then the remaining cells are initialised to zero. It is illegal to declare more initialisation values than there are cells in an array. The declaration of the maximum number of cells in the array can be omitted if initialisation values are present.

int table[ ] = {16, 21, 8, 3, -7, 9};

The contents of the array can be accessed and printed as follows.

```
{
    int     index;

    for (index=0; index < 6; ++index)
        printf("%d\n", table[index]);
}
```

The subscript can be a constant, variable or expression, as long as it evaluates to a non-negative integer in the range 0 to (maximum number of cells - 1). In this example the legal range of a subscript is 0 to 5, since the maximum number of cells is given as 6 in the array declaration.

Warning! C does not require that the range of a subscript is checked. If the subscript (index) was allowed to go out of bounds then the results will be unpredictable when the program is executed.

4.2 Multi-dimensional arrays

Multi-dimensional arrays are repetitive structures. For example a two-dimensional array is a repetition of one-dimensional arrays. In figure 4.2 the two-dimensional array named matrix is composed from three one-dimensional arrays similar to table in the previous section.

		0	1	2	3	4	5
	0	16	21	8	3	-7	9
matrix	1	-3	11	0	5	9	7
	2	13	7	-64	19	14	2

Figure 4.2 An illustration of a two-dimensional array

The declaration of the two-dimensional array in figure 4.2, is given as:

int matrix[3][6];

Access to any element in the two-dimensional array is through a row subscript, followed by a column subscript. For example matrix[0][5] = 9; matrix[2][0] = 13; matrix[1][2] = 0, etc

The contents of the two-dimensional array can be initialised in a similar way to one-dimensional arrays:

int matrix[3][6] = { {16, 21, 8, 3, -7, 9},
                      {-3, 11, 0, 5, 9, 7},
                      {13, 7, -64, 19, 14, 2}};

where the first row of initialisation values corresponds to the first row of the array, the second row of initialisation values corresponds to the second row of the array, and so on.

If a row of initialisation values does not contain enough values then the remaining elements are set to zero.

If there are not enough rows of initialisation values then the remaining rows in the array are set to zero.

The contents of a two-dimensional array can be accessed and printed, using a double loop, as follows:

```
                          for (row=0; row < 3; ++row)
                          {
                                  for (column=0; column < 6; ++column)
                                          printf("%d\t",matrix[row][column]);
                                  printf("\n");
                          }
```

4.3 Pointers

In the previous sections subscripts were used to access elements in an array. However, it is also possible to use pointers to access the contents of an array. In figure 4.3 a pointer ptr has been declared and is made to point at the first cell of the array named table.

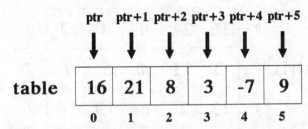

Figure 4.3 An illustration of using a pointer to access a one-dimensional array, where ptr = &table[0]

```
int     table[6] = {16,21,8,3,-7,9};
int     *ptr;
ptr = &table[0]; /* the pointer, which is an address, is assigned the address of the first cell in the array */
```

It is possible to access the first cell through the pointer ptr, thus: printf("%d", *ptr); would display 16, the contents of cell 0.

In order to allow the pointer ptr to traverse the addresses of the cells of the array, it is possible to perform arithmetic on a pointer.

An integer can be added to a pointer to get it to point to another address, for example:

ptr = &table[1]; /* address of the second cell in the array */

ptr = ptr + 1; /* the address held by ptr (&table[1]) has been increased by 1, allowing the pointer to point at the third cell in the array */

The contents of the one-dimensional array table can be displayed using the following segment of code.

for (ptr=&table[0]; ptr <= &table[5]; printf("%d\n", *ptr), ++ptr);

Similarly an integer value can be subtracted from a pointer, therefore, the contents of table can be output in reverse, as indicated by the following code.

for (ptr=&table[5]; ptr >= &table[0]; printf("%d\n", *ptr), -- ptr);

From these two examples it should be clear to the reader that pointers can be compared using the relational and equality operators.

Two pointers can be subtracted as follows.

int   *ptr1, *ptr2;

ptr1=&table[5];
ptr2=&table[0];

then ptr1 - ptr2 represents the difference in the addresses of &table[5] and &table[0] which is 5.

Continuing with the theme of pointers, it is worth noting that when an array is declared, the name of the array is actually a pointer to the first element in the array. Therefore, by writing the array name table (a pointer) it is the same as writing &table[0] (a pointer to the first element). The declaration of int table[6]; implies that *(table+0) = 16. Similarly the pointer *(table+1) = 21, *(table+2) = 8, etc. But table[0] = 16, table[1] = 21, table[2] = 8, etc. Therefore, *(table+i) is the same as table[i], implying that a pointer may be subscripted.

Warning! Do not attempt to modify, using pointer arithmetic, the name of an array. This value is a constant pointer and not a pointer variable.

The two for statements given earlier, can be simplified, as follows. Notice that the value of the pointer table has not changed, only the value of the pointer variable ptr has been modified by pointer arithmetic.

        for (ptr=table; ptr <= table+5; printf("%d\n", *ptr), ++ptr);

        for (ptr=table+5; ptr >= table; printf("%d\n", *ptr), -- ptr);

4.4 Strings

A string literal is stored as an array of characters with a null character being appended to the end of the string. The name of the string literal points to the first element of the array. For example:

        char   *alphabet = "abcdefghijklmnopqrstuvwxyz"

then alphabet = a, alphabet+1 = b, alphabet+2 = c, etc, and alphabet+26 = 00 (null character).

Similarly alphabet[0] = a, alphabet[1] = b, alphabet[2] = c, etc, and alphabet[26] = 00 (null character).

The following code illustrates three methods of displaying the alphabet on the screen.

```
/* declaration of a string literal using a pointer */
{
        char    *alphabet = "abcdefghijklmnopqrstuvwxyz";
        char    *ptr;
        int     index;

        printf("%s\n\n",alphabet);
        for (ptr=alphabet; *ptr != 00; ++ptr)
                printf("%c",*ptr);
        printf("\n\n");
        for (index=0; alphabet[index] != 00; ++index)
                printf("%c",alphabet[index]);
}
```

If the string was declared as a one-dimensional array and initialised with the alphabet

```
                char alphabet[ ] = "abcdefghijklmnopqrstuvwxyz";
```

then the same code can be used to display the alphabet on the screen.

Despite the same code being used to access the string there are differences in the manner in which the string and name of the string can be used. In the array declaration of the string the contents of the string can be modified, however, in the pointer version no attempt should be made to modify the string. In the array declaration alphabet is the name of an array and it cannot point to a different array, by contrast the pointer variable can be changed in the program so that it contains a different address and hence points to a different string!

Strings can be input and output using scanf and printf, where %s is used in the control format. Since the name of a string is a pointer to the first character of the string there is no need to use the address of the string in the scanf statement. The name of the string is already an address.

Scanf will ignore any leading white-space characters in a string and input the string up to the next white-space character. The string will be appended with a null character provided there is enough storage space declared for the string. If the maximum number of character to be input is known in advance, n say, then the control format can be modified to %ns. This acts as a safeguard in storing characters in a fixed-length array, otherwise it is possible for scanf to continue to input and store characters beyond the bounds of an array.

Printf will output the characters in a string until the null character is detected. If there is no null character in the string the printf function will continue to output the contents of memory addresses until a null character is eventually detected.

Warning! Never use scanf if a string is to be input that contains white space-characters.

An alternative to scanf is the function gets. This will allow the characters in a string to be input and stored in an array. All the white-space characters in a string will be stored until a newline character is input as a string terminator.

A string can also be output using the function puts. This function will output the characters in a string up to the first null character, the function then outputs a newline character. The following example illustrates the use of the functions gets and puts.

```
{
      char    string[81];

      printf("input a string\n");
      gets(string);
      printf("you have just input the string\n");
      puts(string);
}
```

4.5 String library

A string is an array of characters. Unlike numbers, C does not allow the use of equality or relational operators in comparing two strings. However, all is not lost! ANSI C does contain a string library that allows for a variety operations on strings that does include string comparison. The following extract is taken from the Jensen & Partners TopSpeed C <string.h> header file, and lists some of the major functions found in the string library.

```
.
.
char    * strcat(char * _dest, const char * _source);
int     strcmp(const char * _s1, const char * _s2);
char    * strcpy(char * _dest, const char * _source);
size_t  strlen(const char * _s);
char    * strset(char * _s, int _ch);
.

char    * stpcpy(char * _dest, const char * _source);
char    * strchr(const char * _s, int _c);
int     strcoll(const char * _s1, const char * _s2);
size_t  strxfrm(char * _s1, const char * _s2, size_t _n);
size_t  strcspn(const char * _s1, const char * _s2);
char    * strdup(const char * _s);
char    * strerror(int _errnum);
int     stricmp(const char * _s1, const char * _s2);
char    * strlwr(char * _s);
char    * strncat(char * _dest, const char * _source, size_t _n);
int     strncmp(const char * _s1, const char * _s2, size_t _n);
char    * strncpy(char * _dest, const char * _source, size_t _n);
int     strnicmp(const char * _s1, const char * _s2, size_t _n);
char    * strnset(char * _s, int _ch, size_t _n);
char    * strpbrk(const char * _s1, const char * _s2);
char    * strrchr(const char * _s, int _c);
char    * strrev(char * _s);
size_t  strspn(const char * _s1, const char * _s2);
char    * strstr(const char * _s1, const char * _s2);
char * strtok(char * _s1, const char * _s2);
```

```
char   * strupr(char *_s);
char   * _strerror (const char *_s);
.
.
```

It is left to the reader to consult the C library reference manual to obtain the meaning of each function listed. However, whenever a string function is used in an example program in the text, a full description of the purpose of the function will be given.

4.6 Dynamic arrays

When a pointer variable is declared, the declaration only allocates storage space for the pointer and does not allocate storage space for the information being pointed at by the pointer.

For example when a pointer variable to a string is declared as char *string; only the address of the pointer variable is allocated. Memory space needs to be allocated to store the characters in the string.

The function malloc found in the header file <stdlib.h> allocates memory, it requires one argument which represents the number of bytes requested, and returns a pointer to the first byte. For example:

```
                    char *string;
                    string = malloc(256);
```

allocates 256 bytes to the character array and points to the first character in this array.

The storage space is allocated from an area of memory known as the heap. The size of the heap is finite, and clearly too many requests for storage space from the heap will exhaust the amount of memory available for allocation. For this reason whenever allocated memory space is no longer required it should be returned to the heap by using the function free. In this example the 256 bytes of storage needed to accommodate the characters of string would be returned to the heap by the statement free(string).

The following program indicates how memory space is allocated to a character array being pointed at by string. A value for the string array is input using get(string). A further area of memory is allocated to a second array of characters pointed at by copy. The amount of memory allocated to the character array copy is determined by the length of string. Note the function strlen returns the length of a string. The string array is then copied into the copy array and the contents of this new array is output. The storage space allocated to string and copy is then returned to the heap using the function free.

```
#include <stdio.h>
#include <stdlib.h>
#include <string.h>

char *string, *copy;

main()
{
        string=malloc(256);
        printf("input string ");
        gets(string);
```

```
        copy=malloc(strlen(string)+1);
        strcpy(copy,string);
        printf("string input was ");
        puts(copy);
        free(string);
        free(copy);
}
```

Space allocation for arrays other than strings is achieved through the function calloc, also found in header <stdlib.h>. This function requires two parameters, the first represents the size of the array, and the second represents the size of the data held in each cell of the array.

If a one-dimensional array pointed at by table, is to store integers it could be declared as:

$$int *table;$$

However, if the number of integers that table will hold is not known in advance, memory allocation for the array can be postponed until the size of the array is known. During program execution if the size of the array is found to be n, say, then memory can be allocated by using:

table = calloc(n, sizeof(int));

If the reader cares to investigate the format of malloc and calloc in the library reference manual then the formats for these functions are:

$$void *malloc(size\_t size), and$$

$$void *calloc(size\_t nmemb, size\_t size)$$

respectively. Notice the use of void * for the return type in both functions. In ANSI C, void * is a generic pointer type, used when the type being pointed to is not known. Note also that the type size_t is implementation dependant, some compilers will use unsigned int, as in the case of TopSpeed C, and others will use unsigned long int. The amount of storage space to be allocated will depend upon the type of data being stored in the array. The value of size can be either a constant, for example 256, an expression (strlen(string) + 1) or the size of the data type being stored (sizeof(int)). Note that sizeof is an operator in C that returns the number of bytes that a data type needs for storage.

The generic pointer returned by malloc is automatically converted to the required type when the assignment is performed.

The format of free is described in the library reference manual as:

$$void free(void *ptr);$$

Since the pointer (ptr) has been described as a generic pointer type a pointer of any type may appear as an actual parameter For example:

free(table); /* table points to data of type int */

free(string); /* string points to data of type char */

4.7 Structures

A structure is a collection of one or more variables, which may be of different types, grouped together under a single name. In other high-level languages a structure would be known as a record. For example a postal address containing street, town and postcode could be represented as a structure.

```
struct {
        char    street[20];
        char    town[20];
        char    postcode[8];
    } abode;
```

Individual components in this structure are accessed by the variable name abode, followed by the required component. Thus abode.street; abode.town; abode.postcode;

An alternative approach is to give the structure a name or tag,

```
struct address       {
                char street[20];
                char town[20];
                char postcode[8];
            };
```

and use the tag to declare a variable: struct address abode;

It is also possible to combine both definitions, so that the structure is given a tag and a variable. In addition to defining the type for abode, it is possible to use the type struct address in later variable declarations.

```
struct address       {
                char street[20];
                char town[20];
                char postcode[8];
            } abode;
```

Structure variables can be initialised at the point of declaration. In the previous example abode can be initialised as follows.

struct address abode = {"23 Sea View", "Southampton", "SO2 9QT"};

Individual components of a structure can be accessed by using the variable name followed by the name of the component, with both names being separated by a full stop. Here individual components of struct address are initialised.

abode.street = "23 sea View";
abode.town = "Southampton";
abode.postcode = "SO2 9QT";

If two variables have the same structure then it is possible to assign the contents of one variable to another. For example if two variables are defined as:

struct address Fred, Mary;

then the assignment Mary = Fred is legal, and implies that Fred's postal address is now the same as Mary's postal address!

A complete variable with a structure can be passed across to a function, for example the function labels would be called using labels(abode);

```
void labels(struct address    abode)
{
      printf("%s\n", abode.street);
      printf("%s\n", abode.town);
      printf("%s\n", abode.postcode);
}
```

A complete structure can also be returned from a function.

```
struct address GetAddress(void)
{
      struct address         abode;

      printf("input street "); scanf("%s", abode.street);
      printf("input town "); scanf("%s", abode.town);
      printf("input postcode "); scanf("%s", abode.postcode);
      return abode;
}
```

An alternative means of dealing with structures is to define the structure as a type. This essentially gives a type name (not a tag) to a structure. In the next example address has been defined as a type having the following structure.

```
typedef struct         {
                       char street[20];
                       char town[20];
                       char postcode[8];
               } address;
```

The type address can be used to define a component within another structure.

```
typedef struct         {
                       char surname[15];
                       char initial;
                       address abode;
               } people;
```

The type people can be used to define the type of information held in say, a one-dimensional array. For example: people AddressList[100]; defines the array AddressList that can hold up to one hundred structures of type people.

4.8 Example programs

The first of the example programs in this chapter simulates the throwing of a die (singular for dice) for a different number of trials. The number of occurrences over a trial, of each face of the die depicted by numbers of spots (_1, _2, _3, _4, _5, _6), is stored in a one-dimensional array. Since all arrays in C have the first cell subscripted at zero it makes sense to describe the six subscripts as enumerated constants, where the first constant _1 equates to subscript 0, the second constant _2 equates to subscript 1, etc. Because enumerated constants are evaluated to their position in the enumeration list, the constants can be treated as integers and be used as a control variable in a for loop, as well as a subscript in an array.

To simulate the throw of a die a random number generator function is used. The function rand() is found in the header file <stdlib.h> and returns a pseudo-random number in the range 0 - RAND_MAX.

```
/* program to simulate throwing a die for different numbers of trials and record the frequency that each
side (number of spots) of the die appears in each trial */

#include <stdio.h>
#include <stdlib.h>

main()
{
        enum{_1,_2,_3,_4,_5,_6} spots;
        int     trials, roll;
        float   RandomNumber;
        int     frequency[6];

        printf("\ninput number of trials (0 to exit) ");
        scanf("%d", &trials);
        while (trials > 0)
        {
                for (spots = _1; spots <= _6; frequency[spots]=0, ++spots);

                for (roll = 1; roll <= trials; ++roll)
                {
                        /* generate a number in the range 0 <= number < 1 */
                        RandomNumber = (float)(rand()/((float)(RAND_MAX) + 1));
                        spots = (int)(10000 * RandomNumber) % 6;
                        frequency[spots] = frequency[spots] + 1;
                }
                printf("\nnumber of spots\t1 2 3 4 5 6\nfrequency\t");
                for (spots = _1; spots <= _6; ++spots)
                        printf("%-6d", frequency[spots]);
                printf("\n\ninput number of trials (0 to exit) ");
                scanf("%d", &trials);
        }
}
```

The next example program allows the user to type a sentence at the keyboard, and records the number of vowels in the sentence. Once again enumerated constants a,e,i,o,u are used as subscripts to the one-dimensional array that holds the frequency of occurrence of each vowel.

```
/* program to count the number of vowels in a sentence */

#include <stdio.h>
#define FullStop '.'

main()
{
        enum {a,e,i,o,u} vowel;
        int     character;
        int     frequency[5] = {0,0,0,0,0};

        printf("input a sentence - terminate with a full stop\n\n");
        character = getchar();
        while (character != FullStop)
        {
                switch (character)
                {
                        case 'a': case 'A':     frequency[a] = frequency[a] + 1; break;
                        case 'e': case 'E':     frequency[e] = frequency[e] + 1; break;
                        case 'i': case 'I':     frequency[i] = frequency[i] + 1; break;
                        case 'o': case 'O':     frequency[o] = frequency[o] + 1;break;
                        case 'u': case 'U':     frequency[u] = frequency[u] + 1;
                }
                character = getchar();
        }
        printf("\n\nvowels\t\ta e i o u \nfrequency\t");
        for (vowel = a; vowel <= u; ++vowel)
                printf("%-4d", frequency[vowel]);
}
```

The third program demonstrates the use of a two-dimensional array to simulate a crossword.

```
/* program to build a crossword */

#include <stdio.h>
#define yes 'y'
#define null 00
char    crossword[15][15];

void clear(void)
{
        int     across, down;
        for (across=0, down=0;  (across <= 14 && down <= 14);
                                crossword[across][down] = null, ++across, ++down);
}
```

```
void GetWord(void)
{
        int    column, row, across, down, index;
        char   word[16], position;

        printf("\nis word a(cross) or d(own)? ");
        position = getchar(); getchar(); /* clear buffer */
        printf("position of first letter (row column) ? ");
        scanf("%d%d", &row, &column);
        printf("what is the word? ");
        scanf("%s", word); getchar(); /* clear buffer */
        if (position == 'a')
                for    (across=column, index = 0 ;      word[index] != null ;
                       crossword[row][across] = word[index], ++index, ++across);
        else
                for    (down = row, index = 0; word[index] != null ;
                       crossword[down][column] = word[index], ++index, ++down);
}

void display(void)
{
        int    column, row;

        printf("\n\n 0 1 2 3 4 5 6 7 8 9 10 11 12 13 14");
        for (row=0; row <= 14; ++row)
        {
                printf("\n%-3d", row);
                for (column=0; column <= 14; ++column)
                        printf("%-3c", crossword[row][column]);
        }
        printf("\n\n");
}

main()
{
        int    reply;

        clear();
        display();
        do
        {
                GetWord();
                display();
                printf("another word? y(es) or n(o) ");
                reply = getchar(); getchar();
        }
        while (reply == yes);
}
```

The fourth program demonstrates the use of a one-dimensional array defined dynamically, and the insertion sort algorithm. A random number determines the number of cells in the array, after which memory can be allocated for storing a stream of pseudo- random numbers. The contents of the unsorted array is then displayed.

The insertion sort orders the first two integers in the array, then orders the next three integers, followed by the next four integers, and so on until all the integers have been sorted into ascending order.

The contents of the sorted array is then displayed.

```c
/* program to create an array of integers, sort the integers into ascending order, display the integers */

#include <stdio.h>
#include <stdlib.h>
int      *table;

/* determine the size of the array, then fill the array with integers */
void GetData(int *size)
{
       int index;

       randomize();
       *size = (rand() % 100) + 1;
       table = calloc(*size, sizeof(int));
       printf("size of table is %d\n", *size);
       for (index = 0; index <= *size-1 ; table[index] = rand(), ++index);
}

/* output the contents of the array printing ten numbers per line */
void display(int *size)
{
       int index, counter = 0;

       printf("\n");
       for (index=0; index <= *size-1; ++index)
       {
              if (counter == 10)
              {
                     printf("\n");
                     counter = 0;
              }
              printf("%6d", table[index]);
              ++counter;
       }
       printf("\n");
}
```

```
/* insertion sort */
void sort(int *size)
{
        int     current, location, index;

        for (index = 1; index < = *size-1; + +index)
        {
                current = table[index];
                location = index;
                while (location > 0 && table[location - 1] > current )
                {
                        table[location] = table[location - 1];
                        --location;
                }
                table[location] = current;
        }
}

main()
{
        int     size;

        GetData(&size);
        display(&size);
        sort(&size);
        display(&size);
        free(table);
}
```

The fifth program serves the purpose of demonstrating string processing and a structure. The user is invited to type a message at the keyboard, and this in turn is translated into Morse code. The coded translation is displayed on the screen.

```
/* program to translate a phrase in English into Morse code */
#include <stdio.h>
#include <stdlib.h>
#include <string.h>
#include <ctype.h>

#define null 00
#define space 040
#define yes 'y'

typedef struct          {
                                char encryption[5];
                        } code;
code MorseCode[26];

char    *message;
```

74

```
/* function to store the Morse code in an array of records */
void initialise(void)
{
        char *MorseData = ".- -...-.-.-.. ...-.--. ......"
                          ".----.- .-..-- -. --- .--.-.-.-. ... - ..- ...-.-- -..--.----..";
        char string[5];
        int index;

        for (index = 0 ; index <= 25 ; ++index, MorseData = MorseData + 4)
        {
                strncpy(string,MorseData,4);
                string[4] = null; /* append null character to string */
                strncpy(MorseCode[index].encryption, string, 5);
        }
}

/* function to inspect each character in the message and convert the character into Morse Code */
void convert(void)
{
        char character;

        for (; *message != null; ++message)
        {
                character = toupper(*message);
                if ( character == space )
                        printf("\n");
                else if ( character >= 'A' && character <= 'Z' )
                {
                        printf("%s", MorseCode[character - 65].encryption);
                        printf("%c", space);
                }
                else
                        printf(" ? \a");
        }
}

main()
{
        char reply;

        initialise();
        message = malloc(256); /* allocate 256 bytes of storage for the string */
        do
        {
                printf("What is your message?\n\n");
                gets(message);
```

75

```
                convert();
                printf("\n\nIs there another message y(es) or n(o)? ");
                reply = getchar(); getchar();
        }
    while (reply == yes);
    free(message);
}
```

The final program in this section builds an array of structures containing the name, date of birth and current age of a person. The array is sorted on the age as primary key, and the contents of the array is then displayed.

```
/* program to create an array of records containing the fields name, date of birth and age today, sort the
records into ascending order on age today, and display the records */
#include <stdio.h>
#include <stdlib.h>

typedef struct         {
                            int     dd;
                            int     mm;
                            int     yy;
                        } date;

typedef struct         {
                            char    name[16];
                            date    DOB;
                            int     age;
                        } PersonsAge;

    PersonsAge  *table;
    date        today;

/* function to calculate and return an age from a date of birth */
int GetAge(date DOB)
{
    if (DOB.yy < today.yy)
    {
        if (DOB.mm < today.mm || (DOB.mm = today.mm && DOB.dd <= today.dd))
            return today.yy - DOB.yy;
        else
        {
            if ((DOB.mm = today.mm && DOB.dd > today.dd) || DOB.mm > today.mm)
                return today.yy - DOB.yy - 1;
        }
    }
    else
        return 0;
}
```

76

```
/* determine the size of the array, then fill the array with records */
void GetData(int *size)
{
      int      entries, index;

      printf("How many entries? ");
      scanf("%d", &entries);
      *size = entries;
      table = calloc(*size, sizeof(PersonsAge));
      for (index=0; index < *size; ++index)
      {
            printf("input name of person ");
            scanf("%s",table[index].name);
            printf("input birthday in format dd mm yy ");
            scanf("%d%d%d",&table[index].DOB.dd, &table[index].DOB.mm, &table[index].DOB.yy);
            table[index].age = GetAge(table[index].DOB);
      }
}


/* display the names and ages of the people in the order youngest to eldest */
void display(int *size)
{
      int      index;
      for (index=0; index <= *size-1; ++index)
            printf("%s\t%d\n",table[index].name, table[index].age);
}

/* sort the contents of the array on the age field using an insertion sort */
void sort(int *size)
{
      PersonsAge   current;
      int          location, index;

      for (index = 1; index <= *size-1; ++index)
      {
            current = table[index];
            location = index;
            while (location > 0 && table[location - 1].age > current.age)
            {
                  table[location] = table[location - 1];
                  --location;
            }
            table[location] = current;
      }
}
```

```
main()
{
    int     size;

    printf("input today's date in format dd mm yy ");
    scanf("%d%d%d", &today.dd, &today.mm, &today.yy);
    GetData(&size);
    sort(&size);
    display(&size);
    free(table);
}
```

4.9 Summary

● Arrays have the first cell subscripted at zero, therefore, an array containing N cells will have subscripts in the range 0 .. (N-1).

● An array can be initialised at the time of declaration.

● The name of an array is a pointer to the first element in the array.

● Access to the elements in an array can be through subscripts or pointers.

● Strings are one-dimensional character arrays, with a null character appended to the (N+1)th cell.

● The C library contains many functions for manipulating strings that include copying, concatenating, comparing and finding the length of a string.

● The size of an array can be declared during program execution. The memory required to store the data in the array is allocated from the heap at run-time.

● The contents of an array is not confined to characters and numbers it can contain structures which themselves contain variables of different data types.

4.10 Questions   *answers begin on page 256*

1. Write a program to store the alphabet as characters in an array. The program should display:

(a) the entire alphabet;
(b) the first six characters of the alphabet;
(c) the last ten characters of the alphabet;
(d) the tenth character of the alphabet.

2. Write a program to play noughts and crosses against the computer. Use a two-dimensional array to store the noughts and crosses. Let the computer be the cross and the position of play by the computer is created using a random number generator. Display the board on the screen and the final result of the game.

3. A palindrome is a word that is spelt the same backwards as forwards e.g. RADAR, POOP, etc. Write a program to input a word and analyse whether it is a palindrome or not.

4. A computerised minefield is divided into a 10x10 matrix. Write a game program to generate the random position of mines in the field. The number of mines is also a random number in the range 1 to 10. Invite a player to input pairs of coordinates of a path through the minefield. The computer generates the starting position in the South, and the only legal move a player can make is to any adjacent position in the matrix. The object of the game is to trace a path through the field, without stepping on a mine, and to finish at the Northern perimeter. Only at the end of the game should the computer reveal the position of the mines.

5. Write a program to store two twenty digit integers as characters of a string and perform the operations of addition and subtraction on the two integers. Output the answer as a string of digits.

6. Write a program to store in an array, ten structures that contain the names of telephone exchanges and their corresponding STD codes. For example Oxford 0865 might be one entry in the array. Sort the array on the STD code as key. Write a routine to search for the exchange when given the STD code. Display the results of the search.

5.
Files

In the previous chapters input was confined to entering data through a keyboard, and output to displaying information on a screen. When there is a requirement to permanently store data there is a need to create files. Data can be written to or read from files held on magnetic disc or tape. This chapter covers the use of text and binary files and the methods of accessing the information held in the files.

Contents

5.1 Streams

The term stream is used to define any input source or output destination for data. The only streams that have been used in the previous chapters are from keyboard input and screen output. However, it is possible to define further streams that use other devices, such as a printer or a disc unit.

A stream is represented by a file pointer which is a value of type FILE *, and in ANSI C there are three standard streams whose file pointers have the following names:

stdin	standard input from a keyboard;
stdout	standard output to a screen;
stderr	standard output of error messages to a screen.

The standard input and output streams can be regarded as files. The functions scanf and printf that relate to keyboard input and screen output have equivalent functions for respective input and output from files held on other devices. The format of these new functions is:

        fscanf(FILE *stream, const char *format, [arguments] ...);

and

        fprintf(FILE *stream, const char *format, ...);

However, since stdin and stdout are file pointers it is possible to substitute scanf and printf with fscanf and fprintf respectively, and retain input from the keyboard and output to the screen as if scanf and printf were being used.

The following program reads numbers input at the keyboard (stdin), displays on the screen (stdout) a running total for the numbers input and calculates and displays the average of all the numbers input.

```
/* program to demonstrate input and output from the standard streams stdin and stdout */
#include <stdio.h>
main()
{
        int integer;
        int sum = 0;
        int counter = 0;
        int mean;
        fscanf(stdin, "%d", &integer);
        while (integer != 0)
        {
                sum = sum + integer;
                fprintf(stdout, "sum of integers so far .. %d\n", sum);
                ++counter;
                fscanf(stdin, "%d", &integer);
        }
        mean = sum / counter;
        fprintf(stdout, "mean value of integers is %d\n", mean);
}
```

5.2 Redirection

The use of a keyboard as a source, and a screen as a destination, can be modified by redirecting the standard input and output. In both MSDOS and UNIX it is possible to redirect standard input and standard output to other devices. For example in MSDOS data can be input and output to a disc unit. If the source of data is to come from a disc-based file named a:numbers.txt, and the output is to be written to a file called a:results.txt then redirection is possible by modifying the command line statement used for running the program. The command line to redirect input and output for a program named Streams would be defined as:

C> **Streams < a:numbers.txt > a:results.txt**, where C> is the MSDOS prompt.

The following program is similar to the previous example. The functions fscanf and fprintf have been substituted by scanf and printf, respectively, and the program is run using the command line given above.

```
/* program to demonstrate redirection for input and output */
#include <stdio.h>
main()
{
        int integer;
        int sum = 0;
        int counter = 0;
        int mean;
        scanf("%d", &integer);
        while (integer != 0)
        {
                sum = sum + integer;
                printf("sum of integers so far .. %d\n", sum);
                ++counter;
                scanf("%d", &integer);
        }
        mean = sum / counter;
        printf("mean value of integers is %d\n", mean);
}
```

The contents of the text file numbers.txt, created using an editor, and stored on disc drive (a) was:

8   4   2   9   2   0

and after the command **Streams < a:numbers.txt > a:results.txt** and the program had been executed, the contents of the text file results.txt, stored on disc drive a was:

sum of integers so far .. 8
sum of integers so far .. 12
sum of integers so far .. 14
sum of integers so far .. 23
sum of integers so far .. 25
mean value of integers is 5

5.3 Opening and closing files

In using standard input and output streams as files it was not necessary to open or close the streams, since this is performed automatically by the system. However, when the programmer defines new streams it is necessary to open a file before it can be used. Similarly when a file is no longer required, or the mode of access is to change, then it should be closed.

A file can be opened using the function fopen, whose declaration in the library reference manual is described as:

FILE *fopen(const char *path, const char *type);

where the function opens the file specified by path, and associates a stream with that file. The character string type specifies the access mode for the file, and can be any of the following.

"r"	Read only - file must exist
"w"	Write only - file need not exist
"a"	Write only from the end of the file - file need not exist
"r+", and "w+"	Read and write starting at the beginning of the file
"a+"	Read and append.

In addition to these values the characters 't' or 'b' may be added after the first character of mode to specify text or binary files respectively.

The function fopen returns a pointer to the open stream. If the stream could not be successfully opened a NULL pointer is returned.

There are three ways in which the name of a file can be input into a program.

(i) The name can be implicitly contained in the fopen statement, for example:

```
FILE *text;
text = fopen("a:text.txt", "r");
```

where a:text.txt implies that a file with the name text.txt may exist in the directory of the disc held on drive a.

(ii) The name of the file can be input at run-time, prior to the file being opened, for example:

```
FILE *text;
char *filename;
{
        filename = malloc(30);
        printf("input the path and name of the file ");
        gets(filename);
        text = fopen(filename, "r");
        .
        .
```

(iii) The names of files can be passed as arguments in a command line when giving the command to run a program. For example if a program file called *prog.exe* had been created that required the names of the data files *file1.txt, file2.txt and file3.txt* to be passed to the main program as parameters, the command line would be input as:

>   prog   file1.txt   file2.txt   file3.txt

To accommodate these program parameters the function main must contain the parameters argc and argv, as follows:

>   main (int argc, char *argv[])

where argc is the number of command line parameters including the name of the program, in this example argv is 4; argv[] is an array of pointers to the command line parameters, in this example argv[0] points to prog, argv[1] points to file1.txt, argv[2] points to file2.txt, argv[3] points to file3.txt and argv[4] is a null pointer.

During run-time if a program attempted to open a file that did not exist the program would be suspended. To overcome this problem it is possible to check whether the number of command line arguments is correct and whether the files exist if they are to be read.

The following segment of code will check whether the correct number of parameters in the command line

>   prog   file1.txt   file2.txt   file3.txt

are present.

```
main ( int argc, char *argv[])
{
        FILE *filename1, *filename2, *filename3;
        if (argc != 4)
        {
                fprintf(stderr, "ERROR - command line arguments\a\n");
                exit(errno);
        }
        .
```

The next segment of code can be used to check whether a file can be opened for reading.

```
        filename1 = fopen(argv[1], "r");
        if (filename1 == NULL)
        {
                fprintf(stderr, "ERROR - file %s cannot be opened\a\n", argv[1]);
                exit(errno);
        }
        .
        fclose(filename1); fclose(filename2); fclose(filename3);
        .
}
```

Warning! When defining a path for a particular file be careful of the use of backslash. The compiler will treat \ in a string literal as the beginning of an escape character. For example in the statement fopen("a:\book\text.txt", "w"); the compiler would treat \b and \t as escape characters and return a null pointer. When a backslash is required use \\, hence the statement is changed to fopen("a:\\book\\text.txt", "w").

In these segments of code the function exit(errno), defined in the header file <stdlib.h>, causes a program to terminate, where errno is a global variable that can be set by library functions. The value of errno indicates the type of error that has occurred. A value of zero implies no error.

A file is closed by using the fclose function. In the previous segment of code fclose(filename1), fclose(filename2), and fclose(filename3) close the streams filename1, filename2 and filename3, respectively.

5.4 Text files

A text file is a collection of ASCII characters, written in lines, with a specific end of line marker, and an end of file marker. Text files can be created using an editor, in the same way as programs are created. Alternatively, a text file can be created from within a program, by writing information to a file that has been opened in the appropriate mode.

The following library functions, found in the header file <stdio.h> are used to create text files.

int fputc(int c, FILE *stream); writes a character c to stream, if an error occurs it returns a negative integer constant EOF, otherwise it returns the ASCII code for the character.

int fputs(const char *s, FILE *stream); writes the string s to stream; note fputs does not write a new line character unless one is present in s; if an error occurs it returns a negative integer constant EOF, otherwise it returns a non-negative integer.

int fprintf(FILE *stream, const char *format, ...); writes a variable number of data items to an output stream, using a format string to control the appearance of the output; if an error occurs it returns a negative value, otherwise it returns the number of characters that were written

The following functions, found in the header file <stdio.h> are used to read from text files.

int fgetc(FILE *stream); reads a character from stream; if the end of the input file is reached or an error occurs it returns a negative integer constant EOF, otherwise it returns the ASCII code for the character that was read.

char *fgets(char *s, int n, FILE *stream); reads from stream into the array that s points to, stopping at the first newline character or when n-1 characters have been read. The newline character, if read, is stored in the array. If the end of the input file is reached or an error occurs the function returns a null pointer, otherwise a pointer to the string read is returned.

int fscanf(FILE *stream, const char *format, ...); reads any number of data items from stream, using format to indicate the layout of input. If the end of the file is reached or an error occurs the function returns a negative integer constant EOF, otherwise the function returns the number of items of data read.

In order to explicitly test whether the end of file has been reached there is an end of file function feof which has the format: **int feof(FILE *stream);** and returns a non-zero value if the end of stream has been reached.

In the following example the poem "I watched a blackbird" by Thomas Hardy 1840-1928 has been created using an editor and stored on disc under the filename Hardy.txt. A listing of the poem is given here.

> I watched a blackbird on a budding sycamore
> One Easter Day, when sap was stirring twigs to the core;
> I saw his tongue, and crocus-coloured bill
> Parting and closing as he turned his trill;
> Then he flew down, seized on a stem of hay,
> And upped to where his building scheme was under way,
> As if so sure a nest were never shaped on spray.

The program is to read the text file, and process each line such that:

(i) the number of letters in each word is analysed, and a frequency count is recorded for word size;

(ii) each line of text is written to a second file, and the frequency of word lengths in the line are written on the next line of the file; for example:

> I watched a blackbird on a budding sycamore
> 3 1 0 0 0 0 2 1 1 0 0 0 0 0 0

indicating three one-letter words, one two-letter word, two seven-letter words, one eight-letter word and one nine-letter word.

(iii) when the end of the file is reached, the total frequency of all word lengths in the file is written at the end of the second file.

```
/* program to analyse the size of words in a passage of text */

#include <stdio.h>
#include <stdlib.h>
#define MaxLength 80
#define MaxChar 15
#define null 00
#define space 040
#define hyphen 055
#define comma 054
#define period 056
#define colon 072
#define SemiColon 073
#define CR 015
#define LF 012

int TotalFrequency[MaxChar+1];
FILE *text, *output;
```

```
/* function to initialise the frequency count for each word to zero */
void initialise(int frequency[])
{
        int CharacterCount;

        for (CharacterCount = 1; CharacterCount <= MaxChar;
                frequency[CharacterCount] = 0, ++CharacterCount);
}

/* function to open both files */
void OpenFiles(void)
{
        text = fopen("a:Hardy.txt", "r");
        if (text == NULL)
        {
                fprintf(stderr, "ERROR - file a:Hardy.txt cannot be opened\a\n");
                exit(errno);
        }
        output = fopen("a:analysis.txt", "w");
}

/* function to close both files */
void CloseFiles(void)
{
        fclose(text);
        fclose(output);
}

/* function to count the size of each word in one line of text; the frequencies of word lengths are stored in
an array called LineFrequency; after each line has been processed the frequencies are added to the
cumulative frequencies for all words that have been processed */
void analysis(char line[], int frequency[])
{
        int index, CharacterCount;
        char character;

        index = 0; /* subscript used to process line of text */
        CharacterCount = 0;
        character = line[index];
        while (index <= MaxLength && character != null)
        {
                if (      character != space &&
                          character != hyphen &&
                          character != comma &&
                          character != period &&
                          character != colon &&
                          character != SemiColon &&
                          character != CR &&
                          character != LF      )
```

88

```
                ++CharacterCount;
        else
        {
                ++frequency[CharacterCount];
                CharacterCount = 0;
        }
        ++index;
        character = line[index];
    }
    for (CharacterCount = 1; CharacterCount <= MaxChar;
        TotalFrequency[CharacterCount] =
        TotalFrequency[CharacterCount] + frequency[CharacterCount],
        ++CharacterCount);
}
```

```
/* function to copy a line from the input file to the output file, and write the frequency of word sizes on the
next line of the output file; the first number represents the number of 1 letter words, second number
represents 2 letter words, third number 3 letter words, etc */

void WriteInfo(char line[], int frequency[])
{
    int CharacterCount;
    fprintf(output, "%s", line);
    for (CharacterCount = 1; CharacterCount <= MaxChar;
        fprintf(output, "%3d", frequency[CharacterCount]), ++CharacterCount);
    fprintf(output, "\n");
}
```

```
/* function to read a line from the input file */
void ReadData(void)
{
    char line[MaxLength + 1];
    int LineFrequency[MaxChar + 1];

    initialise(LineFrequency);
    fgets(line, MaxLength, text);
    while (feof(text) == 0)
    {
        analysis(line, LineFrequency);
        WriteInfo(line, LineFrequency);
        initialise(LineFrequency);
        fgets(line, MaxLength, text);
    }
}
```

```
main()
{
    initialise(TotalFrequency);
    OpenFiles();
```

```
        ReadData();
        WriteInfo("", TotalFrequency);
        CloseFiles();
}
```

The results from running this program are stored in the text file analysis.txt, a listing follows.

```
I watched a blackbird on a budding sycamore
3 1 0 0 0 0 2 1 1 0 0 0 0 0 0
One Easter Day, when sap was stirring twigs to the core;
0 1 5 2 1 1 0 1 0 0 0 0 0 0 0
I saw his tongue, and crocus-coloured bill
1 0 3 1 0 2 0 1 0 0 0 0 0 0 0
Parting and closing as he turned his trill;
0 2 2 0 1 1 2 0 0 0 0 0 0 0 0
Then he flew down, seized on a stem of hay,
1 3 1 4 0 1 0 0 0 0 0 0 0 0 0
And upped to where his building scheme was under way,
0 1 4 0 3 1 0 1 0 0 0 0 0 0 0
As if so sure a nest were never shaped on spray.
1 4 0 3 2 1 0 0 0 0 0 0 0 0 0
6 12 15 10 7 7 4 4 1 0 0 0 0 0 0
```

5.5 Binary files

A binary file consists of a sequence of arbitrary bytes that are not in a human-readable form. Such files can only be created by a specific program, they cannot, unlike a text file, be created using an editor.

There are two functions associated with input and output of binary files, fread and fwrite, respectively. The format of fread is:

```
size_t fread(void *buffer, size_t size, size_t nritems, FILE *stream);
```

where the function fread reads a specified number of data elements from a stream;

buffer points to the block in which the data will be stored; size specifies the size (in bytes) of each element being read; nritems specifies the number of items to be read; and stream specifies the stream from which the data will be read.

The function fread returns the number of complete items read. If this value is less than nritems, use feof or ferror to determine whether the end of file was reached or whether another error occurred. The fwrite function has a similar format to fread:

```
int fwrite(const void *buffer, size_t size, size_t num, FILE *st);
```

where the fwrite writes up to num blocks, each of size bytes, from buffer to the stream st. The stream pointer, if there is one, is incremented by the number of bytes written. However, if an error occurs, the position of the stream pointer or the state of a partially written item are undefined.

The function returns the number of complete items actually written. If an error or end of file condition occurs, this number will be less than num. Again the functions ferror or feof should be used to determine which condition caused fwrite to terminate. If either num or size is zero, the return value will be zero and no bytes are written.

In the example that follows, a binary file is to be created that contains records relating to properties. The format of a property record in the file is:

address	50 characters;	
price	long integer;	
type	1 character	coded A semi-detached
		B terraced
		C flat;
number of bedrooms	integer;	
tenure	1 character	coded F freehold
		L leasehold

The data for each field of a record is input at a keyboard, and stored in an array called properties. The maximum size of this array has been set at 100. When no further records are input the contents of the array is sorted into ascending order on the type of property. The contents of the sorted array is then written to the file data.bin on drive a, using the statement:

```
fwrite(properties, sizeof(details), size, data);
```

where sizeof(details) is the number of bytes in a record, size is the number of records stored in the array and data is the name given to the file a:data.bin.

```
/* program to create a binary file of records, sorted into ascending order on type of dwelling */

#include <stdio.h>
#define MaxCapacity 100
#define yes 'y'

typedef     struct {
                    char address[50];
                    long int price;
                    char type;
                    int bedrooms;
                    char tenure;
            } details;

details properties[MaxCapacity];
FILE *data;

/* function to sort the records on the key property type using an insertion sort */
void sort(int size)
{
     details current;
     int index, location;
```

```
        for (index=1; index < size; ++index)
        {
                current = properties[index];
                location = index;
                while (location > 0 && properties[location - 1].type > current.type)
                {
                        properties[location] = properties[location - 1];
                        --location;
                }
                properties[location] = current;
        }
}

/* function to collect data for each record */
int GetRecords(void)
{
        int records = 0;
        char reply;

        printf("input the following details of properties\n\n");
        do
        {
                printf("address ");
                gets(properties[records].address);
                printf("price ");
                scanf("%ld", &properties[records].price); getchar();
                printf("type - A semi, B terraced, C flat ");
                properties[records].type = getchar();
                printf("number of bedrooms ");
                scanf("%d", &properties[records].bedrooms); getchar();
                printf("tenure - F(reehold), L(easehold) ");
                properties[records].tenure = getchar(); getchar();
                ++records;
                printf("\nmore data y(es) or n(o) ? ");
                reply = getchar(); getchar();
        } while (reply == yes);
        return records;
}


main()
{
        int size;
        data = fopen("a:data.bin", "wb");
        size = GetRecords();
        sort(size);
        fwrite(properties, sizeof(details), size, data);
        fclose(data);
}
```

The binary file created in the previous program cannot be examined correctly using either an editor or by using the TYPE command in MSDOS. Another program must be written to open the file, store the records into an array, and display the contents of the array on a screen. The output can of course be redirected to a text file if required.

```c
/* program to access a binary file of records */

#include <stdio.h>
#include <stdlib.h>
#define MaxCapacity 100
#define yes 'y'

typedef         struct {
                        char address[50];
                        long int price;
                        char dwelling;
                        int bedrooms;
                        char tenure;
                } details;

details properties[MaxCapacity];
FILE *data;

main()
{
        int records, index;

        data = fopen("a:data.bin", "rb");
        if (data == NULL)
        {
                fprintf(stderr, "ERROR - file a:data.bin cannot be opened\a\n");
                exit(errno);
        }
        records = fread(properties, sizeof(details), MaxCapacity, data);

        for (index=0; index < records; ++index)
        {
                printf("%s\t",properties[index].address);
                printf("%ld\t", properties[index].price);
                putchar(properties[index].dwelling); printf("\t");
                printf("%d\t", properties[index].bedrooms);
                putchar(properties[index].tenure);
                printf("\n");
        }

        fclose(data);
}
```

The following listing illustrates the output from the program.

93

2 Liberal Walk	45675 A 4 F
69 Church View	44350 A 3 F
3 Hope St	43000 B 3 F
145 River View	36750 B 3 F
27 Ridge Bank	36750 C 3 L

The final program in this section demonstrates how the contents of the property file data.bin can be interrogated. The contents of the file is copied to the array properties and searched according to the criteria: property type A, B or C; or price range; or both property type and price range.

/* program to access a binary file of records, store the information into an array and search the array on categories type or price or both categories */

```c
#include <stdio.h>
#include <stdlib.h>
#define MaxCapacity 100
#define yes 'y'

typedef        struct {
                              char address[50];
                              long int price;
                              char dwelling;
                              int bedrooms;
                              char tenure;
                     } details;

details properties[MaxCapacity];
FILE *data;
int MenuCode;
char PropertyType;
long int LowerPrice, UpperPrice;

/* function to open the property file and read the file and store the records into an array,
then close the file */

void ReadData(details properties[], int *size)
{
     data = fopen("a:data.bin", "rb");
     if (data == NULL)
     {
             fprintf(stderr, "ERROR - file a:data.bin cannot be opened\a\n");
             exit(errno);
     }
     *size = fread(properties, sizeof(details), MaxCapacity, data);
     fclose(data);
}

/* function to display a menu on the screen and capture a user's selection */
int menu(void)
```

94

```
{
        int code;

        printf("Do you want to search on:\n\n");
        printf("1 - property type A, B or C\n");
        printf("2 - price range\n");
        printf("3 - both (1) and (2)\n\n");
        printf("input selection 1, 2 or 3 ");
        scanf("%d", &code); getchar();
        return code;
}
```

/* function to input data according to the menu code chosen */

```
void InputData(int MenuCode, char *PropertyType, long int *LowerPrice, long int *UpperPrice)
{
        long int lower, upper;
        if (MenuCode == 1 || MenuCode == 3)
        {
                printf("input property type ");
                *PropertyType = getchar();
                getchar();
        }
        if (MenuCode == 2 || MenuCode == 3)
        {
                printf("input lower price ");
                scanf("%ld", &lower);
                printf("input upper price ");
                scanf("%ld", &upper); getchar();
                *LowerPrice = lower;
                *UpperPrice = upper;
        }
}
```

/* function to display on the screen one record from the array */

```
void display(details record)
{
        printf("\n\n");
        printf("address: %s\n",record.address);
        printf("price: £%ld\n", record.price);
        printf("type of property ");
        if      (record.dwelling == 'A') printf("semi-detached\n");
        else if (record.dwelling == 'B') printf("terraced\n");
        else    printf("flat\n");

        printf("bedrooms: %d\n", record.bedrooms);
        printf("tenure of property ");
```

```
            if (record.tenure == 'F') printf("freehold\n\n");
            else printf("leasehold\n\n");
}

/* function to search the array for details according to the user's selection */
void search(int MenuCode, int size, details properties[], char PropertyType,
            long int LowerPrice, long int UpperPrice)
{
        int index = 0;
        if (MenuCode == 1)
        while (index < size &&
                properties[index].dwelling <= PropertyType)
        {
                if (properties[index].dwelling == PropertyType)
                display(properties[index]);
                ++index;
        }
        else if (MenuCode == 2)
        while (index < size)
        {
                if (properties[index].price >= LowerPrice && properties[index].price <= UpperPrice)
                        display(properties[index]);
                ++index;
        }
        else
        while (index < size && properties[index].dwelling <= PropertyType)
        {
                if      (properties[index].dwelling == PropertyType &&
                        properties[index].price >= LowerPrice && properties[index].price <= UpperPrice)
                        display(properties[index]);
                ++index;
        }
}

main()
{
        int size;
        char reply;
        ReadData(properties, &size);
        do
        {
                MenuCode = menu();
                InputData(MenuCode, &PropertyType, &LowerPrice, &UpperPrice);
                search(MenuCode, size, properties, PropertyType, LowerPrice, UpperPrice);
                printf("do you want information y(es) or n(o) ");
                reply = getchar(); getchar();
        }
        while (reply == yes);
}
```

96

The following listing illustrates the output when the program was executed.

Do you want to search on:
1 - property type A, B or C
2 - price range
3 - both (1) and (2)
input selection 1, 2 or 3 1
input property type B

address: 3 Hope St
price: £43000
type of property terraced
bedrooms: 3
tenure of property freehold

address: 145 River View
price: £36750
type of property terraced
bedrooms: 3
tenure of property freehold

do you want information y(es) or n(o) y

Do you want to search on:
1 - property type A, B or C
2 - price range
3 - both (1) and (2)
input selection 1, 2 or 3 2
input lower price 44000
input upper price 46000

address: 2 Liberal Walk
price: £45675
type of property semi-detached
bedrooms: 4
tenure of property freehold

address: 69 Church View
price: £44350
type of property semi-detached
bedrooms: 3
tenure of property freehold

do you want information y(es) or n(o) y

Do you want to search on:
1 - property type A, B or C
2 - price range
3 - both (1) and (2)

input selection 1, 2 or 3 3
input property type B
input lower price 40000
input upper price 45000

address: 3 Hope St
price: £43000
type of property terraced
bedrooms: 3
tenure of property freehold

do you want information y(es) or n(o) n

5.6 Random access

The organisation of the text and binary files means that it is necessary to read each record in a file until the required record is located. With a random access file it is possible to go directly to the record that is required without having to search through the records in the file.

The function fseek moves the file pointer associated with the specified stream. The pointer is moved to a location that is offset bytes from the specified origin. The next operation on the stream will take place at the new location.

The format of fseek is **int fseek(FILE *stream, long offset, int origin);**

where stream specifies the file name; offset the number of bytes to move from the origin, and origin specifies the reference location for the move. Origin must be one of the following values:

SEEK_SET	beginning of the file;
SEEK_CUR	current file position;
SEEK_END	end of file.

In the final example of the chapter a text file music.txt stored on drive a, contains lines of text showing the position, title and artist of popular music in the Top Ten. A copy of the file follows.

6 Living Doll Cliff Richard
8 Under the Boardwalk Rolling Stones
3 Ferry across the Mersey Gerry and the Pacemakers
1 Love me tender Elvis Presley
2 Stranger on the Shore Acker Bilk
4 Good Golly Miss Molly Gerry Lee Lewis
5 She Loves You The Beatles
7 Blowing in the Wind Peter, Paul and Mary
9 The Urban Spaceman Bonzo Dog Do Dah Band
10 Puple haze Jimmy Hendrix

Each record in this file is transferred to an array and stored at the Top Ten position indicated in the text file. For example Love me tender by Elvis Presley would be stored at index 1 in the array, Under the Boardwalk by the Rolling Stones would be stored at index 8 in the array. The contents of the array is then written to a binary file. It is then possible to position the file pointer so that any tune from the Top Ten can be selected by using the statement fseek(TopTen, (long int)position * sizeof(information), SEEK_SET)

```c
/* program to demonstrate random access to a binary file */

#include <stdio.h>
#include <stdlib.h>
typedef struct {char record[60];} information;
FILE *data; /* text file */
FILE *TopTen; /* random access file */
information chart[11];

/* function to read a text file and transfer the information to a binary file */
void transfer(void)
{
        int position;
        data = fopen("a:music.txt", "r");
        if (data == NULL)
        {
                fprintf(stderr, "ERROR - file a:music.txt cannot be opened\a\n");
                exit(errno);
        }
        TopTen = fopen("a:pop.bin", "wb");
        fscanf(data, "%d", &position);
        while (feof(data) == 0)
        {
                fgets(chart[position].record, 60, data);
                fscanf(data, "%d", &position);
        }
        fclose(data);
        fwrite(chart, sizeof(information), 11, TopTen);
        fclose(TopTen);
}

/* function to return the tune and performer given the position */
void PopPicker(void)
{
        int position;
        information line[1];

        TopTen = fopen("a:pop.bin", "rb");
        printf("input chart position (zero to exit) ");
        scanf("%d", &position);
        while (position >= 1 && position <= 10)
        {
                fseek(TopTen, (long int) position * sizeof(information), SEEK_SET);
                fread(line, sizeof(information), 1, TopTen);
                printf("%s\n\n", line);
                printf("input chart position (zero to exit) ");
```

```
            scanf("%d", &position);
      }
      fclose(TopTen);
}

main()
{
      transfer();
      PopPicker();
}
```

A sample of the output from this program follows.

input chart position (zero to exit) 1
Love me tender Elvis Presley

input chart position (zero to exit) 5
She Loves You The Beatles

input chart position (zero to exit) 3
Ferry across the Mersey Gerry and the Pacemakers

input chart position (zero to exit) 10
Puple haze Jimmy Hendrix

input chart position (zero to exit) 0

5.7 Summary

• All input and output in C is from streams. A stream can be regarded as a file, however, it is not confined to disc or tape files, but extends to other devices such as keyboard, screen and printer.

• Input and output can be redirected using command line parameters.

• A file can be opened for reading as long as it exists. However, a file opened for writing need not already exist. If it does the original file will be overwritten. A file can also be opened in an append mode, in which case data can be inserted at the end of a file.

• The name of a file can be input into a program implicitly at the time of writing the program; as a text string at run-time; or as a parameter in a command line at run-time.

• A text file is a collection of ASCII characters separated into lines by end of line characters. A text file can be created using either an editor or a program.

• The stdio.h header file lists the following functions for processing text files:

      for output - fputc, fputs and fprintf;
      for input - fgetc, fgets and fscanf;
      for detecting the end of the file - feof.

● Binary files cannot be created using an editor, but are a product of a specific program. Information is read or written to binary files in blocks of data using the functions fread and fwrite respectively.

● Random access files are normally binary files. The position of any record in the file can be specified, thereby making access to the information direct.

5.8 Questions   *answers begin on page 265*

1. Using an editor create a text file containing words, one per line, translated into Morse code. Write a program to read the file and translate the Morse code back into words in English. Display the results of the translation on the screen.

```
A  . -       H  . . . .      O  - - -      V  . . . -
B  - . . .    I  . .          P  . - - .    W  . - -
C  - . - .    J  . - - -      Q  - - . -    X  - . . -
D  - . .      K  - . -        R  . - .      Y  - . - -
E  .          L  . - . .      S  . . .      Z  - - . .
F  . . - .    M  - -          T  -
G  - - .      N  - .          U  . . -
```

The Morse code for the alphabet

2. Create a binary file containing records with the following format for subscribers to a telephone network.

surname and initials	20 characters;
telephone number	20 characters;
previous meter reading	integer;
current meter reading	integer.

Sort the file into alphabetical sequence on surname and initials as the primary key.

Read each record from the file and create a text file report containing the following information. You may assume that units used, is the difference between current and previous meter readings, and the current reading is always greater than the previous reading.

TELEPHONE SUBSCRIBERS

NAME	NUMBER	UNITS USED
Allen P	Abingdon 41937	2719
Brown J	Oxford 2245643	645
Carter F	Banbury 212	1768
.	.	.
.	.	.

3. A building society keeps on file details of its customers holding ordinary share accounts. An account record contains the following information.

branch code	12 characters;
account number	6 characters;
name of account holder	20 characters;
number of £1 shares	integer.

Assume that the file is already sorted on branch code as primary key in ascending order and account number as secondary key also in ascending order. Create a test data file and write a program to read the file and display the following report on a screen.

```
           THE  XYZ  BUILDING SOCIETY
     DETAILS OF ORDINARY SHARE ACCOUNT CUSTOMERS

   BRANCH CODE: OXFORD

   ACCOUNT NUMBER          NAME            £1 SHARES

   114345                 Smith J          1000
   141456                 Jones K          550
   .                      .                .
   .                      .                .

                          TOTAL            23456


   BRANCH CODE:  POOLE

   ACCOUNT NUMBER          NAME            £1 SHARES

   101456                 Brown H          2000
   .                      .                .
   .                      .                .
```

The algorithm to read the shares file and display the report on the screen follows.

open share file for reading
display first two headings
read a record from the share file
WHILE NOT EOF(share file) DO
    store branch code
    display branch code and display sub-heading
    initialise total number of £1 shares to zero
    WHILE NOT EOF(share file) and same branch code DO
        display account number and number of £1 shares
        increase total by number of £1 shares

> *read record from the share file*
> > **END**
> > *display total number of £1 shares in the branch*
> **END**
> *close share: file*

4. In a simplified weekly wages system factory employees are allocated one record per employee on a wages master file. The format of a record on this file is:

employee number	4 characters;
employee name	20 characters;
hourly rate of pay	float;
fixed allowances against pay	float;
total gross income to date	float;
total tax paid to date	float;
total pension contributions to date	float;
total NI contributions to date	float.

For every employee the pension contribution is 6% of the gross income, the National Insurance (NI) is £10.50 and income tax is levied at 30% of the taxable income. Taxable income is calculated as the difference between gross income and pension contributions and fixed allowances.

A transaction file contains records with the following format.

employee number	4 characters;
hours worked per week	float.

Write a program to process the transaction file against the master file and print pay-slips for each employee on the transaction file.

Assume that both files are sorted on employee number as the primary key. For every employee on the transaction file a record exists on the master file, and the number of records on both files is the same.

The format of a payslip is given below.

Employee Number: 3456	**Employee Name: Harris, K.M**	
	Gross wage:	**307.69**
	Pension:	**18.46**
	NI:	**10.50**
	Tax:	**77.77**
Net wage: 200.96		

5. Write a program to store, in a direct-access binary file, the contents of a daily diary for a non-leap year. The key to an entry in the diary is the day number, which is calculated from the date. The diary is used to record a one line entry (maximum of 60 characters), for each day in a non-leap year. The program should be menu driven and allow for:

(a) the creation of a new diary;

(b) the insertion and deletion of entries on a daily basis;

(c) listing the contents of the diary by month.

6.
Further topics

As the penultimate chapter of part one, it serves to bring together a miscellany of features of the language that could not be classified under the headings of the previous chapters.

Contents

6.1 Macro definitions

Simple macros, for example:

```
#define     pi      3.14159
#define     magic   "abracadabra"
```

have already been defined in earlier chapters and have the format

```
#define identifier replacement list
```

An alternative format for a macro will allow parameters to be included in the identifier:

```
#define identifier(p1, p2 ... pn) replacement list
```

where p1, p2 .. pn are the macro's formal parameters.

The reader has already come across function macros such as:

```
#define getchar() fgetc(stdin)
#define putchar(c) fputc((c), stdout)
```

from the opening chapter.

In both the simple macro and parametrised macro the preprocessor scans the source program and replaces the macro identifier with the contents of the replacement list.

In the following program a conditional expression has been used in the replacement list as a means of finding the smallest of two numbers.

To recapitulate, the conditional expression exp1 ? exp2: exp3 is evaluated such that if exp1 is true (1) then exp2 is the value of the conditional expression, otherwise if exp1 is false (0) then exp3 is the value of the conditional expression. The macro expression #define smallest(X,Y) ((X)<(Y) ? (X):(Y)) implies that if X<Y is true the value of X is returned, otherwise if X<Y is false the value of Y is returned.

Using conditional expressions it is possible to define a function that will convert letters of the alphabet to lower case if they appear as upper case.

```
#define ToLower(c) ('A'< = (c) && (c) <='Z' ? (c) + 'a'-'A' : (c))
```

In this macro expression if the parameter (c) is an upper case letter then the expression (c) +'a'-'A' will be evaluated, giving the lower case equivalent of the letter. If the letter is already in lower case then it remains as (c).

Using parametrised macros and conditional expressions it is possible to define a whole range of functions. This example program defines two validation functions. One to validate a digit:

```
#define digit(x) ('0'< =(x) && (x)<='9' ? TRUE : FALSE)
```

and the other to validate a character as being either in the range A-Z or a-z:

#define letter(L) ('a'<=ToLower(L) && ToLower(L) <= 'z' ? TRUE : FALSE)

Notice that it is permissible to include in a macro previously defined macros.

```
/* program to demonstrate the use of macros */
#include <stdio.h>

#define smallest(X,Y) ((X)<(Y) ? (X):(Y))
#define ToLower(c) ('A'<= (c) && (c) <='Z' ? (c) + 'a'-'A' : (c))
#define TRUE 1
#define FALSE 0
#define digit(x) ('0'<=(x) && (x)<='9' ? TRUE : FALSE)
#define letter(L) ('a'<=ToLower(L) && ToLower(L) <= 'z' ? TRUE : FALSE)

int     first, second;
char    letter;
int     character;

main()
{
        printf("input a pair of numbers ");
        scanf("%d%d", &first, &second); getchar();
        printf("smallest number is %d\n", smallest(first,second));
        printf("input a single alphabetic character ");
        scanf("%c", &letter); getchar();
        printf("lower case letter is %c\n", ToLower(letter));
        printf("input a single character ");
        scanf("%c", &character);
        if digit(character)
                printf("digit\n");
        else if letter(character)
                printf("letter\n");
        else
                printf("cannot classify\n");
}
```

results

input a pair of numbers 25 3
smallest number is 3
input a single alphabetic character Q
lower case letter is q
input a single character ;
cannot classify

Using a parametrised macro instead of a function call has the following advantages.

(i) The program code may run slightly faster.

(ii) A macro can be used with parameters of any type, provided the context of the parameters is consistent with the rest of the program.

The disadvantages of using a macro instead of a function are:

(i) Because the replacement list is inserted in-line with the program code, the compiled code will often be larger.

(ii) Macros cannot be passed as parameters in a function call.

(iii) A macro may evaluate its parameters more than once.

The next example program serves to introduce the # operator, and to illustrate that a parametrised macro can be used as a template for code that is used many times in a program.

The # operator converts a macro parameter into a string literal, for example in the definition:

```
#define        printer(x) printf(#x "=%d\n", x)
```

#x will be replaced by the string literal for x. The statement printer(A) would display A = 3, if the value of A was 3.

Notice in the second macro definition of the program:

```
#define        input(y) (printf("input " #y " "), scanf("%d",&y))
```

that it is possible to include more than one statement in a replacement list, provided the statements are separated by the comma operator.

```
/* program to demonstrate the use of the # operator */
#include <stdio.h>

#define printer(x) printf(#x "=%d\n", x)
#define input(y) (printf("input " #y " "), scanf("%d",&y))

int a,b;

main()
{
        input(a);
        input(b);
        printer(a+b);
        printer(a-b);
        printer(a*b);
        if (a != 0) printer(b/a);
}
```

results

input a 15
input b 24
a+b=39
a-b=-9
a*b=360
b/a=1

There also exists a ## operator used to paste symbols together.

For example #define var(i) Y##i when used in float var(0), var(1), var(2) would produce float Y0, Y1, Y2

Finally the scope of a macro normally covers the entire program from the definition of the macro to the end of the program. The scope can be confined by using the statement #undef identifier at the place in the program where the macro is not to be used any further.

6.2 Conditional compilation

There is a group of preprocessor directives that can be used to stipulate which segments of code are to be compiled. The directives are:

#if, #ifdef, #ifndef, #elsif, #else and #endif

The practice of commenting-out source code, that might contain comments, when testing a program cannot be achieved in C, since nested comments are not allowed. However, by using the preprocessor directive #if .. #end, it is possible to delimit a segment of program that should not be compiled.

```
#define FALSE 0

#if FALSE
        lines of code to temporarily omit
#endif
```

Since the expression after #if is (0) all the statements up to #endif will be ignored by the compiler. If the macro definition was re-written as #define FALSE 1 then the expression after #if would be true and the statements after the expression would be compiled.

External variables are declared outside the body of a function and can be shared by several functions in different files.

If the function main, stored in file main.c, contained the code:

```
#define MAIN
#include <definition.h>
int flag; /* global variable */
.
.
```

then the declaration of the integer variable flag would not require to be declared as an external variable in this function. This would be ensured if the header file <definitions.h> contained the statement:

```
#ifndef MAIN
        extern int flag;
#endif
```

#ifndef tests whether a particular identifier is not defined in a macro. In the file main.c, MAIN has been defined, therefore, the declaration of flag as an external integer is not required. However, in other files that include the header file <definition.h> the identifier flag will be declared as an external integer variable.

There are plenty of other examples of the use of conditional compilation directives as illustrated in the following part listing of the header file <stdio.h>.

.

.

```
#ifndef _SIZE_T
#define _SIZE_T
typedef unsigned size_t;
#endif


#ifndef NULL
#ifndef _fptr
#define NULL 0
#else
#define NULL 0L
#endif
#endif


#ifndef _STDARG_INC_
#include <stdarg.h>
#endif
#ifndef _ERRNOS_INC_
#define _ERRNOS_INC_
```

.

.

```
#ifdef _mthread
#define errno * _errno__()
#define _doserrno * _errno__()
int * _errno__(void);
#else
extern int _doserrno; /* global DOS error variable */
extern int errno; /* global error variable */
#endif
```

.

.

6.3 Bit manipulation

There are six operators, which operate on integer and character operands at the bit level.

There are two shift operators.

$<<$ left shift - the value of a $<<$ b is the result when a is shifted left b positions. Zero bits are added at the right end to replace the bits that are shifted out.

For example, if a = 0xFABA (hexadecimal), a = 1111101010111010 (binary); then a $<<$ 5 gives a result 0101011101000000

$>>$ right shift - the value of a $>>$ b is the result when a is shifted right b positions. If a is unsigned or non-negative then zero bits are added to the left of the number. If the number is negative the result is implementation dependent. The JPI TopSpeed compiler propagates the sign bit.

For example, if a = 1111101010111010 then a $>>$ 4 gives the result 1111111110101011

In addition to the shift operators there are bit operators to provide:

$\sim$ complement;	c = 01101110	$\sim$c = 10010001
& and;	c = 00001011 and d = 11111100 then	c & d = 00001000
$\wedge$ exclusive or;	c $\wedge$ d = 11110111	
| inclusive or;	c | d = 11111111	

Warning! The bit operators & and | are not equivalent to the logical operators && and ||.

The following program illustrates the six bit operators described.

```
/* program to illustrate bit manipulation */
#include <stdio.h>

#define print(x) printf(#x "= %d\n", x);

int i=0x00FF, j=0x000F;

main()
{
    print(i);
    print(j);
    print(i << 8); /* shift left by 8 bits */
    print(j >> 2); /* shift right by 2 bits */
    print(~ j); /* take one's complement of j */
    print(i & j); /* bitwise i AND j */
    print(i | j); /* bitwise i inclusive OR j */
    print(i ^ j); /* bitwise i exclusive OR j */
}
```

results

i = 255
j = 15
i < < 8 = -256
j > > 2 = 3
~j = -16
i & j = 15
i | j = 255
i ^ j = 240

The bit operators &, ^ and | can be combined with = to provide compound assignment operators & =, ^ = and | = respectively, where the result is always stored in the first of the binary operands.

The following program illustrates how to modify bits within a number, by using the appropriate bit masks.

For example, the bit mask 0x8000 (hexadecimal) 1000000000000000 (binary) will set the sign bit of a 16-bit number when used with or (i | = 0x8000).

The bit mask 0x7FFF (hexadecimal) 0111111111111111 (binary) will clear the sign bit of a 16-bit number when used with and (j & = 0x7FFF).

Individual bits can be extracted using bit masks, and tested in an if statement where (0) false, (1) true.

A bit field (group of consecutive bits) can be modified by first clearing the field, then setting the required bits. For example

if j =	0x7FFF (hexadecimal)	0111111111111111 (binary)
	0xFFC7 (hexadecimal)	1111111111000111 (binary)
j &	0xFFC7	0111111111000111 (binary)

has cleared bits 3, 4 and 5 (note bit 0 is the least significant bit)

Bit 4 could then be set by using the bit mask 0x0010 in conjunction with inclusive or:

(j & 0xFFC7 | 0x0010); /* modifying a bit field */

Finally a bit field can be retrieved by masking out unwanted bits and shifting the result. For example if bits 12, 13 and 14 are required (bit 15 is the sign bit), the bit mask 0x7000 would be used with & on the number. The result would then be shifted twelve places to the right in order to obtain the value of the bit field.

((j & 0x7000) > > 12); /* retrieving a bit field */

```
/* program to illustrate access to bits and bit fields */
#include <stdio.h>

#define print(x) printf(#x "=%d\n", x)
int i=0x0000, j=0xFFFF;
```

```
main()
{
        print(i);
        print(j);
        print(i | = 0x8000); /* set the sign bit */
        print(j &= 0x7FFF); /* clear the sign bit */

        if (i & 0x8000)
        {
                printf("sign bit set ");
                print(i);
        }

        if ( ~ j & 0x8000)
        {
                printf("sign bit is cleared ");
                print(j);
        }

        print(j & 0xFFC7 | 0x0010); /* modifying a bit field */
        print((j & 0x7000) >> 12); /* retrieving a bit field */
}
```

results

```
i=0
j=-1
i | = 0x8000=-32768
j &= 0x7FFF=32767
sign bit set i=-32768
sign bit is cleared j=32767
j & 0xFFC7 | 0x0010=32727
(j & 0x7000) >> 12=7
```

An alternative method of defining and accessing bit fields is to use a structure. In the following example a six-digit date has been represented by a structure containing bit fields for day, month and year. It is possible to define the number of bits in each field. In this example five bits have been used to represent the day, giving a range from 1 .. 31; four bits to represent the month, giving a range from 1 .. 12; and seven bits to represent the year, giving a range from 0 .. 99. The total number of bits to represent a date is sixteen, or two bytes. If the fields day, month and year had each been coded as short int, the number of bytes required to store a date would have been three. Therefore, defining the number of bits in a field is a useful way in which to compress information.

```
typedef struct         {
                        unsigned int day : 5;
                        unsigned int month : 4;
                        unsigned int year : 7;
                } date;
```

113

6.4 Unions

When information can be represented in more than one format it is possible to define the different formats in a union. A union resembles a structure, however, each type described in the union shares the same area of memory. From the previous example, a date was represented by two bytes of memory, with bit fields being used to store the day, month and year. In the example that follows the format can be redefined to represent an unsigned integer.

```
typedef union        {
                        date today;
                        unsigned int TODAY;
                } alternative;
```

If a variable Dday of type alternative is defined, it is possible to access the date in day, month and year format:

```
                        Dday.today.day
                        Dday.today.month
                        Dday.today.year
```

or as an unsigned integer:

```
                        Dday.TODAY
```

```
/* program to illustrate bit fields in structures and unions */
#include <stdio.h>

typedef struct          {
                        unsigned int day : 5; /* least significant bits */
                        unsigned int month : 4;
                        unsigned int year : 7; /* most significant bits */
                } date;

typedef union           {
                        date today;
                        unsigned int TODAY;
                } alternative;
alternative Dday;

main()
{
        Dday.today.day = 8U; /* 01000 */
        Dday.today.month = 2U; /* 0010 */
        Dday.today.year = 92U; /* 1011100 */
        /* equivalent bit pattern stored in two bytes */
        /* 1011100001001000 or 0xB848 */
        printf("%X\n", Dday.TODAY);
}
```

114

6.5 Recursion

A recursive function is one which contains a function call to itself. For every recursive call a new occurrence of the same function is created. Eventually the recursive calls must lead to a solution which cannot allow for further recursive calls, since a terminating criterion has been reached. This is known as direct recursion.

In the example that follows the function reverse is recursive. In every recursive call a parameter size is passed to the new occurrence of the function. Since size is constantly decreased by one, size eventually becomes negative. The terminating criterion is then reached and the condition (size >= 0) becomes false. In this example every call to the function reverse will cause a character from a string to be displayed, starting with the last character in the string, then the penultimate character, etc. Eventually all the characters in the string will have been displayed, and the string will appear in reverse order.

```
/* program to demonstrate recursion */
#include <stdio.h>
char *alphabet = "abcdefghijklmnopqrstuvwxyz";

/* function to output a string in reverse order */
void reverse(char *word, int size)
{
        if (size >= 0)
        {
                printf("%c", *(word+size));
                reverse(word, size-1);
        }
}

main()
{
        reverse(alphabet, 25);
}
```

result

zyxwvutsrqponmlkjihgfedcba

Indirect recursion is when a function f1, say, calls function f2, which in turn calls function f3, which in turn calls function f1. This is also legal in the C language.

6.6 Self-referential structures

A self-referential structure is a structure containing a field with a pointer to the same structure. For example, the following structure represents the node of a linked list with one field containing a string of characters (word) and the second field a pointer (*link) to another structure of a node.

```
struct node   {
                char *word;
                struct node *link;
        };
```

115

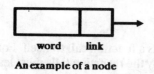

word   link

An example of a node

If a variable is declared as struct node *temp, then *temp.word is the contents of the string in any node, and *temp.link is the pointer to the next node in the linked list. C uses an operator -> which is a combination of the operators * (indirection) and the . (period). The contents of a string in a node can be accessed using:

    temp -> word

and the pointer to the next node in the linked list using:

    temp -> link

The following program builds a linked list of words, placing new words at the head of the linked list. When the list has been created its contents are then displayed.

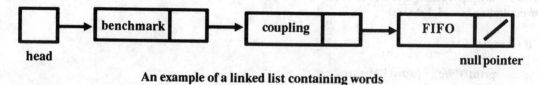

head   null pointer

An example of a linked list containing words

```
/* program to build a linked list containing words */

#include <stdio.h>
#include <stdlib.h>
#include <string.h>

#define sentinel "/"

struct node    {
                char *word;
                struct node *link;
        };

struct node *head=NULL;

struct node *CreateNode(struct node *next, char *string)
{
    struct node *temp;
    temp=malloc(sizeof(struct node));
    temp->word = string;
    temp->link = next;
    return temp;
}
```

```
void CreateList(void)
{
      char *string;
      printf("input one word per line - terminate with /\n");
      string=malloc(256);
      gets(string);
      while (strcmp(string,sentinel)!=0)
      {
            head = CreateNode(head, string);
            string=malloc(256);
            gets(string);
      }
}

void ListOut(void)
{
      struct node *current;
      current=head;
      printf("\n\ncontents of linked list\n");
      while (current != NULL)
      {
            puts(current->word);
            current=current->link;
      }
}

main()
{
      CreateList();
      ListOut();
}
```

results

```
input one word per line - terminate with /
benchmark
coupling
FIFO
clock
Ada
monitor
/
contents of linked list
monitor
Ada
clock
FIFO
coupling
benchmark
```

117

6.7 Pointers to functions

In C it is possible to pass a pointer to a function as an argument in an actual parameter list. For example, if the function Simpson uses Simpson's rule to calculate the area under a curve between the limits x=a and x=b for any curve passed to the function, the formal parameter list would be defined as:

float Simpson(float a, float b, double (*f)(double))

where a and b are the upper and lower limits of integration and (*f) indicates that f is a pointer to a function that requires an argument of type double and returns a value that is of type double. The notation can be simplified, by replacing (*f)(double) with f(double). The function Simpson can be called using a variety of mathematical functions that represent different curves, for example:

Simpson(0, pi/2, sin);
Simpson(0,1, exp);
Simpson(0,9,sqrt);

where the functions sin, exp and sqrt are all described in the header file < math.h > as follows:

double sin(double x);
double exp(double x);
double sqrt(double x);

```
/* program to illustrate a pointer to a function */
#include <stdio.h>
#include <stdlib.h>
#include <math.h>
#define pi 3.14159
#define increment 0.001

float Simpson(float a, float b, double f(double))
{
        float Y0,Y1,Y2, area=0.0;
        do
        {
                Y0=f(a);
                Y1=f(a+increment);
                Y2=f(a+2*increment);
                area=area+(increment/3)*(Y0+4*Y1+Y2);
                a=a+2*increment;
        } while (a<b);
        return (area);
}

main()
{
        printf("integral of sin(x) 0<=x<=pi/2 %f\n", Simpson(0, pi/2, sin));
        printf("integral of exp(x) 0<=x<=1 %f\n", Simpson(0,1, exp));
        printf("integral of sqrt(x) 0<=x<=9 %f\n", Simpson(0,9,sqrt));
}
```

results

integral of sin(x) 0<=x<=pi/2 1.001204
integral of exp(x) 0<=x<=1 1.718282
integral of sqrt(x) 0<=x<=9 17.999997

6.8 Summary

● Macro definitions are either simple or parametrised. Parametrised macros can be used as an alternative to functions. Macros offer the advantages that they are generic (do not specify the data types of the parameters) and the program might run faster.

● A programmer can select the code that is to be included in a program by using preprocessor directives for conditional compilation.

● The language provides six bitwise operators for bit manipulation in low-level programming.

● The fields in a structure can be designated bit-fields, when the type of each fields is replaced by the number of bits in the field. This technique is useful in data compaction.

● A field in a structure can be redefined as a different type if the structure is defined as a union.

● Functions can be directly or indirectly recursive. However, a function cannot be defined within another function.

● By using tagged structures it is possible for the field in a structure to reference the structure. This feature enables self- referential structures such as linked lists and trees to be defined.

● A pointer to a function can be passed as an argument in an actual parameter list such that functions may effectively be passed as arguments.

6.9 Questions   *answers begin on page 272*

1. Write and test parametrised macros to:

(a) Calculate and display the area of a triangle given the lengths of two sides a,b and the included angle C - the formula for the area of the triangle is 1/2*a*b*sin(C).

(b) Rotate 1 bit clockwise the bits of a 16-bit positive integer. Note that a clockwise rotation involves taking the least significant bit, shifting all the remaining bits to the right one place, and inserting the least significant bit in the most significant bit position. TopSpeed C propagates the sign bit when performing a right shift, but this may vary between implementations of C.

(c) Test characters for being hexadecimal digits.

(d) Test whether the second number in a set of three numbers represents a maximum value.

2. Using bit manipulation devise functions to:

(a) Rotate either anticlockwise or clockwise , a specified number of bits, of a 16 bit word.

(b) Multiply two 8 bit binary integers that can be either positive or negative.

3. Use functions passed as parameters to display a table of values for the mathematical functions sine(x), cosine(x) and tangent(x) for $0<=x<=90$ degrees in increments of 5 degrees.

4. Write recursive functions to:

(a) Calculate the factorial value of a number.

(b) Find the largest element in an array of integers.

(c) Implement a selection sort as a recursive procedure. If, say, integers are stored in a one-dimensional array, the selection sort algorithm behaves as follows.

Find the largest number in the array. Exchange this number with the integer stored in the last position. Repeat the process finding the next largest number in the array, and exchange this with the integer in the penultimate position. Continue to find the next largest number and exchange it until all the integers have been stored in ascending order.

5. Modify the program given in section 6.6 to include functions that:

(a) search for a word in the linked list, and

(b) delete a node from the linked list.

7.
Case Study

The final chapter of part one reflects on the language topics that have been introduced in the first part of the book. The chapter not only consolidates the work on C, but explains how the language can be used to build a small software system in the form of a line editor. To help to encourage an active involvement in this chapter the reader is expected to code several of the program files in order to develop a complete working system.

Contents

7.1 Problem

The case study requires that a line editor is built to allow the processing of text stored as a text file. The system is to run on any PC compatible microcomputer under MSDOS.

The line editor should contain the following features.

The editor is invoked by using the command line EDIT followed by the name of the file to be edited, for example EDIT a:prog.c. If the file does not exist then the system allows for a new file to be created. However, if the file is found to exist the contents of the file is displayed on the screen.

After a file has been created it should be possible to perform the following features.

Amend or delete any single line of text in the file; find and replace text either on a specified line or throughout the file; insert new lines of text anywhere in the file; list the contents of the file from any specified line to the end of the file; save the file using either the old filename or a new filename; and quit the line editor and return to MSDOS, without saving the file.

In addition to these features the system should provide an on- line help facility that describes the purpose and use of the line editor commands.

7.2 Functional specification

human computer interface

The line editor uses two windows in which to convey and capture information. The windows are known as screen(1) and screen(2) and are represented as shown in figure 7.1. The coordinates of screen(1) are (0,0) top left-hand corner and (79,18) bottom right- hand corner; and screen(2) are (0,19) top left-hand corner and (79,25) bottom right-hand corner.

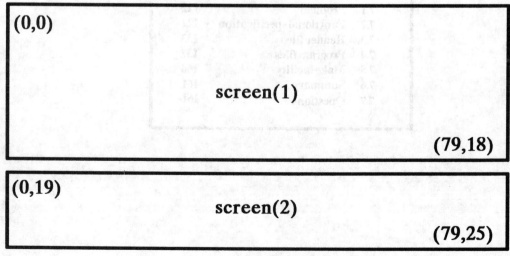

Figure 7.1

After the command line has been input to invoke the editor, if the file has not been created, the system will respond with the prompts NEW FILE, followed by the filename, at screen(2) and enter text - terminate with ~ on a new line at screen(1). Figure 7.2 illustrates the state of the screens after the text for the new file a:prog.c has been entered, and prior to the enter key being pressed after the terminating symbol ~.

```
enter text - terminate with ~ on a new line
#include <stdio.h>
int display(int character)
{
    return putchar(character);
}

main()
{
    int symbol, value;

    symbol = getchar();
    value = display(symbol);
    value = value + 1;
    display(value);
}
~
```

```
NEW FILE a:prog.c
```

Figure 7.2

After the enter key has been pressed, screen(1) displays a listing of the file together with the line number of each line. In addition, an arrowed indicator -> points to the position of the current line. The idea of a current line is to remind the user of the last line to be processed. Screen(2) displays the contents of the main menu. It is from this menu that the user is given the choice of commands of the line editor. These two screens are illustrated in figure 7.3.

When the code A is input to indicate an amendment to a line, the prompt enter line number is displayed in screen(2), as depicted in figure 7.4.

Both screens then change, as shown in figure 7.5. Screen(2) displays to the user the original contents of, in this example, line 13; and screen(1) invites the user to enter a single line of text.

After the line has been entered both screens change again, as shown in figure 7.6. Screen(1) gives a listing of the file with the arrowed indicator pointing to the amended line. Screen(2) displays the main menu.

If the user chooses to delete a line, a prompt is given on screen(2) to enter line number, see figure 7.7. In

```
   1      #include <stdio.h>
   2      intdisplay(int character)
   3      {
   4            return putchar(character);
   5      }
   6
   7      main()
   8      {
   9            int symbol, value;
  10
  11            symbol = getchar();
  12            value = display(symbol);
  13            value = value + 1;
  14            display(value);
->15      }
```

[A]mend   [D]elete   [F]ind   [H]elp   [I]nsert   [L]ist   [Q]uit   [S]ave

enter code

Figure 7.3

[A]mend   [D]elete   [F]ind   [H]elp   [I]nsert   [L]ist   [Q]uit   [S]ave

enter code   A
enter line number: 13

Figure 7.4

---

enter a single line of text
     value + +

->   13   value = value + 1;

Figure 7.5

124

```
     1      #include <stdio.h>
     2      int display(int character)
     3      {
     4            return putchar(character);
     5      }
     6
     7      main()
     8      {
     9            int symbol, value;
    10
    11            symbol = getchar();
    12            value = display(symbol);
->  13            value++
    14            display(value);
    15      }
```

```
[A]mend    [D]elete    [F]ind    [H]elp    [I]nsert    [L]ist    [Q]uit    [S]ave

enter code
```

Figure 7.6

this example line 6 is to be deleted. Screen(1) shows a new listing of the file. The previous line 6, which was a blank line, is removed, and all the lines after line 5 have been automatically renumbered.

If the user chooses to find and replace text, then code F is keyed at the main menu, see figure 7.8.

Screen(2) then changes to a sub-menu that requests the text to be found, in this example symbol; the text to be replaced, in this example letter_from_alphabet; and whether a line or global edit is required, in this example a global edit.

When the edit is complete the contents of the file is displayed in screen(1) and the main menu in screen(2). See figure 7.10.

If a find and replace is required again, the sub-menu re-appears in screen(2) and this time the choice is to find the text, value++ and replace it with the text, value++; (note the inclusion of the semi-colon) on line 12 only. See figure 7.11.

When the edit is complete only the line that has been changed is displayed on screen(1). The main menu appears on screen(2). See figure 7.12.

If the help command is invoked, a listing of the function of each command is displayed on screen(1). The main menu also appears on screen(2). See figure 7.13.

When the code I is input to insert text, screen(2) changes from the main menu to a sub-menu. The

```
     1     #include <stdio.h>
     2     int display(int character)
     3     {
     4          return putchar(character);
     5     }
->   6     main()
     7     {
     8          int symbol, value;
     9
     10         symbol = getchar();
     11         value = display(symbol);
     12         value + +
     13         display(value);
     14    }
```

```
[A]mend     [D]elete     [F]ind     [H]elp     [I]nsert     [L]ist     [Q]uit     [S]ave

enter code  D
enter line number: 6
```

Figure 7.7

```
[A]mend     [D]elete     [F]ind     [H]elp     [I]nsert     [L]ist     [Q]uit     [S]ave

enter code  F
```

Figure 7.8

```
find: symbol
replace with: letter_from_alphabet
[L]ine     [G]lobal  G
```

Figure 7.9

126

```
   1    #include <stdio.h>
   2    int display(int character)
   3    {
   4         return putchar(character);
   5    }
   6    main()
   7    {
   8        int letter_from_alphabet, value;
   9
   10       letter_from_alphabet = getchar();
   11       value = display(letter_from_alphabet);
   12       value + +
   13        display(value);
-> 14    }
```

```
[A]mend    [D]elete    [F]ind    [H]elp    [I]nsert    [L]ist    [Q]uit    [S]ave
enter code  F
```

Figure 7.10

```
find: value + +
replace with: value + +;
[L]ine  [G]lobal  L
enter line number: 12
```

Figure 7.11

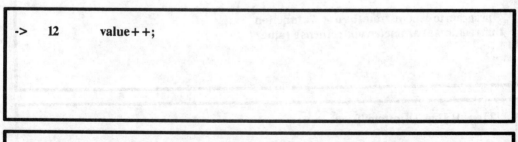

```
-> 12        value + +;
```

```
[A]mend    [D]elete    [F]ind    [H]elp    [I]nsert    [L]ist    [Q]uit    [S]ave
enter code
```

Figure 7.12

```
                              Help

The line editor allows you to make the following edits on text files:

Amend        replace any specified single line in the file
Delete       erase any specified single line in the file
Find         find and replace, either globally or on a specified line, any
             text in the file
Insert       enter any number of new lines either at the top or bottom of the
             file or after any specified line in the file
List         display the contents of the file from any specified line to the
             bottom of the file
Quit         exit from the line editor without saving the file
Save         all changes to the current file are either filed under the new
             filename, if one is given, or under the old filename by default
```

```
[A]mend    [D]elete    [F]ind    [H]elp    [I]nsert    [L]ist    [Q]uit    [S]ave

enter code
```

Figure 7.13

sub-menu prompts where the insertion is to be made, at the top of the file, after a specified line, or at the bottom of the file. In the example shown in figure 7.14, the choice is to insert text at the top of the file. Screen(1) invites the user to enter text - terminate with a ~ on a new line.

```
enter text - terminate with ~ on a new line

/* program to demonstrate the use of a function
that requires a parameter, and returns a value */

~
```

```
[T]op  [L]ine  [B]ottom T
```

Figure 7.14

After the insertion is complete a listing of the file is given on screen(1). Notice in this example, figure 7.15, that screen(1) is too small to list all of the file. In this case the user is prompted, on screen(2), whether to continue listing the file.

The list command will display on screen(1) any part of the file from the line number given to the end of the

```
     1      /* program to demonstrate the use of a function
     2       that requires a parameter, and returns a value */
 ->  3
     4      #include <stdio.h>
     5      int display(int character)
     6      {
     7           return putchar(character);
     8      }
     9      main()
    10      {
    11           int letter_from_alphabet, value;
    12
    13           letter_from_alphabet = getchar();
    14           value = display(letter_from_alphabet);
    15           value++;
    16           display(value);
```

```
continue listing file? [Y]es [N]o
```

Figure 7.15

file. See figure 7.16.

When the command to save the file is given the user is prompted, in screen(2), to enter filename (see figure 7.17). If the name of the file is the same as given in the command line used to invoke the editor, and the file has not yet been saved, it will be saved under the same name. If the user presses the entry key only, the filename is taken by default to be the same as that given in the command line. Alternatively, if the file that has been edited was previously saved, it can now be saved using a different filename.

Screen(2) then displays information that the system is writing the text under the filename that was given. See figure 7.18

When invoking the line editor, if the filename given in the command line already exists, the file is listed on screen(1) and the main menu displayed on screen(2). See figure 7.19.

```
->  9     main()
   10     {
   11          int letter_from_alphabet, value;
   12
   13          letter_from_alphabet = getchar();
   14         value = display(letter_from_alphabet);
   15          value++;
   16          display(value);
   17     }
```

```
[A]mend    [D]elete    [F]ind    [H]elp    [I]nsert    [L]ist    [Q]uit    [S]ave

enter code  L
enter line number: 9
```

Figure 7.16

```
enter filename a:prog.c
```

Figure 7.17

```
writing text to filename a:prog.c
```

Figure 7.18

If the command line parameters are incorrect at the time of invoking the line editor, an error message is displayed on screen(2) and the system returns to MSDOS. See figure 7.20.

```
1      /* program to demonstrate the use of a function
2       that requires a parameter, and returns a value */
3
4      #include <stdio.h>
5      int display(int character)
6      {
7           return putchar(character);
8      }
9      main()
10     {
11         int letter_from_alphabet, value;
12
13         letter_from_alphabet = getchar();
14         value = display(letter_from_alphabet);
15          value++;
16          display(value);
```

```
continue listing file? [Y]es [N]o
```

Figure 7.19

When saving a file under a filename that already exists the user is prompted that the file exists and is given the option to overwrite the file (see figure 7.21). If the option is not taken up the system reverts back to the main menu.

Whenever the commands to amend, delete, find text on a line, insert text after a line or list the file from a line, the user is requested to input a line number. The system must validate the users line number, if it is invalid the user is informed of the error by the prompt shown in figure 7.22.

Finally, if the file is too large to be accommodated in the line editor system a warning message will be displayed on screen(2), as shown in figure 7.23.

```
ERROR - FILENAME PARAMETERS
```

Figure 7.20

131

```
enter filename a:prog.c
WARNING FILE EXISTS OK TO OVERWRITE?
answer [Y]es  [N]o
```

Figure 7.21

```
LINE NUMBER INVALID RE-ENTER
```

Figure 7.22

```
FILE IS FULL NO MORE LINES CAN BE INSERTED
```

Figure 7.23

implementation features

The text file is stored as lines of ASCII characters in a file held on magnetic disc. The operations upon the file are as follows.

Upon invoking the line editor, if the file exists, its contents are copied into a linked list. If the file does not exist the text is built, line by line, and stored in the nodes of a linked list. One line of text is stored in one node.

When the command is given to save the file, the contents of the nodes of the linked list are written to a text file. The text of each node is stored as one line in an ASCII text file.

The commands to amend, delete, find, insert and list operate on the linked list and not upon the text file. The penalty of implementing the commands, to operate directly upon the text file, would be a line editor with a very poor response time.

The size of a text file that can be built is dependent upon the amount of main memory available for building the linked list and the amount of disc space available for storing the contents of the linked list.

The length of a line has been restricted to 70 characters, including the NEW_LINE character. When entering text, any attempt to input more than 70 characters on one line will result in the extra text being inserted onto the next new line. Any attempt to replace a line with more than 70 characters will result in a truncation of the replacement string.

132

For the purposes of printing line numbers the maximum line number has been limited to 9999. This figure is independent of the maximum number of nodes that can be built from available memory. In the design of the system it is assumed that no single file will be built containing more than 9999 nodes.

responses to undesired events

The system should address the following error handling situations.

Whenever an incorrect menu-code is input the system will give an audible warning and re-display the same menu.

Any attempt to amend, delete or insert into an empty linked list, or use a line number that does not exist, will result in the system returning to the main menu without changes to the linked list.

If no more space is available from the heap in allocating new nodes, a warning message appears on screen(1) and the system returns to the main menu.

If the length of text to be found is null, return to the main menu.

If a line number does not contain decimal digits an audible warning is given, followed by an error message on screen(2).

After entering the command line to invoke the line editor, if the command line is incorrect an audible warning is given followed by an error message on screen(1).

In attempting to save a file that has already been created an audible warning is given followed by a warning message on screen(2).

software functions

Since the line editor system is to be implemented using ANSI C advantage can be taken of developing the system using many program files. Each file represents a specific function and can be developed separately. This system uses fourteen program files and one header file. The name of each file and its function is given in figure 7.24.

7.3 Header file

It is normal practice to put the following information in a header file so that it can included in all program files.

> *constant definitions*
> *type declarations*
> *structure declarations*
> *external declarations*
> *function declarations*
> *macros*

A listing of the header file edit.h can be found on page 135.

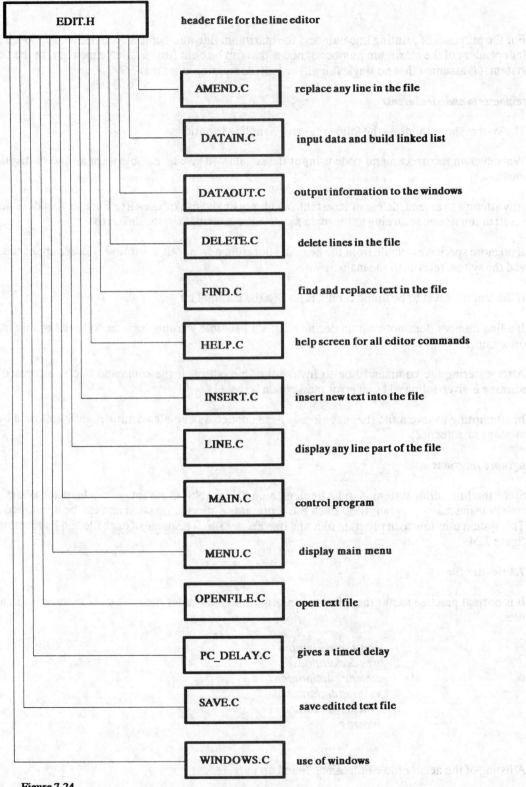

EDIT.H	header file for the line editor
AMEND.C	replace any line in the file
DATAIN.C	input data and build linked list
DATAOUT.C	output information to the windows
DELETE.C	delete lines in the file
FIND.C	find and replace text in the file
HELP.C	help screen for all editor commands
INSERT.C	insert new text into the file
LINE.C	display any line part of the file
MAIN.C	control program
MENU.C	display main menu
OPENFILE.C	open text file
PC_DELAY.C	gives a timed delay
SAVE.C	save edited text file
WINDOWS.C	use of windows

Figure 7.24

```
/********************************** filename EDIT.H **************************************

FUNCTIONALITY

This is the header file for the line editor case study. It contains a list of all the constants, structures, external
declarations, types, and functions associated with the program files which together form the line editor.

ERROR/EXCEPTION HANDLING

None.

PORTABILITY

Not applicable.

*******************************************************************************************/

/******************************* CONSTANT DEFINITIONS ***********************************/

#define AMEND 'A'
#define BOTTOM 'B'
#define CHAR_LENGTH 1
#define DELETE 'D'
#define END_OF_STRING '\0'
#define FILLER ""
#define FIND 'F'
#define GLOBAL 'G'
#define HELP 'H'
#define INSERT 'I'
#define _JPI_WIN_
#define LINE 'L'
#define LINE_LENGTH 70
#define LIST 'L'
#define MAX_LINES 16
#define MAX_LINES_IN_FILE 9999
#define NEW_LINE "\n"
#define NUMBER_LENGTH 4
#define QUIT 'Q'
#define READ_ONLY "r"
#define SAVE 'S'
#define TEXT_END '~'
#define TIME_PERIOD 3000
#define TOP 'T'
#define WRITE_ONLY "w"
#define YES 'Y'

/****************************** TYPE DECLARATIONS *************************************/

typedef enum {false, true} BOOLEAN;
```

```
typedef char CHAR;
typedef unsigned int INT;
typedef void VOID;
```

/***************************STRUCTURE DECLARATION ***************************/

```
struct line      {
                        CHAR text[LINE_LENGTH + 1];
                        struct line      *link;
                 };
```

/***************************EXTERNAL DECLARATIONS ***************************/

```
#ifndef MAIN
      extern struct line *head;
      extern INT current;
      extern CHAR *argument;
      extern INT LinesInFile;
#endif
```

/***************************FUNCTION DECLARATIONS ***************************/

```
BOOLEAN   CheckLineNumber(CHAR *);

CHAR       *GetChar(VOID);
CHAR       *GetNumber(VOID);
CHAR       *GetString(VOID);
CHAR       FindMenu(VOID);
CHAR       InsertMenu(VOID);

struct line      *position(VOID);
struct line      *ReadLine(VOID);

VOID       amend(struct line *);
VOID       build(VOID);
VOID       ClearScreen(VOID);
VOID       CloseWindows(VOID);
VOID       delete(struct line *);
VOID       find(VOID);
VOID       help(VOID);
VOID       insert(VOID);
VOID       list(struct line *);
VOID       menu(VOID);
VOID       OpenFile(INT, CHAR *[]);
VOID       OpenWindows(VOID);
VOID       PC_delay(VOID);
VOID       PrintLine(struct line *);
VOID       save(VOID);
VOID       screen(INT);
```

In the interest of portability never to use C 'raw' data types. For example in this header file under the type declarations the 'raw' C data type unsigned int, has been defined as type INT, similary the 'raw' C data types char and void have been defined as types CHAR and VOID respectively. If this program was ported to a machine with a different representation for unsigned int, only this line in the header file need be changed, and not every type declaration of unsigned int in the program files.

Since functions within program files will use functions from other program files it is necessary to list the prototypes of the functions in the function declaration section of the header file.

The line editor stores all lines of text internally in a linked list. Since this list will be accessed from many different functions, held in many different program files, it is necessary to declare a global pointer variable *head, that is the address of the head of the linked list. Other global variables that are declared in this file are the current line number (current), the number of lines in the file (LinesInFile) and the name of the file (argument).

7.4 Program files

Within this section the program files used to build the line editor will be described. The description will take the form of the functionality of the routines (functions) stored in the file; how the error/exception handling conditions are dealt with; and the portability of the library functions. This last item is useful in defining which header files the library functions can be found under, and ultimately the portability of the program file.

In order to minimise the amount of modifications needed to port programs between computers, all machine dependent functions should be grouped together into machine dependent program files.

AMEND.C

Figure 7.25 illustrates how the node to be amended, in a linked list, is pointed at by position. The line of text is denoted by position->text.

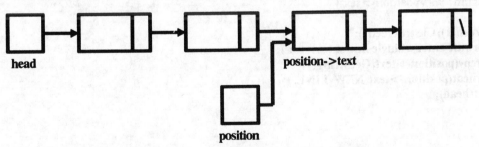

head   **position->text**

position

To amend a node in the linked list, the position of the node is located, and the contents of position -> text replaced by a line of new text.

Figure 7.25

/******************************* filename AMEND.C *******************************

FUNCTIONALITY

The file contains one function - amend, with a formal parameter *position, pointing at the node in the linked list, where the text is to be replaced. The function displays, on screen 2, the line to be amended, and invites the user to enter, on screen 1, the replacement text. After the line has been replaced in the node of the linked list the entire contents of the linked list is displayed on screen 1.

ERROR HANDLING

If the linked list is empty return to the calling function without any changes being made.

PORTABILITY

cprintf - UNIX/DOS/OS2
strcpy - ANSI
strncat - ANSI

***/

```c
#include "edit.h"
#include <conio.h>
#include <string.h>

VOID amend(struct line *position)
{
        if (position == NULL) return;

        screen(2); ClearScreen();
        cprintf("->%4d ", current);
        cprintf("%s", position->text);

        screen(1); ClearScreen();
        cprintf("enter a single line of text\n\n");
        strcpy(position->text, GetString());
        strncat(position->text, NEW_LINE, 1);
        list(head);
}
```

DATAIN.C

/********************************** filename DATAIN.C ************************************

FUNCTIONALITY

This file contains the following five function:

GetString - Purpose to input a string of up to LINE_LENGTH-1 characters at the keyboard and store the characters in the array StringBuffer.

GetChar - Purpose to input a single character at the keyboard and store it in the array CharBuffer.

GetNumber - Purpose to input a string of up to NUMBER_LENGTH characters at the keyboard and store the characters in the array NumberBuffer.

Note all three functions use the conio.h library function cgets, which reads characters from the console until either a carriage return/ line feed combination is read or the specified maximum number of characters is read. If a carriage return/ line feed combination is read, it is replaced by the terminating \0 character. This implies that when the maximum number of characters is read the enter key need not be pressed.

ReadLine - Purpose to return a node containing text, with the pointer to the next node set at NULL. If space cannot be allocated from the heap for the node, then a NULL value is returned. Note a NEW_LINE is appended to a line of text stored in the node. When the length of the text being input is equal to LINE_LENGTH a new line is automatically generated on screen(1), and an audible warning is given.

build - Purpose to build a linked list of nodes containing lines of text. When the TEXT_END marker is input at the beginning of a new line return to the calling function.

ERROR/ EXCEPTION HANDLING:

ReadLine function - If no more space is available, from the heap, for generating new nodes, an audible warning is given, and a warning message appears on screen(2). Control is then returned from the ReadLine function, with a NULL value, to the calling function.

build function - If a new node cannot be created or the number of lines in the file has reached the MAX_LINES_IN_FILE limit, control returns to the calling function. If the TEXT_END terminator is detected the memory allocated to the new node is de-allocated, and control returns to the calling function.

PORTABILITY

cgets - UNIX/DOS/OS2
malloc - ANSI
cprintf - UNIX/DOS/OS2
strcpy - ANSI
strcat - ANSI
strlen - ANSI

**/

```
#include "edit.h"
#include <conio.h>
#include <stdlib.h>
#include <string.h>

CHAR *GetString(VOID)
{
       CHAR StringBuffer[LINE_LENGTH+3];

       StringBuffer[0]=LINE_LENGTH-1;
       return (cgets(StringBuffer));
}

CHAR *GetChar(VOID)
{
       CHAR CharBuffer[CHAR_LENGTH+3];

       CharBuffer[0]=CHAR_LENGTH;
       return (cgets(CharBuffer));
}

CHAR *GetNumber(VOID)
{
       CHAR NumberBuffer[NUMBER_LENGTH+3];

       NumberBuffer[0]=NUMBER_LENGTH;
       return (cgets(NumberBuffer));
}

struct line *ReadLine(VOID)
{
       struct line *p;

       p=malloc(sizeof(struct line));
       if (p == NULL || LinesInFile == MAX_LINES_IN_FILE)
       {
              screen(2);
              cprintf("\aFILE IS FULL NO MORE LINES CAN BE INSERTED\n");
              return NULL;
       }

       screen(1);
       strcpy(p->text, GetString());
       strncat(p->text, NEW_LINE, 1);
       if (strlen(p->text)==LINE_LENGTH) cprintf("\a\n");
       p->link = NULL;
       return p;
}
```

```
VOID build(VOID)
{
        struct line *p, *new;

        screen(1);
        cprintf("enter text - terminate with %c", TEXT_END);
        cprintf(" on a new line\n");
        new=ReadLine();

        if (new==NULL) return;
        if(new->text[0]==TEXT_END)
        {
                free(new);
                return;
        }

        LinesInFile = 1;

        for (head=new, p=new, current=1 ;; p=new, current++)
        {
                new=ReadLine();

                if (new==NULL) return;
                if(new->text[0]==TEXT_END)
                {
                        free(new);
                        return;
                }

                p->link = new;
                LinesInFile++;
        }
}
```

DATAOUT.C

```
/****************************** filename DATAOUT.C *********************************
```

FUNCTIONALITY

The file contains the following two functions:

list - Purpose is to display, on screen(1), the contents of the linked list from any line in the list. Displayed against each line in the list is a line number, with the current line indicated by the -> symbol. When the number of lines in the linked list exceeds the depth (MAX_LINES) of screen(1), the user is prompted, on screen(2), to continue the listing.

PrintLine - Purpose is to display on screen(1) any one line of text.

ERROR/EXCEPTION HANDLING

None.

PORTABILITY

cprintf - UNIX/DOS/OS2
strcpy - ANSI

**/

```c
#include "edit.h"
#include <conio.h>
#include <ctype.h>
#include <string.h>

VOID list(struct line *position)
{
        struct line *p;
        INT count, LineCount=0;
        CHAR reply[CHAR_LENGTH+1];

        screen(1);
        ClearScreen();

        if (position != head)
                for (p=head, count=1; count!=current; p=p->link, count++);
        else
        {
                p=head;
                count=1;
        }

        for (; p!=NULL; p=p->link, count++)
        {
                if (current == count)
                        cprintf("->");
                else
                        cprintf("  ");

                cprintf("%4d ", count);
                cprintf("%s",p->text);

                LineCount++;

                if (LineCount == MAX_LINES)
                {
                        screen(2);
                        ClearScreen();
```

```
            cprintf("continue listing file? [Y]es [N]o ");
            strcpy(reply, GetChar());
            reply[0]=toupper(reply[0]);

            if (reply[0]==YES)
            {
                    LineCount=0;
                    screen(1);
            }
            else
                    return;
        }
    }
}


VOID PrintLine(struct line *position)
{
    screen(1);
    ClearScreen();
    cprintf("->%4d ", current);
    cprintf(position->text);
}
```

DELETE.C

Figure 7.26 illustrates how it is necessary to use two pointers when deleting a node from a linked list. The first marker is necessary in providing the link when the node pointed at by position has been deleted.

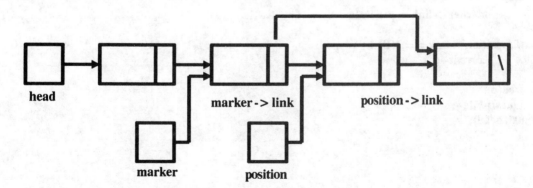

To delete a node from the linked list the previous node to the one to be deleted is located, in this example called marker, and marker -> link is assigned the value of position -> link. If the value of position is head then head is assigned head -> link

Figure 7.26

143

```
/*********************************filename DELETE.C *********************************

FUNCTIONALITY

The file contains one function called delete. The purpose of the function is to remove a specified node from
the linked list. After the node has been deleted the entire contents of the linked list is displayed on
screen(1).

ERROR/EXCEPTION HANDLING

If the linked list is empty or the line does not exist return without change.

PORTABILITY

free - ANSI

*********************************************************************************************/

#include "edit.h"
#include <stdlib.h>

VOID delete(struct line *position)
{
        struct line *p, *marker;

        if (head == NULL || position == NULL) return;

        for (p=head, marker=NULL; position !=p; marker=p, p=p->link);

        if (position == head)
                head = p->link;
        else
                marker->link = p->link;

        if (position->link == NULL)
                current--;

        free(p);
        LinesInFile--;
        list(head);
}
```

FIND.C

The coding of the function find has been deliberately omitted in this section. The reader is encouraged to
write the code from the algorithm given in figure 7.27.

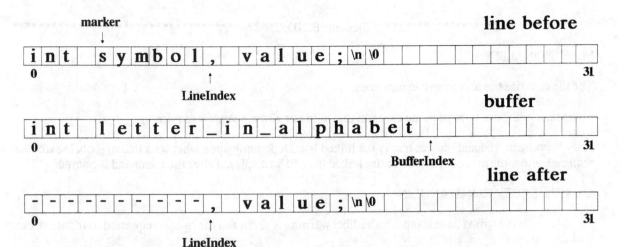

All the characters up to, but not including, the marker are copied from the line to buffer.
After each character has been copied from line it is replaced by the FILLER character (-).
The replace text is then copied into the buffer, leaving the BufferIndex set at the next available position in the array buffer.
The find text in the line is replaced by FILLER characters, leaving the LineIndex at the next available position in the array line.
An attempt is made to locate the next occurrence of the text to be found. If a new position for the marker can be found, the operations necessary to replace the text are repeated. In this example the marker will be set to NULL since the text to be replaced does not occur again in that line.

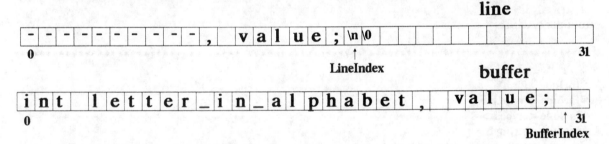

After the marker is set to NULL, the remainder of the text from line is copied to buffer while a NEW_LINE character is not found and the BufferIndex is not at the penultimate end location of buffer.

In this example it would appear that copying of text should continue until both the NEW_LINE and NULL characters have been copied from the line into the buffer. However, if the replace text was very long   or the buffer was almost full the NEW_LINE and NULL characters may never get transferred. For this reason the final operation must be to explicitly copy a NEW_LINE and a NULL character into BufferIndex and BufferIndex + 1 respectively. This ensures that the text held in the buffer is correctly terminated.

buffer

| i | n | t | | l | e | t | t | e | r | _ | i | n | _ | a | l | p | h | a | b | e | t | , | | v | a | l | u | e | ; | \n | \0 |

0   ↑ 31
                                                                                              BufferIndex

Figure 7.27

145

/****************************** filename FIND.C **

FUNCTIONALITY

The file contains the following two functions:

FindMenu - Purpose to prompt the user whether a line or global search is required.

find - Purpose to find and replace text in the linked list. Depending upon whether a line or global search was required, either the amended line or entire linked list will be displayed after the command is obeyed.

ERROR/EXCEPTION HANDLING

FindMenu - If the wrong code is input an audible warning is given and the user is requested to input the data again.

find - If the length of the string to be found is zero, return with no change. If the length of the replacement string causes the line of text to exceed the LINE_LENGTH then characters are deliberately lost from the right-hand end of the string.

PORTABILITY

cprintf - UNIX/DOS/OS2
strcpy - ANSI
strlen - ANSI
strstr - ANSI
toupper - ANSI

***/

```
#include "edit.h"
#include <conio.h>
#include <ctype.h>
#include <string.h>

CHAR FindMenu(VOID)
{
    CHAR MenuCode[CHAR_LENGTH+1];

    for (;;)
    {
        cprintf("[L]ine [G]lobal ");
        strcpy(MenuCode, GetChar());
        MenuCode[0] = toupper(MenuCode[0]);

        switch (MenuCode[0])
        {
            case LINE:      return LINE;
            case GLOBAL:    return GLOBAL;
```

```
        default :      cprintf("\a");
                       ClearScreen();
                       break;
           }
      }
}

VOID find(VOID)
{
      CHAR MenuCode;
      INT count;
      CHAR line[LINE_LENGTH+1];
      CHAR buffer[LINE_LENGTH+1];
      CHAR find[LINE_LENGTH+1];
      CHAR replace[LINE_LENGTH+1];
      CHAR *marker;
      struct line *p;
      INT LineIndex, BufferIndex, temp;

      /* coded algorithm deliberately omitted */

}
```

HELP.C

/********************************** filename HELP.C **

FUNCTIONALITY

The file contains one function help whose purpose is to display on screen(1) on-line help, describing the function of each line editor command.

ERROR/EXCEPTION HANDLING

None.

PORTABILITY

cprintf - UNIX/DOS/OS2

**/

```
#include "edit.h"
#include <conio.h>

VOID help(VOID)
{
        screen(1); ClearScreen();
        cprintf(" Help\n\n");
        cprintf("The line editor allows you to make the following edits on text files:\n\n");
        cprintf("Amend replace any specified single line in the file\n");
        cprintf("Delete erase any specified single line in the file\n");
        cprintf("Find find and replace, either globally or on a specified line, any\n");
        cprintf(" text in the file\n");
        cprintf("Insert enter any number of new lines either at the top or bottom of the\n");
        cprintf(" file or after any specified line in the file\n");
        cprintf("List display the contents of the file from any specified line to the\n");
        cprintf(" bottom of the file\n");
        cprintf("Quit exit from the line editor without saving the file\n");
        cprintf("Save all changes to the current file are either filed under the new\n");
        cprintf(" filename, if one is given, or under the old filename by default\n\n");
}
```

INSERT.C

Figure 7.28 illustrates how to insert a new node into a linked list. Two pointers are again necessary, one to mark the position at which the new node will be inserted (position->link) and the other to mark the position at which the original node in the list will follow from the new node (marker).

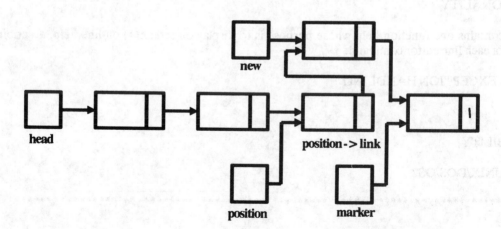

To insert a node into a linked list, the position where the node is to be inserted must be stored, in this example by the pointers position and marker. A new node is generated, and position->link is assigned to new, position is then re-assigned to point at the new node, and the new position->link is assigned to marker, to complete the link.

Figure 7.28

The code for the function insert has been omitted, and it is left as an exercise for the reader to complete the code.

/******************************** filename INSERT.C ********************************

FUNCTIONALITY

The file contains the following two functions:

InsertMenu - Purpose is to give the user a choice of inserting text at the top or bottom of the linked list, or after a specified line in the linked list.

insert - Purpose is to insert extra lines of text into the linked list. The mechanism for inserting text into the linked list is very similar to that described for the function build.

ERROR/EXCEPTION HANDLING

InsertMenu - If the user enters the wrong code an audible warning is given followed by an invitation to re-type the code.

insert - If the linked list is empty and the user requests to insert text at a line or at the bottom of the list, then return without change. If the user requests to insert text after a non-existent line then return without change. The same mechanisms are used for error/exception handling as the function build.

PORTABILITY

cprintf - UNIX/DOS/OS2
strcpy - ANSI
toupper - ANSI
free - ANSI

**/

```c
#include "edit.h"
#include <conio.h>
#include <ctype.h>
#include <stdlib.h>
#include <string.h>

CHAR InsertMenu(void)
{
        CHAR MenuCode[CHAR_LENGTH+1];

        for (;;)
        {
                screen(2); ClearScreen();
                cprintf("[T]op [L]ine [B]ottom ");
                strcpy(MenuCode, GetChar());
                MenuCode[0] = toupper(MenuCode[0]);
```

```
                switch (MenuCode[0])
                {
                        case TOP :          return TOP;
                        case LINE :         return LINE;
                        case BOTTOM :       return BOTTOM;
                        default:            cprintf("\a");
                                            ClearScreen();
                                            break;

                }
        }
}

void insert(void)
{
        struct line *p, *new, *marker, *NewPosition;
        CHAR MenuCode;

        /* coded algorithm deliberately omitted */

}
```

LINE.C

/*************************************** filename LINE.C ***************************************

FUNCTIONALITY

The file contains the following two functions:

CheckLineNumber - Purpose is to inspect each character in a string to ensure that it is a decimal digit. The function returns true if the string contains decimal digits, otherwise returns false.

position - Purpose is to invite the user to specify a line number (n) where text can be found, and convert this number to the position in the linked list of the nth node.

ERROR/EXCEPTION HANDLING

CheckLineNumber - None.

position - If the string does not contain decimal digits an audible warning is given, followed by an error message, and the user must re-enter the string. If the linked list is empty or the line does not exist the function returns a NULL value.

PORTABILITY

atoi - ANSI
cprintf - UNIX/DOS/OS2
isdigit - ANSI

strcpy - ANSI

***/

```
#include "edit.h"
#include <conio.h>
#include <ctype.h>
#include <stdlib.h>
#include <string.h>

BOOLEAN CheckLineNumber(CHAR *number)
{
        INT index;

        for (index=0; index != strlen(number); index++)
                if (isdigit(number[index]) == 0)
                        return false;

        return true;
}

struct line *position(void)
{
        struct line *p;
        INT count, LineNumber;
        CHAR number[NUMBER_LENGTH+1];
        BOOLEAN NoError;

        screen(2);
        cprintf("\nenter line number: ");
        strcpy(number, GetNumber());
        NoError=CheckLineNumber(number);

        while (! NoError)
        {
                ClearScreen();
                cprintf("\aLINE NUMBER INVALID RE-ENTER ");
                strcpy(number, GetNumber());
                NoError=CheckLineNumber(number);
        }

        LineNumber = atoi(number);
        for (p=head, count=1 ;; p=p->link, count++)
        {
                if (LineNumber == count)
                {
                        current = LineNumber;
                        return p;
                }
```

```
        else if (p = = NULL)
                return NULL;
        }
}
```

MAIN.C

/********************************filename MAIN.C ********************************

FUNCTIONALITY

The file contains one function called main. The purpose of the function is to communicate the values of the command line parameters, for the name of the file to be edited, and to control access to the functions of the line editor system.

ERROR/EXCEPTION HANDLING

None.

PORTABILITY

Not applicable.

***/

```
#define MAIN
#include "edit.h"
#include <stdlib.h>

/* declaration of external variables */
struct line      *head = NULL;
INT              current;
CHAR *argument;
INT              LinesInFile;

main(INT argc, CHAR *argv[])
{
        OpenWindows();
        OpenFile(argc, argv);
        menu();
        CloseWindows();
}
```

MENU.C

```
/****************************** filename MENU.C *****************************

FUNCTIONALITY

The file contains one function - menu its purpose is to invite the user to enter, on screen(2), a line editor
command.

ERROR/ EXCEPTION HANDLING:

If the command code is illegal an audible warning is given and the user is invited to enter a code again.

PORTABILITY

cprintf - UNIX/DOS/OS2
strcpy - ANSI
toupper - ANSI

*****************************************************************************/

#include "edit.h"
#include <conio.h>
#include <ctype.h>
#include <string.h>

VOID menu(VOID)
{
        CHAR MenuCode[CHAR_LENGTH+1];

        for (;;) {
                        screen(2);
                        ClearScreen();
                        cprintf("[A]mend [D]elete [F]ind [H]elp ");
                        cprintf("[I]nsert [L]ist [Q]uit [S]ave\n\n");
                        cprintf("enter code ");
                        strcpy(MenuCode, GetChar());
                        MenuCode[0] = toupper(MenuCode[0]);

                        switch (MenuCode[0])
                        {
                        case AMEND:         amend(position());break;
                        case DELETE:        delete(position());break;
                        case FIND:          find();break;
                        case HELP:          help();break;
                        case INSERT:        insert();break;
                        case LIST:          list(position());break;
                        case QUIT:          return;
                        case SAVE:          save();break;
```

```
                        default :        cprintf("\a");
                        }
                }
        }
```

OPENFILE.C

```
/********************************* filename OPENFILE.C ********************************
```

FUNCTIONALITY

The file contains one function whose purpose is to examine the contents of the command line parameter and place the line editor system into a state ready for the next line editor command.

If the filename given in the command line exists on disc, the contents of the text file is copied into the linked list. The mechanism for building the linked list is identical to the build function. However, instead of text being entered at the console it is read from the text file until the end of file is encountered. After the linked list has been built the entire contents of the linked list is displayed on the screen.

ERROR/EXCEPTION HANDLING

If the number of command line parameters are incorrect then an audible warning is followed by an error message, the screens are closed and control returns to the command line of the operating system, in this case MSDOS.

If the filename given in the command line parameter cannot be used to open a file in a READ_ONLY mode, then it is assumed that the file does not exist on the disc; an audible warning is followed by a NEW FILE message, and the user is invited to insert the text to build a new file. At the end of building the file the entire contents is listed to screen(1).

If the line editor is the only editor to be used in building text files, the size of the file being built will depend upon the amount of memory available on the heap. Therefore, in loading an existing file, the memory space available should be sufficient to build the linked list, if it is not sufficient part of the old file will appear to have been truncated.

PORTABILITY

cprintf - UNIX/DOS/OS2
fclose - ANSI
feof - ANSI
fgets - ANSI
fopen - ANSI
free - ANSI
malloc - ANSI

```
**************************************************************************************/
```

```
#include "edit.h"
#include <conio.h>
#include <stdio.h>
#include <stdlib.h>

VOID OpenFile(INT argc, CHAR *argv[])
{
        FILE *filename;
        struct line *p, *new;

        screen(2);
        ClearScreen();

        if (argc != 2)
        {
                cprintf("\aERROR - FILENAME PARAMETERS\n");
                PC_delay();
                CloseWindows();
                exit(errno);
        }

        filename = fopen(argv[1], READ_ONLY);
        argument=argv[1];

        if (filename == NULL)
        {
                cprintf("\aNEW FILE %s\n", argument);
                build();
                list(head);
        }
        else
        {
                new=malloc(sizeof(struct line));
                fgets(new->text, LINE_LENGTH+1, filename);

                while (feof(filename) == 0)
                {
                        new->link=NULL;
                        LinesInFile = 1;
                        for (head=new, p=new, current = 1 ;; p=new, current++)
                        {
                                new=malloc(sizeof(struct line));
                                fgets(new->text, LINE_LENGTH+1, filename);
                                new->link=NULL;
                                if (feof(filename) != 0)
                                {
                                        free(new);
                                        fclose(filename);
                                        list(head);
```

155

```
                                    return;
                            }
                            p->link = new;
                            LinesInFile++;
                        }
                    }
                }
}
```

PC_DELAY.C

```
/******************************* filename PC_DELAY *********************************
```

FUNCTIONALITY

The file contains one function - PC_delay; its purpose is to provide a time delay of TIME_PERIOD milliseconds between the execution of statements.

ERROR/EXCEPTION HANDLING

None.

PORTABILITY

delay - IBM PC or compatible

```
********************************************************************************/

#include "edit.h"
#include <stdlib.h>

VOID PC_delay(VOID)
{
        delay(TIME_PERIOD);
}
```

SAVE.C

Once again the code for this function has been omitted and it is left to the reader to complete the function.

```
/************************************ filename SAVE.C ****************************
```

FUNCTIONALITY

The file contains one function save, whose purpose is to copy the contents of the linked list to a named text file to be stored on disc.

ERROR/EXCEPTION HANDLING

If the file already exists on the disc, the user is given the option to overwrite the file. If the file is not to be overwritten return from the function with no change.

If the file does not exist on the disc then the linked list will be copied to the named file or to the file named in the command line if the user does not input a filename.

Note: This function does not check on the amount of available space on disc prior to copying the file.

PORTABILITY

cprintf - UNIX/DOS/OS2
strcpy - ANSI
toupper - ANSI
fopen - ANSI
fclose - ANSI

```
**********************************************************************************************/

#include "edit.h"
#include <conio.h>
#include <ctype.h>
#include <stdio.h>
#include <string.h>

VOID save(VOID)
{
    struct line *p;
    FILE *filename;
    CHAR reply[CHAR_LENGTH+1];
    CHAR NewFile[LINE_LENGTH+1];

/* function code has been deliberately omitted */

}
```

WINDOWS.C

The TopSpeed window module provides a collection of window management functions. With these functions you can display several virtual screens, or windows, on the physical screen. The window package is designed to integrate with the standard console input/output through generic console input/output routines defined in the conio.h header file.

The following constants and types are defined and used in the window module.

```
typedef enum {    Black, Blue, Green, Cyan, Red, Magenta, Brown, LightGray,
                  DarkGray, LightBlue, LightGreen, LightCyan, LightRed,
                  LightMagenta, Yellow, White      } Color ;
```

```
typedef struct {
                abscoord X1, Y1, X2, Y2; /* outer co-ordinates of opposite corners */
                unsigned char Foreground, Background; /* not Used if Palette */
                unsigned char CursorOn; /* if cursor active */
                unsigned char WrapOn; /* if EOL wrap enabled */
                unsigned char Hidden; /* if window on view */
                unsigned char FrameOn; /* if frame */
                framestr FrameDef; /* only Used if frame */
                unsigned char FrameFore, FrameBack; /* only Used if frame
                                                    and not Palette Window */
        } windef;

typedef enum {   NoTitle, LeftUpperTitle, CenterUpperTitle, RightUpperTitle,
                LeftLowerTitle, CenterLowerTitle, RightLowerTitle   } TitleMode;

extern windef fullscreendef;
extern wintype _fullscreen;

wintype windowopen(windef *WD);

void use(wintype _win);
void windowclose(wintype _win);
void clrscr(void);
void cursoron(void);
void cursoroff(void);
.
.
```

A window is defined by the type windef, and a variable or constant of this type is used to create a window. In windef, X1, Y1 are the coordinates of the upper left-hand corner and X2, Y2 represent the lower right-hand corner of the window.

A window is created using the function windowopen, which returns a handle of type wintype. Any subsequent reference to that window is made by using this handle.

/*********************************** filename WINDOWS.C ***********************************

FUNCTIONALITY:

The file contains the following four functions:

OpenWindows - Purpose to define the windows used by the line editor.

screen - Purpose to assign a screen for input and output.

ClearScreen - Purpose to clear the current screen.

CloseWindows - Purpose to close both windows by removing the windows from the screen, deleting the

158

window descriptors and de-allocating any buffers previously allocated to the windows. The screen is then cleared and the cursor restored to the normal screen.

ERROR/EXCEPTION HANDLING

None.

PORTABILITY

clrscr - TopSpeed DOS/OS2
cursoroff - TopSpeed DOS/OS2
cursoron - TopSpeed DOS/OS2
strcpy - ANSI
window - IBM PC and compatibles

```
************************************************************************************/

#include "edit.h"
#include <string.h>
#include <window.h>

typedef struct          {
                             INT x,y;
                        } WindowCoordinates;

typedef WindowCoordinates windows[2];
windef WindowDef;

const windows TopLeftHandCorner = {{0,0}, {0,19}};

wintype window[2];

VOID OpenWindows(VOID)
{
     clrscr();
     cursoroff();

     WindowDef.Foreground = White;
     WindowDef.Background = Black;
     WindowDef.CursorOn = FALSE;
     WindowDef.WrapOn = FALSE;
     WindowDef.Hidden = FALSE;
     WindowDef.FrameOn=TRUE;
     strcpy(WindowDef.FrameDef,SINGLEFRAME);
     WindowDef.FrameFore=White;
     WindowDef.FrameBack=Black;

     WindowDef.X1=TopLeftHandCorner[0].x;
     WindowDef.Y1=TopLeftHandCorner[0].y;
```

```
        WindowDef.X2 = WindowDef.X1 + 79;
        WindowDef.Y2 = WindowDef.Y1 + 18;
        window[0] = windowopen(&WindowDef);

        WindowDef.X1 = TopLeftHandCorner[1].x;
        WindowDef.Y1 = TopLeftHandCorner[1].y;
        WindowDef.X2 = WindowDef.X1 + 79;
        WindowDef.Y2 = WindowDef.Y1 + 6;
        window[1] = windowopen(&WindowDef);
}

VOID screen(INT number)
{
        use(window[number-1]);
        cursoron();
}

VOID ClearScreen(VOID)
{
        clrscr();
}

VOID CloseWindows(VOID)
{
        windowclose(window[0]);
        windowclose(window[1]);
        clrscr();
        cursoron();
}
```

7.5 Make facility

All the programs in the previous six chapters were compiled, and linked as single entities. However, in the case study there are fourteen different program files, how should we compile and link these?

As each program is developed it could be separately compiled, to ensure that it does not contain any syntax errors. However, if you decide to change a header file, all the programs dependent upon that file will need to be recompiled again!

The make facility requires a makefile, which contains commands to show what files are to compiled and linked. For example, the makefile used in this case study is named EDIT.PR and contains the following information.

```
#system auto exe
#model mthread
#compile
        amend, datain, dataout, delete, find, help, insert, line, main, menu, openfile, pc_delay, save, windows
#link edit
```

160

The first command #system auto exe indicates the target operating system and file type for this makefile. The auto indicates that the target operating system is the same as the development operating system, in this case MSDOS. The exe indicates that an executable file is being built.

The second command #model mthread indicates the memory model.

The third command #compile causes each nominated source file to be compiled.

Finally, the #link command links together all the files listed into the nominated executable file edit.exe.

The make facility calculates dependencies within the file, and automatically recompiles all out-of-date modules within the program. If all compilations are successful, an executable file is created by linking the program objects together.

If after making an executable file, edit.h was changed, then since all fourteen program files are dependent upon the edit.h file, the make facility would automatically re-compile all the program files. However, if only one program file had been changed, then this single file would be recompiled in order to make a new executable file.

7.6 Summary

- Software produced using C is normally spread over many program files.

- Each program file will contain functions related to a specific task.

- Do not use machine dependent functions throughout program files, but group such functions into fewer files, in order to minimise the amount of re-programming when porting software to another computer.

- Do not use 'raw' C data types in the program files since these will hinder the portability of a system.

- Use one or more 'project' header files to define the constants, data types, structures, global variables, macros and prototyped functions that occur in the program files.

- Use the make facility to compile and link all the program files in a project. This will automatically recompile any files that have dependencies upon files that have been changed.

7.7 Questions   *answers begin on page 280*

Code complete functions as answers to:

1. Function find in file FIND.C.

2. Function insert in file INSERT.C.

3. Function save in file SAVE.C.

Compile and link each function using the MAKE facility. Test each function thoroughly before progressing to the next question.

Part Two

Convert to C++

8.
The Transition

*Using the knowledge gained in learning and understanding C,
this chapter focuses the reader's attention upon many of the
differences between C and C++ as a procedural language.*

Contents

8.1 What is C++ ?

C++ has developed from C, and can be regarded as an extension to ANSI C. The language offers improvements upon many of the features of C for procedural programming, but extends the functionality of the language into the realms of data abstraction and object-oriented programming. This chapter concentrates on the differences between C and C++ for procedural programming. The use of C++ for data abstraction and object-oriented programming will be covered in the next two chapters.

If C++ can be regarded as a superset of ANSI C, then it must follow that a program written in C will compile using a C++ compiler. To a large extent this statement is true, however, there are some features of C that will no longer work in C++. These incompatibilities will be explained later in the chapter.

To support the earlier statement that a program written in C will compile using a C++ compiler, consider the following program that generates an array of integers and calculates the sum and average of the numbers in the array.

```
/* program to create an array of integers; calculate the sum and
arithmetic mean of the numbers and display this information */

#include <stdio.h>
#include <stdlib.h>

int *table;
int sum;

/* function to generate the size of the array between 1 and 10,
and fill the array with integers in the range 1 to 25 */

void GetData(int *size)
{
        int index;

        randomize();
        *size = (rand()%10)+1;
        table = calloc(*size, sizeof(int));
        for (index=0; index!=*size; table[index]=(rand()%25)+1, index++);
}

/* function to calculate the arithmetic mean of the numbers in the array */

float mean(int *size, int *sum)
{
        int index;

        for (index=0, *sum=0; index!= *size; index++)
        *sum=*sum+table[index];
        return (float) *sum / (float) *size;
}
```

```
/* function to display the contents of the array */

void display(int *size)
{
      int index;

      for (index=0; index!=*size; index++)
            printf("%4d", table[index]);
      printf("\n");
}

main()
{
      int size;
      float average;

      GetData(&size);
      printf("size of table %4d\n", size);
      display(&size);
      average=mean(&size, &sum);
      printf("sum of numbers %4d\n", sum);
      printf("arithmetic mean %10g\n", average);
      free(table);
}
```

This, without any doubt, is a program written in ANSI C, however, the program filename was given a .cpp extension in place of the .c extension, and compiled using the JPI TopSpeed C++ compiler. The outcome was that it compiled without any errors, was linked and ran correctly.

If C++ offers improvements over C how can this program be improved? In the next section the program has been rewritten using C++, and the differences between the changes are discussed. The line numbers have been included for easy reference and are NOT part of the program.

8.2 Minor differences

Before continuing with the rest of this section read through the following C++ program and write down all the new features that you can find.

```
1       // program to create an array of integers; calculate the sum and
2       // arithmetic mean of the numbers, and display this information
3
4       #include <iostream.hpp>
5       #include <stdlib.h>
6
7       int *table;
8       int sum;
9
10      // function to input the size of the array from 1 to 10,
11      // then fill the array with integers in the range 1 to 25
```

167

```
12
13      void GetData(int &size)
14      {
15              randomize();
16              size=(rand()%10)+1;
17              table = new int[size];
18
19              for (int index=0; index!=size; table[index]=(rand()%25)+1, index++);
20      }
21
22      // function to calculate the arithmetic mean of the numbers in the array
23
24      float mean(int &size)
25      {
26              int sum=0;
27
28              for (int index=0; index!=size; index++)
29              sum=sum+table[index];
30
31              ::sum=sum;
32
33              return float(sum) / float(size);
34      }
35
36      void display(int &size)
37      {
38              for (int index=0; index!=size; index++)
39              {
40                      cout.width(5);
41                      cout << table[index];
42              }
43              cout << endl;
44      }
45
46      main()
47      {
48              int size;
49
50              GetData(size);
51              cout << "size of table " << size << endl;
52              display(size);
53              float average = mean(size);
54              cout << "sum of numbers " << sum << endl;
55              cout.precision(2);
56              cout << "mean of contents " << average << endl;
57              delete [ ] table;
58      }
```

There are a total of sixteen new features in this example, many of them repeated, did you find all of them?

Here is a list of the some of the new features together with an explanation of what they do.

```
1       // program to create an array of integers; calculate the sum and
```

C++ allows single line comments, which begin with // and terminate at the end of the line. Single-line comments are regarded as being safer than the old-style comments, since they cannot accidentally be left unterminated. However, old-style comments can still be used, either style comment delimiter can be commented out using the other. For example:

```
/*
    // these comments
    // are commented out
*/
// /*
    // these comments
    // are commented in
// */
```

```
4       #include <iostream.hpp>
```

There is one unfamiliar header file associated with input/ output <iostream.hpp>. Notice that in JPI TopSpeed C++, the header filename extension is hpp and not h. In the <iostream.hpp> library, the standard input stream is named cin, the output stream is named cout and the error stream is named cerr, all three streams correspond to the stdin, stdout and stderr streams, respectively, found in the C library.

```
13      void GetData(int &size)
```

In C all parameters, except for arrays, are passed by value. Therefore, changing the value of a parameter affects only the function's local copy. For a C function to modify a variable the function must be passed as a pointer to the variable.

C++ provides an alternative way to allow the modification of an actual parameter by declaring the formal parameter only to be a reference by using the symbol &. Notice from line 16 that the reference parameter &size is treated as a variable and not as a pointer.

```
16      size=(rand()%10)+1;
```

Notice also that the actual parameter in the function call, line 50, is not preceded by the & operator, but simply treated as a variable.

```
50      GetData(size);
```

Reference parameters, like pointer parameters, make it possible to pass a large data structure to a function without the extra overhead of making a local copy of the structure. Reference parameters make it possible to code formal parameters in C++ programs in a similar way to, say, Pascal or Modula-2.

```
17      table = new int[size];
57      delete [ ] table;
```

In C dynamic storage allocation for arrays is made by using the functions calloc or malloc, depending upon the type of data being stored. C++ provides an alternative to calloc and malloc through the operator new. The deallocation of memory assigned to an array is possible by using the C++ operator delete, in place of the C function free.

```
19      for (int index=0; index!=size; table[index]=(rand()%25)+1, index++);
```

In C++ the first expression in the for statement, for initialising the loop variable, may contain a type declaration for the loop variable. In this example the type declaration int has been declared with the initialisation of index. This feature allows the for statement to declare its own loop control variable, without the declaration being made outside the loop.

The scope of the declared variable extends to the end of the enclosing block. In this example, the block is the one in which the for statement appears. However, if a for statement is declared in one branch of an if statement the scope of the loop control variable is confined to the if statement, and does not exist outside this statement.

```
31      ::sum=sum;
```

In C, when a declaration inside a block names an identifier that is already visible, the new declaration temporarily hides the old one. In this program sum has been declared on line 8, as a global variable, yet sum has also been declared and initialised, on line 26, in function mean, as a local variable. During the life of this function the global variable sum will not represent any of the values associated with the local variable sum. C++ provides a scope resolution operator :: as a means of access to the hidden identifier, in this example the global variable sum. After the execution of the statement ::sum=sum; the global variable contains the same value as the local variable.

```
33      return float(sum) / float(size);
```

In C, explicit type conversions are performed using cast expressions. C++ allows an alternative notation in which the type name is used as though it were a function. In this example both float(sum) and float(size) convert the type of the variables sum and size, temporarily from integer to floating-point.

```
53      float average = mean(size);
```

In a C++ function, declarations can be mixed with statements. For example the declaration of float appears embedded within the statements of main().

The scope of such a variable extends from its declaration to the end of the enclosing block.

```
40      cout.width(5);
41      cout << table[index];
43      cout << endl;
```

The operator << is similar to printf, in so much as it implies output, it is known as an insertion into the standard output stream cout. Thus the value of table[index] is to be inserted into the standard output stream cout. Prior to this statement being executed the field width for the number has been set to 5 characters, by cout.width. After the number has been displayed, a new line character is inserted into the output stream and the stream emptied (flushed) by cout << endl.

Notice the << operation. This symbol has been used before to represent a bitwise left shift. The use of the same symbol, but in a different context, is known as operator overloading. This is common practice in C++, the compiler resolves the intended use for the symbol by examining the context in which the symbol is being used. But more of this later!

51   cout << "size of table " << size << endl;

Several items can be inserted into the output stream in one statement. In this example, the string constant size of table is output, followed by the value for size and finally terminated with a new line character.

55   cout.precision(2);

The precision function is used to signify the maximum number of figures to display after the decimal point. In this example, a value output to the stream cout, may contain up to two decimal places.

One example is not enough to be able to demonstrate many of the minor procedural differences between C and C++, therefore, a second example follows to demonstrate the changes in the use of structures, initialisation and in-line function.

In this second example a C++ program has been written to calculate income tax according to the following rules.

A tax allowance is given according to marital status; a single person is allowed £3000, a married person £5000, which is only allowed against one salary if both partners are working.

The pension contribution is 6% of the annual gross salary.

Taxable income is the difference between the annual gross salary and the sum of the single/ married allowance and the pension contributions.

Income tax is based upon taxable income, and is levied at the following rates.

The first £5000 of taxable income attracts tax at 0% - tax band 0;
a taxable income of up to £20,000 attracts tax at the rate of 20% for any amount over £5000 - tax band 1;
a taxable income of up to £30,000 attracts tax at the rate of 30% for any amount over £20,000 - tax band 2;
a taxable income of up to £40,000 attracts tax at the rate of 40% for any amount over £30,000 - tax band 3;
and a taxable income in excess of £40,000 attracts tax at the rate of 50% - tax band 4.

The data to be input is the annual gross salary and the marital status of married or single.

The information supplied by the program is the allowance for a married or single person; the annual pension contribution; the annual taxable income; the annual income tax and the net annual salary.

```
1       // program to demonstrate the use of tags, anonymous unions,
2       // initialisers, constants and in-line functions in C++
3
4       // the program computes the personal allowance,
5       // income tax and pension contributions on a person's salary
6
```

```
7       #include <iostream.hpp>
8       #include <limits.h>
9
10      enum answer {no, yes};
11
12      struct income        {
13                                  float AnnualSalary;
14                                  char status;
15                                  union {
16                                              int single;
17                                              int married;
18                                  };
19                       };
20
21      struct PayDetails     {
22                                  float TaxableIncome;
23                                  float pension;
24                                  float tax;
25                                  float salary;
26                       };
27
28      const int MarriedAllowance = 5000;
29      const int SingleAllowance = 3000;
30      const float superannuation = 0.06;
31      const float BasicRateTax = 0.20;
32      const int NumberOfTaxBands = 4;
33      const int LowestThreshold = 5000;
34
35      // function that receives status of a person and returns the allowance
36
37      int allowance(income &person)
38      {
39              if (person.status == 'M' || person.status == 'm')
40              {
41                      person.married = MarriedAllowance;
42                      return MarriedAllowance;
43              }
44              else
45              {
46                      person.single = SingleAllowance;
47                      return SingleAllowance;
48              }
49      }
50
51      // function to input the annual salary and marital status
52
53      void DataIn(income &person)
54      {
55              cout << "input annual salary ";
```

```
56          cin > > person.AnnualSalary;
57          cout < < "married or single? ";
58          cin > > person.status;
59      }
60
61      // function to calculate the taxable income, pension, income tax and net salary
62
63      void calculations(income &person, PayDetails &wages)
64      {
65          const float b=BasicRateTax;
66          long int threshold = LowestThreshold;
67
68          float TaxRate[NumberOfTaxBands] = {b, 1.5*b, 2.0*b, 2.5*b};
69          long int TaxBand[NumberOfTaxBands+1] =
70          {threshold, 4*threshold, 6*threshold, 8*threshold, LONG_MAX};
71
72          // calculate pension
73
74          wages.pension = superannuation * person.AnnualSalary;
75
76          // calculate taxable income
77
78          wages.TaxableIncome = person.AnnualSalary - allowance(person) - wages.pension;
79
80          // calculate income tax
81
82          wages.tax = 0;
83
84          if (wages.TaxableIncome > TaxBand[0])
85          {
86          for (int index=0; index != NumberOfTaxBands; index++)
87                  if (wages.TaxableIncome > TaxBand[index+1])
88                  wages.tax = wages.tax + (TaxBand[index+1]-TaxBand[index]) * TaxRate[index];
89                  else
90                  {
91                  wages.tax = wages.tax + (wages.TaxableIncome-TaxBand[index]) * TaxRate[index];
92                  break;
93                  }
94          }
95
96          // calculate net salary
97
98          wages.salary = person.AnnualSalary - wages.tax - wages.pension;
99      }
100
101     // function to set the format for printing numbers
102
103     inline void OutStream(void)
104     {
```

```
105              cout.precision(5);
106              cout.width(12);
107     }
108
109     // function to display details of allowance, deductions and wage
110
111     void InfoOut(income &person, PayDetails &wages)
112     {
113              cout << "allowance ";
114              OutStream();
115              cout << allowance(person) << endl;
116              cout << "pension contribution ";
117              OutStream();
118              cout << wages.pension << endl;
119              cout << "taxable income ";
120              OutStream();
121              cout << wages.TaxableIncome << endl;
122              cout << "income tax ";
123              OutStream();
124              cout << wages.tax << endl;
125              cout << "net salary ";
126              OutStream();
127              cout << wages.salary << endl;
128     }
129
130     // function to capture a yes/no reply
131
132     answer MoreData(void)
133     {
134              char reply;
135
136              cout << "\n\nMORE DATA? [Y]es [N]o ";
137              cin >> reply;
138              cout << endl;
139              return (reply=='Y' || reply=='y') ? yes : no;
140     }
141
142     main()
143     {
144              income person;
145              PayDetails wages;
146
147              do
148              {
149                       DataIn(person);
150                       calculations(person, wages);
151                       InfoOut(person, wages);
152              }
153              while (MoreData()==yes);
154     }
```

In C++, unlike C, tags are automatically visible as type names. Therefore, with the following enumerated type

```
10      enum answer {no, yes};
```

the tag answer can be used to declare a variable or function of type answer, for example:

```
132     answer MoreData(void)
```

Similarly, a structure such as:

```
21      struct PayDetails    {
22                  float TaxableIncome;
23                  float pension;
24                  float tax;
25                  float salary;
26                  };
```

could be used to define a variable of type PayDetails, for example:

```
63      void calculations(income &person, PayDetails &wages)
```

In C, a union variable or union member must always have a name, in C++, provided there is no ambiguity, this restriction is lifted. A union with no name is anonymous.

```
12      struct income          {
13                  float AnnualSalary;
14                  char status;
15                  union {
16                              int single;
17                              int married;
18                          };
19                  };
```

The members of the union are directly accessible as illustrated by the following code.

```
39      if (person.status == 'M' || person.status == 'm')
40      {
41              person.married = MarriedAllowance;
42              return MarriedAllowance;
43      }
44      else
45      {
46              person.single = SingleAllowance;
47              return SingleAllowance;
48      }
```

The input of data is from the standard input stream cin, is accomplished by using the extraction operator >>, for example:

                56   cin > > person.AnnualSalary;

will allow a value for the annual salary to be input via the keyboard. Notice there is no need to specify the type for the data being input as was the case when using scanf.

                68   float TaxRate[NumberOfTaxBands] = {b, 1.5*b, 2.0*b, 2.5*b};

In C++, a constant can appear in a constant expression, for example TaxRate[NumberOfTaxBands].

In C++, all initialisers may contain references to previously declared variables and functions, for example {b, 1.5*b, 2.0*b, 2.5*b}.

                103   inline void OutStream(void)
                104   {
                105   cout.precision(5);
                106   cout.width(12);
                107   }

In C, it is common practice to write small functions as macros, either with or without parameters. In C++ the preferred method is to define an inline function. This is a suggestion to the compiler that a particular function should be generated as an inclusion within the calling function, without the overhead of a function call. The compiler is not obliged to honour the request, especially if the inline function contains loops or selections.

A general rule is to restrict inline function to no more than two or three statements.

8.3 Functions revisited

In C++, the formal parameters of a function can be initialised. For example the following function prototype has the three default values, operation = '+', a=10 and b=5. Although these values are constants, the default arguments can be expressions, they do not have to be a constant value.

                int calculator(char operation = '+', int a=10, int b=5)

In this example all three arguments have default values, however, not all arguments may have default values, in which case these arguments must appear in the formal parameter list before those arguments having default values. For example,

                int calculator(int a=10, char operation, int b=5)

would be wrong, and would need to be rewritten as:

                int calculator(char operation, int a=10, int b=5)

Function calls may omit parameters with default values, starting from the right-hand end of the formal parameter list. For example using the function:

                int calculator(char operation = '+', int a=10, int b=5)

it is legal to call calculator with the following actual parameter lists.

```
calculator();                    // all three defaults assumed
calculator('*');                 // operation '*', a and b use defaults
calculator('/', 30);             // operation '/', a=30, b uses default
calculator('*', 30, 40);         // operation '*', a=30 and b=40
```

The following program illustrates some of the function calls that are possible using default arguments.

// **program to demonstrate the use of default arguments**

```
#include <iostream.hpp>

int calculator(char operation = '+', int a=10, int b=5)
{
        switch (operation)
        {
                case '+': return a+b;
                case '-': return a-b;
                case '*': return a*b;
                case '/':       if (b==0) return 0;
                                else return a/b;
                default : cout  << "ILLEGAL OPERATOR"; return 0;
        }
}

main()
{
        cout << calculator() << endl;
        cout << calculator('-') << endl;
        cout << calculator('*', 20) << endl;
        cout << calculator('/', 32767, 128) << endl;
}
```

The results from running this program are:

```
15
5
100
255
```

Default values for the same parameter cannot appear more than once in the same file, even if the values of the parameters are the same. However, multiple declarations of a function in the same file may supply additional default values. Therefore,

```
int calculator(char operation = '+', int a, int b);
int calculator(char operation, int a=10, int b);
int calculator(char operation = '+', int a, int b=5);
```

are the same as:

    int calculator(char operation = '+', int a=10, int b=5).

An alternative strategy for declaring default values is to put them in a header file. For example if the contents of the header file "a:p4.hpp" is:

    int calculator(char operation = '/', int a=99, int b=11);

then if it is included in a modified version of the previous program as follows.

// program to demonstrate the use of default arguments using a
// header file containing a declaration of the default values

#include <iostream.hpp>
#include "a:p4.hpp"

int calculator(char operation, int a, int b)
.
.

The results from running the program are:

9
88
220
255

In a C program, functions within the same scope must be given unique names, however, this restriction is lifted in C++. When two or more functions within the same scope have the same name the function name is said to be overloaded.

The reader may wonder how the compiler can resolve calls to an overloaded function. The answer is by examining the types in the formal parameter list. For example in the two prototypes for the function calculator, that follow:

    long int   calculator(char operation, long int a, long int b = 1)
    double   calculator(char operation, float a, float b)

the types in the formal parameter lists are quite different. A call of calculator('+', 47567, 69856) would be to the first function since the actual parameters are both long integers (greater than 32767); whereas a call of calculator('*', 32767.0F, 128.0F) would be to the second function since the actual parameters are both explicitly stated as floating-point values. It is worth noting that if the suffix F was omitted from each real number, then the numbers would be implicitly converted to double precision and a parameter match would not be possible.

If overloaded functions have a different number of formal parameters then argument matching is straightforward. However, when the number of parameters is the same then the compiler attempts to find the best match for any one parameter by using the following rules in the order given.

(i) Exact match - is the actual parameter the same type as the formal parameter?

(ii) Match with promotions - the compiler attempts to convert the actual parameter by applying integral promotions; float to double to long double or int to unsigned int to long int to unsigned long int.

(iii) Match with standard conversions - the compiler attempts to convert the actual parameters to other numeric or character types, for example long to int, char* to void*.

(iv) Match with user-defined functions - the compiler attempts to apply a conversion function provided by a user-defined class.

(v) Match with ellipsis - the compiler matches the actual parameter with an ellipsis in the formal parameter list. Note functions that take an unlimited number of parameters are declared with an ellipsis ... This is the worst case and will not be used if there is any other match. If two or more formal parameter lists are equally as good then the function call is illegal.

The following program gives an example of overloaded functions.

```
// program to demonstrate the use of overloading functions
#include <iostream.hpp>
#include <stdlib.h>

long int calculator(char operation, long int a, long int b = 1)
{
        switch (operation)
        {
                case '+':       return a+b;
                case '-':       return a-b;
                case '*':       return a*b;
                case '/':       return a/b;
        }
}

double calculator(char operation, char *stringA, char *stringB)
{
        char *endchar; long int a, b;

        a=strtol(stringA, &endchar, 10);
        b= strtol(stringB, &endchar, 10);
        switch (operation)
        {
                case '+':       return a+b;
                case '-':       return a-b;
                case '*':       return a*b;
                case '/':       return a/b;
        }
}
```

179

```
main()
{
        cout << calculator('+', 47567, 69856) << endl;      // uses first function answer 117423
        cout << calculator('*', 32767.0F, 128.0F) << endl;   // uses second function answer 4.194176e6
        cout << calculator('-', 32768) << endl;              // uses first function answer 32767
}
```

8.4 Incompatibilities

C++ is a superset of C, however, there are some features in C which will no longer operate correctly under C++. There are also cases where a C program can have a different meaning when compiled using a C++ compiler.

A list of the known incompatibilities between the two languages follows.

The linkage of a variable determines the extent to which it may be shared. A variable with external linkage may be shared by all files in a program. However, a variable with internal linkage is restricted to a single file. In C, constants defined by const have external linkage by default. In C++ such constants have internal linkage by default. As a result, a C file that refers to a const in another file will not link using C++. The program can be fixed by qualifying the definition of the constant with extern.

In C, character constants have type int, in C++ character constants have type char. Thus sizeof('A') in C is sizeof(int), sizeof('A') in C++ is sizeof(char). These changes will affect the meaning of a C program.

In C, an external variable can be defined more than once in a source file; in C++ a variable can be defined only once.

In C, a character array can be initialised by a string of the same length; in C++ the array must be at least one character longer than the string to store the terminating null character.

In C, values of an enumerated type are freely convertible to and from integers; in C++, values of an enumeration type are automatically converted to integers when necessary, however, integers are not automatically converted to enumeration values. For example,

```
                enum answer {no, yes}
                answer reply(void);
                return yes;              // legal in C and C++
                return 1;                // legal in C but not C++
```

This last case can be fixed by using an explicit type conversion.

```
                return answer (1);
```

C allows a function to be called without a prior declaration or definition; C++ does not.

C allows a goto statement to jump over any declarations at the beginning of a block; in C++, a goto statement may not jump over a declaration that contains an initialiser, however, it can bypass an entire block.

In C, structure, union and enumeration tags must be preceded by the words struct, union or enum respectively, for the tags to become visible. In C++, tags are visible without being preceded by struct, union or enum.

In C, a pointer of any type can be assigned to a variable of type void*, and void* pointers can be assigned to variables of other pointer types. In C++, any pointer can be assigned to a variable of type void* only.

Finally, the following C++ keywords are not part of C.

asm	friend	private	try
catch	inline	protected	this
class	new	public	throw
delete	operator	template	virtual

C programs that use any of these keywords as identifiers (variable names, constants, types, function names, etc) will not compile using a C++ compiler.

8.5 Summary

• C programs will compile using a C++ compiler, however, there are some features of C that will no longer operate under C++. In some instances, C programs may take a different meaning when compiled as a C++ program.

There are many minor differences between the C and C++ languages, these include the following areas.

• Single line comments using //.

• Input/output library <iostream.hpp>, using streams cin, cout.

• Memory allocation and deallocation from the heap with new and delete.

• Format of the for loop including a declaration of the type of loop variable.

• Declarations can occur anywhere in a block, provided there is no attempt to use the identifier before it is declared.

• Formal parameters can be reference parameters.

• Variables that would normally be hidden can be made visible using the scope resolution operator.

• Explicit type conversion by using the type in a similar manner to a function name.

• Tags for structures, unions and enumerations can be used to define types without the need to precede the tag with struct, union or enum.

• Unions do not need to be tagged, they can be anonymous.

• Inline functions are preferred to macros.

● Formal parameters can be given default values. Defaults can be omitted from the actual parameter list when the function is called.

● Default values can be changed by using different actual parameters in a function call, or by using header files containing prototypes of the function with different default values.

● Functions can have the same names within the same scope. The names are overloaded, and the compiler uses a set of rules based on the formal and actual parameters in resolving which function to use.

8.6 Questions   *answers begin on page 283*

1. Return to chapter 4 on arrays, and convert the final program in section 4.8 to a program written using as many features of C++ as possible. The program listing, starting on page 76, is to create an array of records, sort the records on ascending order of age and display the sorted array.

2. What are the errors in the following segments of code?

(a)

```
float alpha(void)
{
        int a, b;
        c = a+b;
        return float(c);
}
```

(b)

```
int j, n=10;
if (n > 0)
        for (int i = 1; i != n; i++)
                cout << i;
else
        j=i;
```

(c)

```
// file X.cpp
int alpha(float x)
{
        .
        .
}
```

```
// file Y.cpp
int alpha(int);
```

(d)
```
void beta(int i = 0, float j);
```

(e)

void gamma(char a, int b = 10, float c = 3.14);

      (i)   gamma(,,);
      (ii)   gamma(*, , 3.14159);
      (iii)   gamma(67);

3. Comment on the following use of references as:

(a) return values

```
int a[10];
int& alpha(int i)
{
        return a[i]
}
```

(b) variables

```
int i;
int & p = i;
```

4. Comment on the legality of the following statements.

(a)

```
void alpha(int, char);
void alpha(float, int);
```

      (i)   alpha(1, 2);
      (ii)   alpha(1.0, 2);
      (iii)   alpha(1, 2.0);
      (iv)   alpha(1.0, 2.0);

(b)

```
void beta(const int *);
void beta(int *);
int *p;
const int *q
```

      (i)   beta(p);
      (ii)   beta(q);

(c)

```
void gamma(int&);
```

183

```
void gamma(float);
int i;
double d;

        gamma(i);
        gamma(d);
```

(d)

```
void epsilon(signed char);
void epsilon(unsigned char);
char c;

        epsilon(c);
```

5. Write a program to demonstrate overloading the function name area, for the calculation of the area of a triangle given:

(a) the lengths of three sides (a, b and c) - area = sqrt(s(s-a)(s-b)(s-c)) where s is the semi-perimeter;

(b) base length (b) and perpendicular height (h) - area = 0.5 b h;

(c) two sides (a and b) and an included angle C - area = 0.5 a b sin C.

9.
Data Abstraction

This chapter highlights one of the major enhancements of C++ over C, in the introduction of features that permit the use of abstract data types.

Contents

9.1 Introduction

Data abstraction is the technique of combining a data type with a set of operations on data of the same type. This concept is not new. Consider for a moment the data type integer. Data of type integer can have the operations of addition (+), subtraction (-), multiplication (*), division (/) and remainder (%), applied to the data. The method of implementing the data type integer is hidden from the user. The integer could be represented in either pure binary or binary coded decimal, without resorting to a manual there is no way of knowing.

Similarly the implementations of the operations +, -, *, /, and % are hidden from the user, there is no direct way of inspecting how these operations are carried out.

The integer example demonstrates the necessary properties encountered in the data abstraction model. The abstraction has created a data type (integer). The type contains a minimal set of properties (+, -, *,/, and %). The implementation of the type, behind the scenes, uses whatever data and functions are necessary. User access to the type is through a restricted interface with the implementation details being hidden from the user of the type.

9.2 Classes

A class is essentially a new data type. The format of a class, in its simplest form, is similar to a structure definition. For example, two operands A and B, and a result could be represented as part of the structure:

```
struct arithmetic    {
                    int A;
                    int B;
                    int result;
            };
```

or as part of the class:

```
class calculator    {
                    int A;
                    int B;
                    int result;
            };
```

Variables could be declared as:

```
    arithmetic data_1;
    calculator data_2;
```

Access to members of data_1 would be through data_1.A, data_1.B, data_1.result. However, here is where the similarity between a struct and a class finishes, since it is not possible to access the data items A, B and result in the class structure calculator, by using the dot (.) notation, or even the (->) notation, if it were appropriate.

The three items of data in class calculator, are by default, private, and cannot be accessed outside the class. An alternative notation for the calculator class could be:

```
class calculator      {
                 private:
                        int A;
                        int B;
                        int result;
                 };
```

emphasising that access to the data is restricted by using the word private. The reader may wonder how such data can be accessed if it is private? The answer is to introduce functions that access the data, inside the class. Since the functions themselves are to be accessed by the user, in order to change the protected data, the functions must be made public. The class calculator has been re-coded to include functions that access the private data.

```
class calculator
{
       private:
              int A;
              int B;
              int result;
       public:
              void ADD(void);
              void SUBTRACT(void);
              void MULTIPLY(void);
              void DIVIDE(void);
              void create(void);
              void display(void);
};
```

The functions ADD, SUBTRACT, MULTIPLY, DIVIDE, create and display are all capable of accessing the private data and are known as member functions of the class calculator. This definition of the abstract data type calculator, could be stored in a file under the name, calc.hpp, say. This definition should be made visible to the user in order to show how data of the type calculator can be accessed.

The implementation of the class should have restricted access, and is of no consequence to the user. The implementation of the member functions follow and are stored in the file calc.cpp.

```
#include <iostream.hpp>
#include "a:calc.hpp"

void calculator :: ADD(void)
{
       result = A+B;
}

void calculator :: SUBTRACT(void)
{
       result = A-B;
}
```

```
void calculator :: MULTIPLY(void)
{
        result = A*B;
}

void calculator :: DIVIDE(void)
{
    if (B!=0)
            result = A/B;
    else
            result = 0;
}

void calculator :: create(void)
{
        cout << "A? "; cin >> A;
        cout << "B? "; cin >> B;
}

void calculator :: display(void)
{
        cout << result << endl;
}
```

Notice that calculator :: precedes the name of each member function. Without this notation a C++ compiler would regard the functions as ordinary functions that did not belong to the class calculator.

An alternative method of implementing the member functions would be to code them in the file calc.hpp, after the prototype of each function, making each function in-line by default.

The following program uses the abstract data type calculator.

```
#include "a:calc.cpp"
main()
{
        calculator data; // declare an instance of the calculator class

        data.create();
        data.ADD();
        data.display();
        data.SUBTRACT();
        data.display();
        data.MULTIPLY();
        data.display();
        data.DIVIDE();
        data.display();
}
```

In this program the variable data has been declared as type calculator, which causes the compiler to set aside space for the three data members A, B and result. The variable data calls function create, which effectively initialises A and B to values input at the keyboard. The variable data has then been operated upon by the member functions, and after each operation the value of the operation is displayed.

It is possible to create instances of the same class, in the same way as declaring variables of a given type, for example:

calculator X,Y;

X and Y are known as objects. Objects can be copied, provided one object has already been initialised to a value.

X.create();
Y=X;

Copying an object is equivalent to copying its data members; Y=X is equivalent to:

Y.A = X.A;
Y.B = X.B;
Y.result = X.result;

Similarly, one object can be used to provide an initial value to another object.

calculator X;
X.create();
calculator Y = X;

Since objects can be passed as parameters or returned by functions it is possible to re-write the member functions of the class calculator so that each function is called in a more natural way.

As an extension of the last example, consider the following definition of a new class, number.

```
class number
{
    private:
        double value;
    public:
        number ADD(number);
        number SUBTRACT(number);
        number MULTIPLY(number);
        number DIVIDE(number);
        number PERCENT(number);
        number sqrt(void);
        void create(double num);
        void display(void);
};
```

Notice that only one item of data exists for this class, a floating-point double variable called value. Notice also that two extra member functions have been included in this class, PERCENT and sqrt (square root).

The declaration of the member functions do not appear to take binary operators. However, by inspecting the implementation of ADD, say, these first impressions will be dispelled.

```
number number :: ADD(number B)
{
        number X;
        X.value = value + B.value;
        return X;
}
```

Clearly from this code it would appear that B is one of the numbers to be added, but where is the other? In a declaration of:

```
        number A,B,C;        C=A.ADD(B);
```

is interpreted as follows.

A.ADD implies that value contains the number from A.create(double num); for example A.create(15.0) initialises value to 15. A is taken as an implicit parameter to ADD. The object B is passed as an actual parameter to ADD; the sum value+B.value is then assigned to the temporary object X, and the function returns the value of the sum A+B, which is copied to object C.

The full implementation of the member functions for class follows. These have been filed under the name "a:calc1.cpp".

```
#include <iostream.hpp>
#include <math.h>
#include "a:calc1.hpp"

number number :: ADD(number B)
{
        number X;
        X.value = value + B.value;
        return X;
}

number number :: SUBTRACT(number B)
{
        number X;
        X.value = value - B.value;
        return X;
}

number number :: MULTIPLY(number B)
{
        number X;
        X.value = value * B.value;
        return X;
}
```

```
number number :: DIVIDE(number B)
{
        number X;
        if (B.value !=0)
                X.value = value / B.value;
        else
                X.value = 0;
        return X;
}

number number :: PERCENT(number B)
{
        number X;
        X.value = value/100.0 * B.value;
        return X;
}

number number :: sqrt(void)
{
        number X;
        X.value = :: sqrt(value);
        return X;
}

void number :: create(double num)
{
        value = num;
}

void number :: display(void)
{
        cout << value << endl;
}
```

Notice that the member function sqrt uses the function sqrt from the C library math.h. To resolve the conflict in names between the local class sqrt function, and the global function sqrt, the scope resolution operator is used.

An example program that uses objects of class number follows. This is similar in format to the program that used an object of type calculator. However, the use of the functions appears more natural, in that C=A.ADD(B) is to be preferred to data.ADD().

```
#include "a:calc1.cpp"
main()
{
        number A, B, C;

        A.create(5.0);
        B.create(7.0);
```

191

```
        C=A.ADD(B);
        C.display();
        C=A.SUBTRACT(B);
        C.display();
        C=A.MULTIPLY(B);
        C.display();
        C=A.DIVIDE(B);
        C.display();
        C=A.PERCENT(B);
        C.display();
        C=A.sqrt();
        C.display();
}
```

9.3 Constructors

Up to now, the only method of initialising data of a class has been through a create member function. C++ offers an alternative technique that conforms to the syntax of the language.

A constructor is used for class data initialisation, it looks like a function and has the same name as the class. The definition of the class number has been modified to include three constructors as follows.

```
class number
{
        private:
                double value;
        public:
                // constructors
                number();
                number(double);
                number(char *);

                // functions
                number ADD(number);
                number SUBTRACT(number);
                number MULTIPLY(number);
                number DIVIDE(number);
                number PERCENT(number);
                number sqrt(void);
                void display(void);
};
```

The first constructor, number(), is the default constructor, and is used to initialise objects to some default value. The second constructor number(double), is used to initialise the object to a specified value through a member initialisation list. The third constructor number(char *), serves the same function as the second, however, the initial value of the object is a string, and will be converted to a double value by the constructor. The third constructor has in effect been used as a type conversion function.

A constructor has a dual purpose; to declare an object and initialise the data of the object. For example, the declaration:

    number A(1234), B("9876"), C;

uses all three constructors, in which objects A, B and C are declared with respective initial values of 1234, 9876 and 0. A study of the implementation of the constructors will reveal how this is possible.

```
number :: number()
{
      value = 0;
}

number :: number(double num)
{
      value = num;
}

number :: number(char *string)
{
      char *terminator;
      value = strtod(string, &terminator);
}
```

Notice in this last constructor that the string parameter has been converted into a double precision floating-point number by using the function strtod from the library string.h

Observe also that the function names of the constructors have been overloaded and the correct function is obtained through argument matching.

It is also possible to use the practice of default arguments when invoking constructors, although this is not possible with this example.

By introducing constructors into the class number there is no further requirement for the member function create, and for this reason it has been deleted.

The only modification to the earlier test program is the insertion of the line, number A(1234), B("9876"), C; and the deletion of the lines A.create(5.0); B.create(7.0). Apart from the values of A and B being different the program will run without further modification.

Before leaving the topic of classes it is worth mentioning, that class members that do not belong to individual instances of a class, but to the class itself, are called static members. These can be static data members and function members.

In the last example it is possible to include a static data member in the class number that keeps a running total (sum) of all the numbers input via the constructors. A static member function (SUM) can also be included that returns the value of this running total.

The modified class would appear as follows.

```
class number
{
        private:
                double value;
                static double sum;
        public:
                .

                .
                static double SUM() {return sum;}
};
```

Notice that the static member function has been treated as an in-line function since it only requires one line of code.

The file a:calc2.cpp would then need to be modified to change the value of sum for each instance of the class number.

```
        .
        .


double number::sum=0; // definition and initialisation of sum
        .
        .

number :: number(double num)
{
        value = num;
        sum = sum + value; // sum increased
}

number :: number(char *string)
{
        char *terminator;
        value = strtod(string, &terminator);
        sum = sum + value; // sum increased
}
```

The appearance of a static data member in a class definition only declares the member, it must be defined and initialised in the implementation of the class. Notice that sum has been declared and initialised in the implementation file a:calc2.cpp, and that it is necessary to use the scope resolution operator to indicate the class to which sum belongs. Despite sum being private it is possible to access it outside of a member function only for the purpose of declaration and initialisation.

Declaring a member function to be static allows it to be called without referring to an object of the class. As with static data members the scope resolution operator is required. The test program could be modified to include the following line to output the value of sum.

```
                cout << "total of numbers " << number :: SUM();
```

9.4 Operator overloading

If overloading of function names implies that several functions, in the same scope, have the same name; then operator overloading means that the same operator can serve different purposes, depending on the types of the operands.

The previous examples in this chapter are just right to demonstrate operator overloading. How much better to replace the function names ADD, SUBTRACT, MULTIPLY, DIVIDE and PERCENT with the respective operators +, -, *, /, and %.

The definition of the class number has been modified and is listed as follows.

```
class number
{
            friend number operator + (const number&, const number&);
            friend number operator-(const number&, const number&);
            friend number operator*(const number&, const number&);
            friend number operator/(const number&, const number&);
            friend number operator%(const number&, const number&);
        private:
            double value;
        public:
            // constructors
            number();
            number(double);
            number(char *);

            // functions
            number sqrt(void);
            void display(void);
};
```

There are clearly a few major changes. The functions for ADD, SUBTRACT, MULTIPLY, DIVIDE and PERCENT have not only been replaced by their respective operators, but they have been moved out of the public section, to the beginning of the class definition and have had several new reserved words of friend and operator appended to them!

A friend mechanism is provided in C++ to allow the programmer to bypass class access restrictions. Since this goes against the spirit of data abstraction it should be used sparingly.

A friend is NOT a member function. However, a function that is defined as a friend, has access to all members of the class, including private members, as though it were a member itself. A friend declaration can be placed into either the private or public section of a class. By convention, friends are declared at the beginning of a class definition.

Binary and unary operators differ slightly in the classes and functions within which their methods can be defined. A binary operator, such as +, -, *, / or % can be defined by either a member function taking one argument, or a friend function taking two arguments. Generally only operators with zero or one operand can be defined as member functions, and operators with two operands must be defined as functions with a friend qualifier.

If an overloaded operator has a predefined type as its first operand, the operator cannot be a member function but must be a friend function.

All C++ operators may be overloaded except for ::, ., sizeof, .* and ?: The =, [], () and -> operators, if overloaded, must be member functions and not friends.

Overloaded operators retain their original number of operands as well as their original precedence and associativity.

The implementation of the class number follows, notice that the operands for the overloaded functions have been passed by reference and not copied.

```
#include <iostream.hpp>
#include <math.h>
#include "a:calc3.hpp"

// overloaded operators
number operator+(const number& A, const number& B)
{
        number C;
        C.value = A.value + B.value;
        return C;
}


number operator-(const number& A, const number& B)
{
        number C;
        C.value = A.value - B.value;
        return C;
}


number operator*(const number& A, const number& B)
{
        number C;
        C.value = A.value * B.value;
        return C;
}


number operator/(const number& A, const number& B)
{
        number C;
        if (B.value !=0)
                C.value = A.value / B.value;
        else
                C.value = 0;
        return C;
}
```

```
number operator%(const number& A, const number& B)
{
      number C;
      C.value = A.value/100.0 * B.value;
      return C;
}

// constructors
number :: number()
{
      value = 0;
}

number :: number(double num)
{
      value = num;
}

number :: number(char *string)
{
      char *terminator;
      value = strtod(string, &terminator);
}

// functions
number number :: sqrt(void)
{
      number C;
      C.value = :: sqrt(value);
      return C;
}

void number :: display(void)
{
      cout << value << endl;
}
```

The following program represents a simple calculator in which numbers can be added, subtracted, multiplied, divided, and the percentage and square root of a number calculated. The numbers are input as strings and converted to double-precision floating point before being used as operands. The program uses the abstract data type number with overloading on the operations of +, -, *, /, and %.

```
// program to demonstrate the use of class number with overloaded operators
#include <stdlib.h>
#include <iostream.hpp>
#include "a:calc3.cpp"

char a[30], b[30];
char reply;
```

```
main()
{
      for (;;)
      {
              cout << "\ncalculator options\n"
              << "+ add\n"
              << "- subtract\n"
              << "* multiply\n"
              << "/ divide\n"
              << "% percentage\n"
              << "s square root\n"
              << "e exit calculator\n\n";
              cin >> reply;

              if (reply == 'e' | reply == 'E') exit(errno);
              cout << "enter number --> ";
              cin >> a;
              if (reply != 's' && reply != 'S')
              {
                      cout << "enter number --> ";
                      cin >> b;
              }

              number A=a, B=b, C;

              switch (reply)
              {
              case '+'      : C=A+B; break;
              case '-'      : C=A-B; break;
              case '*'      : C=A*B; break;
              case '/'      : C=A/B; break;
              case '%'      : C=A%B; break;
              case 's'      : C=A.sqrt();
              }

              cout << "answer --> ";
              C.display();
      }
}
```

9.5 Copy constructors

The constructors defined in section 9.3, were used in initialising numeric class data. When the data is a character string a copy constructor is required. A copy constructor will allocate enough memory to copy the string associated with the argument.

The following code illustrates the class string.

class string

```
{
            // friends
            // string comparisons
            friend int operator > (const string&, const string&);
            friend int operator < (const string&, const string&);
            friend int operator = = (const string&, const string&);
    private:
            char *characters;
            int length;
    public:
            // constructors
            string();
            string(char *);

            // functions
            // string assignment
            string& operator = (const string&);
            // string concatenation
            string& operator + (const string&);
            // display string on screen
            void display(void) const;
};
```

This class provides member functions for string assignment, concatenation and output, together with friend functions for string comparisons. The implementation of the constructors follows.

```
string :: string()
{
        characters = NULL;
        length = 0;
}

string :: string(char *s)
{
        length = strlen(s);
        characters = new char[length+1];
        strcpy(characters, s);
}
```

Notice that the default constructor sets the string to NULL and the length of the string to zero. Whereas the copy constructor calculates the length of the argument string and allocates enough memory to store the string. The characters from the argument are then copied into the data string for the class.

The complete implementation of the class string follows.

Notice that the code for the string comparisons >, < and == respectively, have been defined as in line code. This is perfectly acceptable since the each block of code is only a short length.

Observe that both the assignment operator and concatenation operator only require single arguments. For this reason they have been coded as member functions and not friends.

The reader will notice a new reserved word, this, in both the assignment and concatenation member functions. The reserved word, this, refers to a special pointer, which always points to the object that called the function, and represents the implicit parameter that is passed to a member function. This implicit parameter is always present for operator functions defined as class methods.

```
#include <iostream.hpp>
#include <string.h>
#include "a:string.hpp"

inline int operator > (const string&a, const string&b)
{
        if (strcmp(a.characters, b.characters) > 0)
                return 1;
        else
                return 0;
}

inline int operator < (const string&a, const string&b)
{
        if (strcmp(a.characters, b.characters) < 0)
                return 1;
        else
                return 0;
}

inline int operator = = (const string&a, const string&b)
{
        if (strcmp(a.characters, b.characters) == 0)
                return 1;
        else
                return 0;
}

string :: string()
{
        characters = NULL;
        length = 0;
}

string :: string(char *s)
{
        length = strlen(s);
        characters = new char[length+1];
        strcpy(characters, s);
}

string& string :: operator = (const string &s)
```

```
string& string :: operator = (const string &s)
{
       delete characters;
       length = s.length;
       characters = new char [length + 1];
       strcpy(characters, s.characters);
       return *this;
}

string& string :: operator + (const string&a)
{
       char *s;
       length = length + a.length;
       s = new char [length + 1];
       strcpy(s, characters);
       strcat(s, a.characters);
       strcpy(characters, s);
       return *this;
}

void string :: display(void) const
{
       cout << characters << endl;
}
```

9.6 Destructors

If a copy constructor dynamically allocates memory from the heap for storing an object's data then a destructor returns the memory to the heap when the object ceases to exist.

A class is allowed only one destructor, which has no return type, and no formal parameters.

The name of the destructor is the same name as the class, with a preceding tilde ~ symbol. Hence the name of the destructor can be thought of as the complement of the name of the constructor.

The destructor is automatically called when an object ceases to exist. Note that a static object (global variable), exists throughout the execution of a program, so its destructor will not be called until the program terminates. An automatic object (variable in a function), ceases to exist when its enclosing block completes execution. A dynamic object ceases to exist when it is deallocated using delete.

If a class has user defined types as members and these types have destructors, then the member type destructors will be called under circumstances which would cause any host class destructor to be called. The overall sequence of events from construction to destruction is:

    (i) construct the member instances;
    (ii) construct the host class;
    (iii) destroy the host class;
    (iv) destroy the member instances.

The order of construction of the member instances is the order in which they are defined in the class. Destruction is in the reverse order.

In the definition of the class string a destructor could be introduced into the public section as:

```
// destructor
~ string(void);
```

The implementation of this destructor could be:

```
string :: ~ string(void)

{
        delete characters;
}
```

9.7 Worked examples

The first example uses the class string developed in section 9.5. The program shows how an array of objects of class string can be built. The objects are then sorted into ascending order using the insertion sort, and the contents of the array is displayed on the screen before and after the sorting process. This example emphasises the overloading of the operators + for concatenation, > for string comparison and = for string assignment. These three operations are normally carried out using the appropriate string functions from the library string.h.

```
// program to demonstrate the string class
#include <iostream.hpp>
#include "a:string.cpp"

const int size=5;
string array[size];

void input(void)
{
        char name[20], telephone[20];

        cout << "enter the following details\n\n";
        for (int index=0; index!=size; index++)
        {
                cout << "name ";
                cin.getline(name,19);
                cout << "telephone number ";
                cin.getline(telephone,19);
                // declare strings
                string Name(name), spaces(" "), Telephone(telephone);
                // concatenate strings
                array[index]=Name+spaces+Telephone;
        }
}
```

```
void sort(void)
{
      string current;
      int location;

      for (int index=1; index!=size; index++)
      {
            current=array[index];
            location=index;
            while (location > 0 && array[location-1] > current)
            {
                  array[location]=array[location-1];
                  location--;
            }
            array[location]=current;
      }
}

void output(void)
{
      for (int index=0; index!=size; index++)
            array[index].display();
      cout << endl << endl;
}

main()
{
      input();
      output();
      sort();
      output();
}
```

In the second example a new class is developed for a stack (last in first out queue) using a linked list with access to the list from one end only. The class stack is used to store single characters, and the only operations allowed on the stack are to test whether it is empty (head or stacktop pointer is null), insert or push a character on the top of the stack and to delete or pop a character from the top of the stack. The definition and implementation of the class stack follow.

```
// contents of file stack.hpp
class node
{
            friend class stack;
      private:
            char datum;
            node* link;
};
```

```
class stack
{
      private:
            node* stacktop;
      public:
            stack();
            int empty(void);
            void push(char value);
            char pop(void);
};

// contents of file stack.cpp
#include <stdlib.h>
#include "a:stack.hpp"

stack :: stack()
{
      stacktop=NULL;
}

int stack :: empty(void)
{
      return (stacktop==NULL);
}

void stack :: push(char value)
{
      node* temp;
      temp=new node;
      temp->datum = value;
      temp->link = stacktop;
      stacktop = temp;
}

char stack :: pop(void)
{
      node* temp;
      char value=stacktop->datum;
      if (! empty())
      {
            temp=stacktop;
            stacktop=stacktop->link;
            delete temp;
            return value;
      }
}
```

The demonstration program that uses the abstract data type stack converts infix mathematical expresssions to reverse Polish expressions.

In compiler writing it is more convenient to evaluate arithmetic expressions written in reverse Polish notation than it is to evaluate arithmetic expressions written in infix notation. The following algorithm can be used to convert infix notations to reverse Polish notations. For example, the expression a*(b+c/d) in infix notation is written as abcd/+* in reverse Polish notation. The algorithm uses operator priorities as defined in figure 9.1. The operators [and] are used to delimit the infix expression. For example, the expression a*(b+c/d) will be coded as [a*(b+c/d)].

operator	priority
^	6
*	5
/	4
+	3
-	2
(	1
[	0

Figure 9.1 Operator priorities

Using figure 9.2 in the explanation of the algorithm. If brackets [or (are encountered, each is pushed on to the stack. All operands that are encountered, for example a, b and c, are displayed on the screen. When an operator is encountered its priority is compared with that of the operator priority at the top of the stack. If when comparing priorities the operator encountered is not greater than the operator on the stack, the stack operator is popped and displayed. This process is repeated until the encountered operator has a higher priority than the stack top operator. The encountered operator is then pushed on to the stack. When a) is encountered all the operators up to, but not including (, are popped from the stack one at a time and displayed. The operator (is then deleted from the stack. When the operator] is encountered all the remaining operators, up to but not including [, are popped from the stack one at a time and displayed. The string of characters that is displayed will be the reverse Polish string.

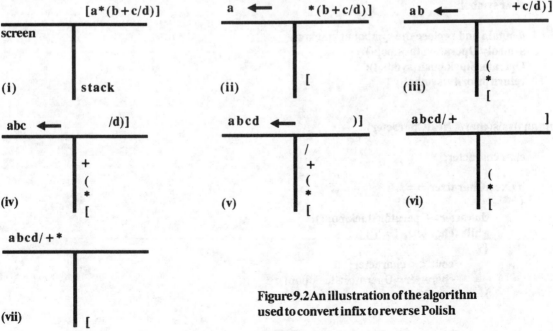

Figure 9.2 An illustration of the algorithm used to convert infix to reverse Polish

```
// program to convert an infix expression to a reverse Polish expression
#include <iostream.hpp>
#include "a:stack.cpp"

const int MaxOperators=7;
const int MaxData=7;
const int MaxString=15;
const char operators[MaxOperators] = {'[','(','-','+','/','*','^'};
const char* InfixData[MaxData] = {    "[a*b+c]",
                                      "[a*(b+c/d)]",
                                      "[a*b+c/d]",
                                      "[u+f*t]",
                                      "[b^2-4*a*c]",
                                      "[h*(a+4*b+c)/3]",
                                      "[w*1-1/(w*c)]"};

stack OperatorStack;

// function to find the priority of a symbol
int priority(char symbol)
{
        for (int index=0; index!=MaxOperators; index++)
                if(symbol==operators[index])
                        return index;
}

// function to find the priority of the symbol at stacktop
int priority_stacktop(void)
{
        char symbol;

        // obtain and replace the symbol at stacktop
        symbol=OperatorStack.pop();
        OperatorStack.push(symbol);
        return priority(symbol);
}

void analysis(char& NextCharacter)
{
        char character;

        if (NextCharacter == ')')
        {
                character=OperatorStack.pop();
                while (character != '(')
                {
                        cout << character;
                        character=OperatorStack.pop();
                }
```

```
        }
        else if (NextCharacter == ']')
        {
                character=OperatorStack.pop();
                while (character != '[')
                {
                        cout << character;
                        character=OperatorStack.pop();
                }
        }
        else if (NextCharacter == '(' || NextCharacter == '[')
                OperatorStack.push(NextCharacter);
        else if (NextCharacter == '^' || NextCharacter == '*' ||
                NextCharacter == '/' || NextCharacter == '+' ||
                NextCharacter == '-')
        {
                while (priority(NextCharacter) <= priority_stacktop())
                {
                        character=OperatorStack.pop();
                        cout << character;
                }
                OperatorStack.push(NextCharacter);
        }
        else
                cout << NextCharacter;
}

main()
{
        char temp[MaxString+1];
        char NextCharacter;

        for (int index=0; index!=MaxData; index++)
        {
                strcpy(temp, InfixData[index]);
                for (int position=0; position!=strlen(temp); position++)
                {
                        NextCharacter=temp[position];
                        analysis(NextCharacter);
                }
                cout << endl;
        }
}
```

207

9.8 Input/Output library

The <iostream.hpp> header file contains three classes for input streams, output streams and input/output streams, known as istream, ostream and iostream respectively. Where the standard stream cin belongs to the istream class, and the standard streams cout, cerr and clog belong to the ostream class. Note clog is a new standard stream and provides for buffered standard error output.

By now the reader should have realised that C++ input/output uses overloaded versions of the left and right shift operators << and >> respectively, for stream insertion (output) and stream extraction (input). Furthermore, these operators are overloaded many times to provide for the input and output of all the standard data types. The following partial listing from the file <iostream.hpp> shows the extent to which the classes istream and ostream cater for the input and output of standard data types.

```
        .
        .

istream& operator>> (signed char*);
istream& operator>> (unsigned char*);
istream& operator>> (char*);
istream& operator>> (signed char&);
istream& operator>> (unsigned char&);
istream& operator>> (char&);
istream& operator>> (short&);
istream& operator>> (int&);
istream& operator>> (long&);
istream& operator>> (unsigned short&);
istream& operator>> (unsigned int&);
istream& operator>> (unsigned long&);
istream& operator>> (float&);
istream& operator>> (double&);
istream& operator>> (long double&);

        .
        .


ostream& operator<< (signed char);
ostream& operator<< (unsigned char);
ostream& operator<< (char);
ostream& operator<< (signed short);
ostream& operator<< (unsigned short);
ostream& operator<< (signed int);
ostream& operator<< (unsigned int);
ostream& operator<< (signed long);
ostream& operator<< (unsigned long);
ostream& operator<< (float);
ostream& operator<< (double);
ostream& operator<< (long double);
ostream& operator<< (const signed char *);
ostream& operator<< (const unsigned char *);
ostream& operator<< (void *);
```

Clearly C++ input/output is to be preferred over C input/output. Reflect for a moment on the use of scanf to read, say, a double precision floating-point number. The statement in C might appear as:

```
double YourMoney;
scanf("%lf", &YourMoney);
```

Remember to use l in a scanf format string and not a printf format string. Remember to precede the numeric variable with an &, otherwise the value to be read from the input will not be stored in the variable. Contrast this with the equivalent C++ statement:

```
cin >> YourMoney;
```

In a similar manner, consider the output of a long double. The statement in C might appear as:

```
long double BigOne;
printf("%Lf", BigOne);
```

Remember to use the symbol L to precede e, f or g in the format string. By way of a contrast, in C++ the equivalent statement might appear as:

```
cout << BigOne;
```

I think the message is loud and clear! Although C++ will allow the use of the C input/output library, the programmer gains far more in terms of clarity, ease of use and safety, from using the C++ input/output library.

The programmer can define additional overloaded versions of >> and << to allow objects of a user-defined class to be inserted and extracted.

If the operators << and >> are to be included in the class rational (fraction), the following code would be necessary.

```
class rational
{
        friend ostream& operator<<(ostream&, const rational&);
        friend istream& operator>>(istream&, rational&);
.
.


        private:
                int numerator;
                int denominator;
        public:
                .
                .

};
```

```
ostream& operator < < (ostream& output, const rational& f)
{
        if (f.denominator == 1)
                return output < < f.numerator;
        else
                return output < < f.numerator < < "/" < < f.denominator;
}

istream& operator > > (istream& input, rational& f)
{
        return input > > f.numerator > > f.denominator;
}
```

The code used to read a fraction would be cin > > f; and the code to write a fraction would be cout < < f;

A further inspection of the class istream and ostream from the library header <iostream.hpp> will reveal that C++ also supports a number of input and output functions.

```
istream& seekg(streampos);
istream& seekg(streamoff, ios::seek_dir);
streampos tellg();
istream& get( signed char*, int, char = '\n');
istream& get(unsigned char*, int, char = '\n');
istream& get( char*, int, char = '\n');
istream& read( signed char*, int);
istream& read(unsigned char*, int);
istream& read( char*, int);
istream& getline( signed char*, int, char = '\n');
istream& getline(unsigned char*, int, char = '\n');
istream& getline( char*, int, char = '\n');
istream& get(streambuf&, char = '\n');
istream& get( signed char&);
istream& get(unsigned char&);
istream& get( char&);
int get();
int peek();
int gcount();
istream& putback(char);
istream& ignore(int = 1, int = EOF);


ostream& seekp(streampos);
ostream& seekp(streamoff, ios::seek_dir);
streampos tellp();
ostream& put(char);
```

```
ostream& write(const signed char*, int);
ostream& write(const unsigned char*, int);
.
.
```

Use the get and getline functions whenever input is required that does not skip over white space characters. The get function reads a single character and the getline function reads an entire line.

There are two forms of get, both of which in this example, will store the character being input in the char variable symbol.

```
                symbol = cin.get();
                or
                cin.get(symbol);
```

There are two forms of getline. The first reads characters into a string until a specified number of characters-1, in this example 19 (20-1), have been read or a new-line character is encountered.

```
        cin.getline(name, 20);
```

The second reads characters until a specified character is encountered, in this example the letter 'X'.

```
        cin.getline(name, 20, 'X');
```

The following functions perform as described.

put	- outputs one character;
write	- outputs a sequence of characters of known length;
read	- reads a block of characters of a specified length;
gcount	- returns the number of characters read;
peek	- returns the next input character without actually reading it;
putback	- puts back the last character read;
ignore	- reads and ignores characters;
seekg	- used with an input or input/output stream, it sets a file to the position specified by its parameter;
tellg	- used with an input or input/output stream, returns the current file position;
seekp and tellp	- used with an output or input/output stream, and have the same functionality as for seekg and tellg.

File input/output requires the inclusion of the <fstream.hpp> header file. This header defines the classes, ifstream for input files, ofstream for output files and fstream for input/output files.

File reading and writing is performed in the same way as for standard streams. Any operation on cin is legal for an ifstream of fstream object, similarly any operation on cout is legal for an ofstream or fstream object.

Files are opened for input or output using the appropriate ifstream or ofstream constructor. For example,

```
        ifstream InputFile("a:input.dat");
        ofstream OutputFile("a:output.dat");
```

or alternatively by using the open member function. For example,

```
ifstream InputFile;
ofstream OutputFile;
InputFile.open("a:input.dat");
OutputFile.open("a:output.dat");
```

Streams can be tested as though they were boolean values, therefore, it is possible to check whether a file is successfully opened as follows.

```
if (!InputFile)
{
        cerr << "ERROR - file a:input.dat cannot be opened ";
        exit(EXIT_FAILURE);
}
```

Files are closed automatically by destructors. The member function close is only used if the same stream object will be reused with a different file, for example.

```
OutputFile.close();
```

9.9 The ios class

All stream classes are derived from the ios class. The data members of the ios class control input/output formatting and keep track of the status of the stream. From the header file <iostream.hpp> a partial listing of the ios class follows.

```
class ios {
        public:

                enum io_state {
                                goodbit = 0x00,
                                eofbit = 0x01,
                                failbit = 0x02,
                                badbit = 0x04,
                                hardfail = 0x80
                        };

                enum open_mode {
                                in = 0x01,
                                out = 0x02,
                                ate = 0x04,
                                app = 0x08,
                                trunc = 0x10,
                                nocreate = 0x20,
                                noreplace = 0x40,
                                binary = 0x80
                        };
```

```
enum {
        skipws = 0x0001,
        left = 0x0002,
        right = 0x0004,
        internal = 0x0008,
        dec = 0x0010,
        oct = 0x0020,
        hex = 0x0040,
        showbase = 0x0080,
        showpoint = 0x0100,
        uppercase = 0x0200,
        showpos = 0x0400,
        scientific = 0x0800,
        fixed = 0x1000,
        unitbuf = 0x2000,
        stdio = 0x4000
};


long flags();
long flags(long _fl);
long setf(long _setbits, long _fld);
long setf(long _fld);
long unsetf(long _fld);
int width();
int width(int _w);
char fill();
char fill(char _f);
int precision();
int precision(int _p);


int rdstate();
int eof();
int fail();
int bad();
int good();


int state;
long x_flags;
int x_precision;
int x_width;
int x_fill;


}
```

A file stream constructor may have a second parameter. This is a collection of mode bits taken from the enumeration open_mode in class ios. When a file is opened, one or more of these mode bits can be combined to specify the mode of the file. For example,

ofstream OutputFile("a:output.dat", ios::out | ios::noreplace);

This implies open the file "a:output.dat" for output, and fail to open if the file already exists.

When a file is to be opened for both input and output use the fstream constructor, for example.

fstream IO_file("a:inout.dat", ios::in | ios::out | ios::trunc);

The error status of a stream is stored in the state member as depicted by the enumeration io_state.

The error bits in the state member can be tested by either using the appropriate member functions in the ios class rdstate(), eof(), fail(), bad(), good().

The error bits can be reset in an attempt to recover from an error by using the ios function clear(). A call to clear without parameters clears the state. For example,

cout.clear();

Clear can also be used to set specified error bits, for example

cout.clear(ios::failbit);

sets specified bit for failbit, and resets the remaining bits.

A streams current format conventions are recorded in its format flags, as defined in the unnamed enumeration in the partial listing of the ios class.

A protected variable long x_flags records the status of the format flags. The value of flags can be saved by using, say

long f = cout.flags();

x_flags can be changed by calling flags with one parameter, say

cout.flags(f);

Individual format flags can be changed by calling the ios member function setf. For example,

cout.setf(0, ios::dec); // clears the ios::dec bit
cout.setf(ios::dec, ios::dec); // sets the ios::dec bit

The x_width state variable controls the field width for input and output.

The width function with no parameters returns the current width. For example,

```
int FieldWidth = cout.width();
```

The width function with one parameter sets the width and returns the old value, for example.

```
int OldWidth = cout.width(20); // set new field with to 20
```

The x_fill data member of the ios class contains the filler character, which by default is a space.

The fill member function with no parameters returns the current width. The fill member function with one parameter sets x_fill with another character and returns the old filler character. For example,

```
cout.fill('*'); // sets fill character to *
```

The x_precision data member of the ios class controls the number of digits after the decimal point in a floating-point number. The precision function with no parameters returns the current precision. The precision function with one parameter sets x_precision and returns the old value. For example,

```
cout.precision(6); // set precision to 6 decimal places
```

9.10 Manipulators

This section concludes by examining a set of functions that are inserted or extracted to affect the behaviour of a stream. The reader has already encountered one manipulator for inserting a new line character and flushing a stream, this was endl. The header file <iostream.hpp> contains other manipulators, these are:

```
ends    - insert a null character to terminate a string (ostream only);
flush   - flush a stream (ostream only);
ws      - skip white space (istream only);
dec     - set the ios::dec format flag;
oct     - set the ios::oct format flag;
hex     - set the ios::hex format flag.
```

The following examples show how the manipulators can be used.

```
cout << "a new line follows " << endl;
cout << "this string is terminated" << ends;
cout << "avoid buffering output now" << endl << flush;
cin >> hex >> HexNumber; // read number in hexadecimal format
cout << oct << OctalNumber; // display number in octal format
```

In addition the <iomanip.hpp> header file contains further parametised manipulators, as indicated in the partial listing. If these manipulators are required the header file must be included after <iostream.hpp>.

.
.

```
smanip_int    setbase(int _b); // set base to either 0, 8, 10 or 16
smanip_long   resetiosflags(long _b); // clear ios flags, e.g. ios::skipws
smanip_long   setiosflags(long _b); // set ios flags
smanip_int    setfill(int _f); // set the fill character
```

smanip_int   setprecision(int _n); // set the precision
smanip_int   setw(int _n); // set the field width

.

.

The six manipulators can be used with both the input and output streams, their purpose should be clear from the name of each function.

9.11 Summary

- Data abstraction is the technique of combining a data type with a set of operations on data of the same type.

- A class is a data type that contains both data members and function members. Access to the data members is through the function members.

- A class can contain at least two sections, private and public. Outside the class, access to the private members is prohibited and only access to public members is permissible.

- A data abstraction is normally organised into two header files. The first header, appended with the abbreviation .hpp, should be made accessible to the user of the class. This file contains the definition of the members of the class. The second file, appended with the abbreviation .cpp, should be given restricted access. This file contains the implementation of the members of the class and is not intended to be made visible to the user of the class.

- The implementation of class member functions can be made in the definition file for the class, in which case the functions are treated as in line. In the case of functions longer than two or three lines this is not advisable. A preferred method is to implement the member functions in a separate .cpp file. Each function in this file needs to be qualified with a scope resolution operator, otherwise, the C++ compiler will not associate it as a class member.

- All instances of a class are known as objects of the class.

- Objects can be copied and used for initialisation, and passed as parameters or returned by functions. In the latter case it is advisable to declare the formal parameter or function return type as a reference to avoid the overhead of copying the object.

- An object is initialised through constructors.

- Constructors can have an empty initialisation list, and are known as default constructors; contain default parameters in the initialisation list, or in the case of strings be defined as copy constructors.

- Constructors can also act as a type conversion function.

- Constructors, as functions, can be overloaded.

- Whenever, a copy constructor is used to allocate memory from the heap, a destructor to re-allocate memory back to the heap should be defined.

• A friend is not a class member function, but a means of bypassing the class access restrictions to access all the members of a class.

• Operators as well as functions can be overloaded.

• Only operators with zero or one operand can be defined as overloaded operators implemented as member functions. If an overloaded operator has a predefined type as its first operand, the operator cannot be a member function but must be a friend function.

• The C++ input/output library uses heavy overloading of the insertion and extraction operators. To this end input and output in C++ is easy to use, clearer and safer!

• There are three classes of stream defined in the header file <iostream.hpp> - istream, ostream and iostream. cin belongs to istream and cout, cerr and clog belong to ostream.

• There are a number of predefined functions that help simplify stream input and output.

• All stream classes are derived from the ios class. The data members of this class control input/output formatting and keep track of the status of the stream. There are many predefined functions and manipulators that control the formatting of a stream.

9.12 Questions   *answers begin on page 287*

1. Devise a class for the addition, subtraction, multiplication and division of rational numbers (fractions). The class should also contain a function to display a rational number. Use operator overloading for the symbols +, -, * and /, and << to output to the ostream.

In this question you will need to find the greatest common divisor (gcd) between two integers m and n. This is achieved by using Euclid's algorithm as follows.

> *divide m by n and find remainder*
> *while remainder not zero*
> > *assign n to m*
> > *assign remainder to n*
> > *divide m by n and find remainder*
> *end*
> *assign n to gcd*

Euclid's algorithm is used in a private function that converts a numerator and denominator into a rational number by dividing both by the greatest common denominator and adjusting the sign of the fraction according to the signs of the numerator and denominator.

Write a program to test the validity of the class rational.

2. Devise a class for the addition, subtraction, multiplication and division of complex numbers. The class should also contain a function to display complex numbers. As with the previous question, overload the operators +, -, *, / and <<.

A complex number has two parts (A, iB), where A is the real part, B is the imaginery part, and i=sqrt(-1).

The following expressions show how arithmetic can be performed on two complex numbers, such that a real part (R) and an imaginery part (I) are evaluated.

addition	R = A.real + B.real
	I = A.imaginery + B.imaginery
subtraction	R = A.real - B.real
	I = A.imaginery - B.imaginery
multiplication	R = (A.real * B.real) - (A.imaginery* B.imaginery)
	I = (A.real * B.imaginery) + (A.imaginery * B.real)
division	T = A * (B.real - B.imaginery)
	N = B.real * B.real - B.imaginery * B.imaginery
	R = T.real / N
	I = T.imaginery / N

3. If floating-point computations are performed on amounts of money, inaccuracies can occur in the results. Devise a class money that will cater for arithmetic using the overloaded operators +, -, *, /, and % (remainder); comparisons using the overloaded operators ==, !=, >, <, >=, and <=, and the overloaded operator << on ostream for displaying an amount of money.

10.
Object-oriented Programming

This final chapter extends the work on classes, and serves as an introduction to the topic of object-oriented programming. Only the features of C++ that enable object-oriented programming to be performed are considered here.

Contents

10.1 Introduction

The basic mechanisms of object-oriented programming are objects, messages and methods, classes and instances, and inheritance.

A *traditional* program consists of procedures and data, an object-oriented program consists only of objects that contain both procedures and data. Objects can be thought of as self- contained units that comprise both data and the instructions that operate upon the data.

Unlike the passive data items in *traditional* systems, objects have the ability to act. Action occurs when an object receives a message, that is, a request asking the object to behave in some way. Functions, known as methods, reside in the object and determine how the object acts when it receives a message. An object will contain instance variables that store information or data local to the object. An objects methods execute in response to messages and manipulate the values of the instance variables.

Many different objects may act in very similar ways. A class is a description of a set of nearly identical objects. A class consists of methods and data that summarize common characteristics of a set of objects. Classes contain the blueprints for creating objects, where an object is an instance of a class.

Objects are created when a message requesting creation is received by the parent class. The new object takes its methods and data from its parent class. Data are of two forms, class variables and instance variables. The former have values stored in a class and the latter have values associated uniquely with each instance or object created from a class.

Subclasses can be referred to as derived classes where a parent child relationship exists between the class and subclass. Parent classes are located above child classes in the hierarchy between classes. A class can summarize common elements for a set of subclasses. Common methods and data are elevated as high as possible so that they are accessible to all relevant subclasses.

Inheritance is the mechanism for automatically sharing methods and data among classes, subclasses and objects. Inheritance allows programmers to create new classes by programming only the difference from the parent class. In the declaration of a child class or subclass, all the methods and instance variables associated with the parent class are automatically inherited by the subclass or child. If the parent class contains methods that are inappropriate to the child subclass, then the programmer can override these methods by writing new methods and storing them as a part of the child subclass.

There are two types of inheritance. Single inheritance where a subclass may inherit data and methods from a single parent class, as well as providing additional methods, and multiple inheritance where a subclass inherits data and methods from more than one class.

To quote from Grady Booch in his book on Object Oriented Design with Applications "...object-oriented programming is a method of implementation in which programs are organised as cooperative collections of objects, each of which represents an instance of some class, and whose classes are all members of a hierarchy of classes via inheritance relationships ..."

C++ is suitable as an object-oriented programming language because it offers features to:

> represent abstractions;
> encapsulate abstractions into objects;

pass on the structure and properties of an object to another derived object - inheritance;
allow functions to behave 'intelligently' depending on the type of object for which it is invoked - polymorphism.

In the previous chapter the reader was introduced to abstraction and encapsulation, in the remainder of this chapter the techniques of inheritance and polymorphism are described in the context of C++.

10.2 Inheritance

Inheritance is the process by which one class inherits the characteristics of another class. A class becomes a descendant of one or more other classes when it is designed as an extension or specialization of these classes.

In the following example a class is described for a point, represented as an illuminated pixel on a screen.

```
class point
{
        protected:
                short int x,y;
        public:
                // constructors
                point() {x=0; y=0;}
                point(const short int &X, const short int &Y) {x=X; y=Y;}

                // functions
                void plot();
                void erase();
                short int GetX();
                short int GetY();
                void move(const short int &toX, const short int &toY);
};
```

Upon the inspection of this class the reader should notice one new feature, the introduction of the reserved word protected. Members of a class can be declared as protected when access is permitted to member functions, friends and any classes derived from the base class. If x and y had been declared as private then access would be denied to any derived subclass of point.

In the class, point, x and y represent the graphical coordinates of a point (pixel) on a screen; the methods plot and erase enable a pixel to be illuminated or blacked-out; GetX and GetY enable the position of a point to be obtained; and move enables a point to be moved from the current position to the graphical coordinates (toX, toY).

A new class, cross, is to be created that inherits all the characteristics of a point.

```
class cross: public point
{
        public:
                //constructors
                cross() {x=0; y=0;}
```

221

```
            cross(const short int &X, const short int &Y) {x=X; y=Y;}
            void plot();
            void erase();
};
```

The syntax for inheritance permits a derivation list to be included in the definition of the derived class.

```
class cross: public point
{
    .
    .
    .
};
```

In multiple inheritance a class is derived from several base classes.

```
class derived: public base1, ... , public baseN
{
    .
    .
    .
};
```

The class, derived, inherits the members of all its base classes, base1 through baseN. Multiple inheritance allows a class to have all the properties of two or more other classes.

Notice that the protected variables x,y are not declared again, since they have been inherited and are accessible by default. There has been a need to declare new constructors for the class cross. Constructors and destructors are never inherited. The methods to plot and erase a point have been inherited, however, these function names have been overloaded, since plotting and erasing a cross requires a different implementation to plotting and erasing a point.

The two classes point and cross are stored under a filename point.hpp. The implementation of the methods in these classes is stored under the filename point.cpp. A listing of this file follows.

```
#include <graph.h>
#include "point.hpp"

void point :: plot()
{
    _setcolor(_getcolor());
    _setpixel(x,y);
}

void point :: erase()
{
    short colour;

    colour= _getcolor();
    _setcolor(_getbkcolor());
    _setpixel(x,y);
```

```
        _setcolor(colour);
}

short int point :: GetX()
{
        return x;
}

short int point :: GetY()
{
        return y;
}

void point :: move(const short int &toX, const short int &toY)
{
        erase();
        x=toX;y=toY;
        plot();
}

void cross :: plot()
{
        _setcolor(_getcolor());
        _moveto(x-2,y);
        _lineto(x+2,y);
        _moveto(x,y-2);
        _lineto(x,y+2);
}

void cross :: erase()
{
short colour;

        colour=_getcolor();
        _setcolor(_getbkcolor());
        _moveto(x-2,y);
        _lineto(x+2,y);
        _moveto(x,y-2);
        _lineto(x,y+2);
        _setcolor(colour);
}
```

The functions _setpixel, _setcolor, _getcolor, _getbkcolor, _moveto, and _lineto are taken from the Jensen and Partners TopSpeed C Graphics library. The meaning of each function should be obvious from the function name.

Before leaving the topic of inheritance it is worth noting that a base class may be declared as private instead of public.

class derived: private base
```
{
       .
       .
}
```

However, objects of a derived class cannot be assigned to objects of a private class. The inherited members of a base class become private members of the derived class. This implies a member that is accessible in its base class is not accessible in its derived class.

What is the point of declaring a base class as being private when it restricts the access to members of the derived class? When a base class helps implement a derived class then private derivation should be used. In such a case the derived class does not exhibit all the behaviour, if any, of the base class. Such a technique is known as layering. In true inheritance the derived class represents a more specialized version of the base class and public derivation should be used.

10.3 Virtual methods

The following program was used to test the implementation of the methods for the classes point and cross. The program plots a point at coordinates (100,100) and plots a cross at coordinates (200,200). There is a delay of 5 seconds and the point is moved to a new position at coordinates (100,150) and the cross to a new position at coordinates (200,250). There is a further 5 seconds delay before the program terminates.

```
#include <graph.h>
#include <stdlib.h>
#include "point.cpp"

main()
{
       point A(100,100);
       cross B(200,200);

       _setvideomode(_VRES16COLOR);

       A.plot();
       B.plot();
       delay(5000);
       A.move(100,150);
       B.move(200,250);
       delay(5000);

       _setvideomode(_DEFAULTMODE);
}
```

When the program was executed the point and cross were both plotted at their initial positions, but after the first 5 seconds delay, only point A was correctly moved. The cross remained at its original position of (200,200) and a second point appeared, where the cross should have moved to, at position (200,250). What went wrong?

Despite cross inheriting all the methods from point, when B.move(200,250) was executed, the methods plot and erase from point were executed and not the overloaded methods of plot and erase from cross!

One way of overcoming this problem would be to overload the method move in the class cross. Notice that move has not been defined in the class cross. The compiler would then use the overloaded methods plot and erase from the class cross and not the methods plot and erase from the class point. This solution is far from satisfactory since it requires coding the same procedure twice. There would be no difference in the coding between cross.move and point.move. In other examples the amount of extra coding might be excessive!

The class methods described so far are static. the compiler allocates them and resolves all references to them at compile time. This is known as early-binding. That is why B.move in the last example, was executed using point :: move. In order to overcome the problems stated, class methods should be defined as being virtual. If point :: plot, point :: erase, cross :: plot and cross :: erase are defined as being virtual then the references to plot and erase in the method point :: move will be resolved at run-time through the object being used (known as dynamic-binding); B.move(200,250) will automatically use cross :: plot and cross :: erase in the inherited method point :: move.

C++ provides a special mechanism, virtual, that allows a function declared in a base class to be implemented differently in derived classes. The following listing shows how methods in the class definitions for point and cross have been qualified by the reserved word virtual. Notice that once an ancestor method is tagged as virtual all the descendant types that implement a method of the same name must tag that method as virtual.

```
class point
{
        protected:
                short int x,y;
        public:
                // constructors
                point() {x=0; y=0;}
                point(const short int &X, const short int &Y) {x=X; y=Y;}
                // functions
                virtual void plot();
                virtual void erase();
                short int GetX();
                short int GetY();
                void move(const short int &toX, const short int &toY);
};

class cross: public point
{
        public:
                //constructors
                cross() {x=0; y=0;}
                cross(const short int &X, const short int &Y) {x=X; y=Y;}
                virtual void plot();
                virtual void erase();
};
```

225

The implementation of these functions is unchanged, and the same listing as given earlier still applies.

Virtual functions are invoked through a pointer or reference. In the modified program to plot and move a point and a cross, two pointers have been declared, *p and *q. The pointer of type class point (*p) is assigned to point at A, p=&A; the appropriate function is then called using p->plot(), p->move(), etc. Similarly, a pointer of type class cross (*q) is assigned to point at B, q=&B; the appropriate function is then called using q->plot(), q->move(), etc.

Although not shown in this example a pointer or reference of type base class can refer to either a base class or a derived class. Thus p=&B; p->plot() is valid, however, q=&A; q->plot() is illegal.

```
#include <graph.h>
#include <stdlib.h>
#include "point.cpp"

main()
{
        point A(100,100), *p;
        cross B(200,200), *q;

        _setvideomode(_VRES16COLOR);

        p=&A;
        p->plot();
        q=&B;
        q->plot();
        delay(5000);
        p->move(100,150);
        q->move(200,250);
        delay(5000);

        _setvideomode(_DEFAULTMODE);
}
```

The use of virtual functions requires dynamic binding. Calls of virtual functions cannot be resolved by the compiler but must be resolved during program execution. For example, the determination of which method must be called in the statement p->plot() must wait until the program is executed.

Ever class of object has only one virtual method table (VMT) in the data segment of memory. This table contains the size of the object and pointers to the code for each virtual method associated with the class of object. A constructor establishes a link between the instance of the object calling the constructor and the class of object's VMT.

Figure 10.1 illustrates the internal representation of instances of objects (i) with static methods, (ii) with virtual methods and (iii) on instances of a single class.

Dynamic binding allows for the creation of data structures containing objects of different classes, provided all the classes are derived from a common base class. It also makes it possible to add new classes and remove old classes without modifying the code for processing the data structure.

(i) Static Methods

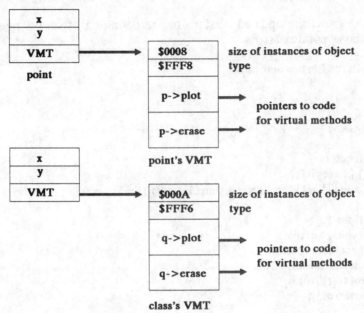

The fields of an object are stored in the order of declaration as a contiguous
sequence of variables in the program's data segment.

(ii) Virtual methods

The link between the instance of the object's VMT field and the VMT is established
by the constructor.

(iii) Instances of a single class (cross)

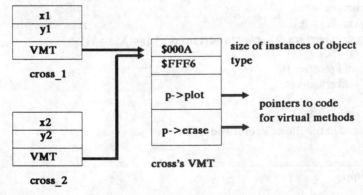

Every instance of an object must be initialised by a separate constructor call,
otherwise the link between the VMT field entry and the VMT cannot be made.

Figure 10.1

227

10.4 Polymorphism

Polymorphism is a way of giving an action one name that is shared up and down an object hierarchy, with each object in the hierarchy implementing the action in a way appropriate to itself. Virtual functions are used to support polymorphism in C++.

As an extension of the last worked example a program is created to move either a point or a cross to any position on the screen by using the 'arrowed' keys on a keyboard. The methods plot, erase and move are all polymorphic. Notice however, that move does not need to be declared as virtual.

The following listing shows the updated versions of the definition of classes point and cross and the implementation of classes point and cross.

```
// definitions stored in the file newpoint.hpp
class point
{
        protected:
                short int x,y;
        public:
                // constructors
                point() {x=0; y=0;}
                point(const short int &X, const short int &Y) {x=X; y=Y;}

                // functions
                virtual void plot(void);
                virtual void erase(void);
                short int GetX(void);
                short int GetY(void);
                void move(void);
};

class cross: public point
{
        public:
                //constructors
                cross() {x=0; y=0;}
                cross(const short int &X, const short int &Y) {x=X; y=Y;}

                virtual void plot(void);
                virtual void erase(void);
};

// implementation stored in the file newpoint.cpp
#include <graph.h>
#include <conio.h>
#include "newpoint.hpp"

void point :: plot(void)
{
```

228

```
        _setcolor(_getcolor());
        _setpixel(x,y);
}

void point :: erase(void)
{
        short colour;

        colour=_getcolor();
        _setcolor(_getbkcolor());
        _setpixel(x,y);
        _setcolor(colour);
}

short int point :: GetX(void)
{
        return x;
}

short int point :: GetY(void)
{
        return y;
}

enum boolean {false, true};
```

The boolean function is not a method of the class point. The purpose of the function is to capture the movement of the arrowed keys on the keyboard. Arrowed keys use extended two byte codes, therefore, it is necessary to read a first character and if the code is zero read a second character. If the second character is code 72 the up-arrow key was pressed, code 80 down-arrow key pressed, code 75 left-arrow key pressed or code 77 right-arrow key was pressed. The variable Yinc is set at -1 for upward movement and +1 for downwards movement. The variable Xinc is set at -1 for movement left and +1 for movement right. Both Xinc and Yinc are set at zero for no movement of arrowed keys. Only when the return or enter key is pressed (code 13) will this signal that the movement of the object has stopped.

```
boolean direction(short int &Xinc, short int &Yinc)
{
        int key;
        boolean quit, dirn;

        Xinc=0; Yinc=0;
        dirn=true;
        do
        {
                key=getch();
                quit=true;
                switch (key)
                {
                        case 0: {
```

```
                                    key=getch();
                                    switch (key)
                                    {
                                            case 72: Yinc=-1; break;
                                            case 80: Yinc= +1; break;
                                            case 75: Xinc=-1; break;
                                            case 77: Xinc= +1; break;
                                            default: quit=false;
                                    } break;
                            }
                            case 13: dirn=false; break;
                            default: quit=false;
                    }
            } while (!quit);
            return dirn;
    }


void point :: move(void)
{
        const displacement=5; // distance travelled by object after each key press
        short int Xinc, Yinc;

        while (direction(Xinc,Yinc))
        {
                erase();
                x=x+(Xinc*displacement);
                y=y+(Yinc*displacement);
                plot();
        }
}

void cross :: plot(void)
{
        _setcolor(_getcolor());
        _moveto(x-2,y);
        _lineto(x+2,y);
        _moveto(x,y-2);
        _lineto(x,y+2);
}

void cross :: erase(void)
{
        short colour;

        colour=_getcolor();
        _setcolor(_getbkcolor());
        _moveto(x-2,y);
        _lineto(x+2,y);
        _moveto(x,y-2);
```

230

```
        _lineto(x,y+2);
        _setcolor(colour);
}
```

Demonstration program that plots a point at coordinates (100,100), and plots a cross at coordinates (200,200), then allows the user to move the point to anywhere on the screen, followed by moving the cross to anywhere on the screen.

```
#include <graph.h>
#include "newpoint.cpp"

main()
{
        point A(100,100), *p;
        cross B(200,200), *q;

        _setvideomode(_VRES16COLOR);

        p=&A;
        q=&B;
        p->plot();
        q->plot();
        A.move();
        B.move();

        _setvideomode(_DEFAULTMODE);
}
```

10.5 Example

This example is a continuation of the previous example. It serves to bring together many of the features found in object-oriented programming.

The example is to produce a sketch-pad where predefined shapes can be drawn. An illustration of the sketch pad is given in figure 10.2. Notice that four icons appear on the left-hand side of the screen, a straight line, triangle, rectangle and ellipse. A cross wire appears on the bottom of the screen. The user moves the cross wire to the level only of the appropriate icon, and presses the return or enter key. The system acknowledges the chosen shape, and displays the name of the shape at the top of the sketch-pad. The user must now move the cross wire, and press return or enter at every corner of the shape visited. When the correct number of corners have been input (from left to right), the chosen figure is drawn.

The system will allow the user to draw as many shapes on the sketch-pad screen as are necessary for sketching a picture. The system terminates when the user fails to select an icon yet presses the return or enter key.

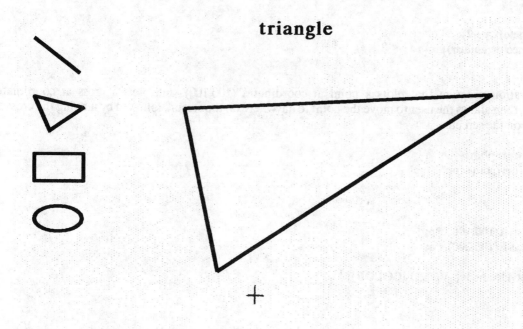

Figure 10.2 An illustration of the graphical output from the sketch-pad program

```
// definition of classes stored in the file shapes.hpp
class point
{
        protected:
                short int x,y;
        public:
                // constructors
                point() {x=0; y=0;}
                point(const &X, const &Y) {x=X; y=Y;}

                // functions
                virtual void plot(void);
                virtual void erase(void);
                short int GetX(void);
                short int GetY(void);
                void move(void);
};

class cross: public point
{
        public:
                // constructors
                cross() {x=0; y=0;}
                cross(const &X, const &Y) {x=X; y=Y;}
```

232

```
                virtual void plot(void);
                virtual void erase(void);
};

class line: public point
{
        protected:
                short int x1,y1;
        public:
                // constructors
                line() {x=0; y=0; x1=0; y1=0;}
                line(const &X, const &Y, const &X1, const &Y1)
                {
                        x=X; y=Y; x1=X1; y1=Y1;
                }

                virtual void plot(void);
                virtual void erase(void);
};

class triangle: public line
{
        protected:
                short int x2, y2;
        public:
                // constructors
                triangle() {x=0; y=0; x1=0; y2=0; x2=0; y2=0;}
                triangle(const &X, const &Y, const &X1, const &Y1, const &X2, const &Y2)
                {
                        x=X; y=Y; x1=X1; y1=Y1; x2=X2; y2=Y2;
                }

                virtual void plot(void);
                virtual void erase(void);
};

class rectangle: public line
{
        public:
                // constructors
                rectangle() {x=0;y=0;x1=0;y1=0;}
                rectangle(const &X, const&Y, const &X1, const &Y1)
                {
                        x=X; y=Y; x1=X1; y1=Y1;
                }

                virtual void plot(void);
                virtual void erase(void);
};
```

```
class ellipse: public line
{
        public:
                // constructors
                ellipse() {x=0; y=0; x1=0; y1=0;}
                ellipse(const &X, const &Y, const &X1, const &Y1)
                {
                        x=X; y=Y; x1=X1; y1=Y1;
                }

                virtual void plot(void);
                virtual void erase(void);
};

// implementation of class methods stored in file shapes.cpp
#include <graph.h>
#include <conio.h>
#include "shapes.hpp"

void point :: plot(void)
{
        _setcolor(_getcolor());
        _setpixel(x,y);
}

void point :: erase(void)
{
        short int colour;

        colour=_getcolor();
        _setcolor(_getbkcolor());
        _setpixel(x,y);
        _setcolor(colour);
}

short int point :: GetX(void)
{
        return x;
}

short int point :: GetY(void)
{
        return y;
}

enum boolean {false, true};
```

```
boolean direction(short int &Xinc, short int &Yinc)
{
        int key;
        boolean quit, dirn;

        Xinc=0; Yinc=0;
        dirn=true;

        do
        {
                key=getch();
                quit=true;
                switch (key)
                {
                        case 0: {
                                key=getch();
                                switch (key)
                                {
                                        case 72: Yinc=-1; break;
                                        case 80: Yinc=+1; break;
                                        case 75: Xinc=-1; break;
                                        case 77: Xinc=+1; break;
                                        default: quit=false;
                                } break;
                        }
                        case 13: dirn=false; break;
                        default: quit=false;
                }
        } while (!quit);
        return dirn;
}

void point :: move(void)
{
        const displacement=10;
        short int Xinc, Yinc;

        while (direction(Xinc,Yinc))
        {
                erase();
                x=x+(Xinc*displacement);
                y=y+(Yinc*displacement);
                plot();
        }
}

void cross :: plot(void)
{
        _setcolor(_getcolor());
```

```
        _moveto(x-2,y);
        _lineto(x+2,y);
        _moveto(x,y-2);
        _lineto(x,y+2);
}

void cross :: erase(void)
{
        short int colour;

        colour=_getcolor();
        _setcolor(_getbkcolor());
        _moveto(x-2,y);
        _lineto(x+2,y);
        _moveto(x,y-2);
        _lineto(x,y+2);
        _setcolor(colour);
}

void line :: plot(void)
{
        _setcolor(_getcolor());
        _moveto(x,y);
        _lineto(x1,y1);
}

void line :: erase(void)
{
        short int colour;

        colour=_getcolor();
        _setcolor(_getbkcolor());
        _moveto(x,y);
        _lineto(x1,y1);
        _setcolor(colour);
}

void triangle :: plot(void)
{
        _setcolor(_getcolor());
        _moveto(x,y);
        _lineto(x1,y1);
        _lineto(x2,y2);
        _lineto(x,y);
}

void triangle :: erase(void)
{
        short int colour;
```

```
        colour=_getcolor();
        _setcolor(_getbkcolor());
        _moveto(x,y);
        _lineto(x1,y1);
        _lineto(x2,y2);
        _lineto(x,y);
        _setcolor(colour);
}

void rectangle :: plot(void)
{
        _setcolor(_getcolor());
        _rectangle(_GBORDER,x,y,x1,y1);
}

void rectangle :: erase(void)
{
        short int colour;

        colour=_getcolor();
        _setcolor(_getbkcolor());
        _rectangle(_GBORDER,x,y,x1,y1);
        _setcolor(colour);
}

void ellipse :: plot(void)
{
        _setcolor(_getcolor());
        _ellipse(_GBORDER,x,y,x1,y1);
}

void ellipse :: erase(void)
{
        short int colour;

        colour=_getcolor();
        _setcolor(_getbkcolor());
        _ellipse(_GBORDER,x,y,x1,y1);
        _setcolor(colour);
}

// program used to generate the sketch-pad
#include <stdlib.h>
#include "shapes.cpp"

cross Xwire(320,400), *p;

// the function of the shapes menu is to display the icons on the
// left-hand side of the screen and display the cross-wire ready
```

```
// for the user to move it and select a particular item
char ShapesMenu(void)
{
        short int y;
        point *q;

        // define positions of shapes
        line L(10,10,60,60);
        triangle T(10,100,35,75,60,120);
        rectangle S(10,150,60,180);
        ellipse E(10,210,60,250);

        // plot icons
        q=&L; q->plot();
        q=&T; q->plot();
        q=&S; q->plot();
        q=&E; q->plot();

        // move cross wire to chosen icon
        Xwire.move();
        y=Xwire.GetY();

        // prepare screen ready to display name of shape
        _settextposition(2,35);
        _outtext("        ");
        _settextposition(2,35);

        // select icon from the position of the cross wire
        // display the name of the shape and return the type of shape
        if (y>=10 && y<=60) {_outtext("line"); return 'L';}
        else if (y>=75 && y<=120) {_outtext("triangle"); return 'T';}
        else if (y>=150 && y<=180) {_outtext("rectangle"); return 'S';}
        else if (y>=210 && y<=250) {_outtext("ellipse"); return 'E';}
        else if (y>250) {_outtext("exit"); return 'X';}
}


// the purpose of function draw is to capture the positions of the
// cross wire in determining the corners of the shape and draw the
// chosen shape
void draw(char &shape)
{
        short int x,y,x1,y1,x2,y2;
        point *q;

        // capture coordinates of shape
        Xwire.move();
        x=Xwire.GetX(); y=Xwire.GetY();
        Xwire.move();
```

```
        x1=Xwire.GetX();y1=Xwire.GetY();
        if (shape=='T')
        {
                Xwire.move();
                x2=Xwire.GetX();y2=Xwire.GetY();
        }

        // select and draw shape
        switch (shape)
        {
                case 'L':{line L(x,y,x1,y1); q=&L; q->plot(); break;}
                case 'T':{triangle T(x,y,x1,y1,x2,y2); q=&T; q->plot(); break;}
                case 'S':{rectangle S(x,y,x1,y1); q=&S; q->plot(); break;}
                case 'E':{ellipse E(x,y,x1,y1); q=&E; q->plot(); break;}
        }
}

main()
{
        char shape;

        _setvideomode(_VRES16COLOR);

        p=&Xwire;
        p->plot();
        for (;;)
        {
                shape=ShapesMenu();
                if (shape=='X')     {delay(2000);_setvideomode(_DEFAULTMODE);return(0);}
                draw(shape);
        }
}
```

10.6 Summary

• Objects can be thought of as self-contained units that comprise both data and the instructions that operate on the data.

• Action occurs when an object receives a message. An objects methods execute in response to messages and manipulate the values of the instance variables.

• In C++ objects are implemented as instances of classes.

• A sub-class (child) may be derived from a base class (parent), allowing all the protected and public members of the base class to be available to the derived class - inheritance.

• Inherited methods can be overloaded in the derived class.

- A derived class may inherit from more than one base class.

- Virtual methods allow methods declared in a base class to be implemented differently in derived classes.

- Polymorphism is a way of giving an action one name that is shared up and down an object hierarchy, with each object in the hierarchy implementing the action in a way appropriate to itself.

- Virtual functions are used to support polymorphism in C++.

It is claimed that the following benefits are to be gained by using object-oriented programming techniques.

- OOP encourages the use of libraries of objects. Software can be reusable and can also be extended, which in turn should help to reduce development costs.

- The maintainability of software is improved in terms of better standards of documentation and changes to software can take place at a local level.

- Software development time is shorter and development costs are lower.

- Reliability of software is meant to be improved.

- OOP is useful for the rapid prototyping of systems.

10.7 Questions *answers begin on page 293*

1. Adapt the methods in the files shapes.hpp and shapes.cpp to provide for a class GunSight and a class EnemyPlane. The shapes can be drawn from straight lines, circles and points as depicted below.

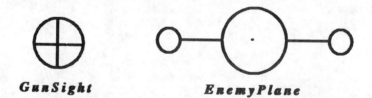

GunSight   **EnemyPlane**

2. Using the classes defined in the previous question, invent a game of space invaders. Program the gun-sight to move around the screen in response to the arrowed keys being pressed. Enemy planes appear at random positions on the screen, and at random intervals, only when the gun-sight is being moved. Only when the gun-sight cross hair is centralised over the centre-point of an enemy plane can an invader be zapped! Use sound effects with the sound(frequency), delay(mS) and nosound() functions. Display on the screen the number of enemy planes shot down.

Use the clock function from <time.h> to generate the passing of time, in the following algorithm that determine when to generate an enemy plane.

// produce a random number between 0 and 49 using the clock to generate elapsed time since Midnight
elapsed seconds = clock() % difficulty (where difficulty is a value between 1 and 50)

// produce a second random number in the range 0 - 49
LastTime = rand() % difficulty

// if both random numbers match then generate the coordinates of an enemy plane and plot the plane

3. Derive a class window, which represents a rectangle containing text, and has a marker > pointing at any line in the window. A typical window is depicted below.

Code methods to display a window and its contents, insert text into the window, select text from the window, show and erase the marker, move the marker to any item in the window using the arrowed keys, and make a window active (by showing the marker), or not active (by hiding the marker).

Write a program to display several windows as objects, and be able to inspect the contents of any window.

4. Derive a class notes, which represents a musical note. Use inheritance to define new classes for a quaver, crotchet and minim. Devise methods to display a single note, show the value of the note, play the note and display the note on a stave. The following illustration demonstrates the graphical output that is expected in this question.

The approximate frequency of the notes in the octave containing middle C are as follows.

C = 262, D = 294, E = 330, F = 349, G = 392, A = 440, B = 494

The tempo for playing notes will range from largo (delay factor 27); adagio (delay factor 16); moderato (delay factor 10); to presto (delay factor 6). The duration of a single note is quaver (1 beat); crotchet (2 beats) and minim (4 beats), where each beat is represented by a fixed unit of time.

Write a program to test the class notes, by creating objects of type note, storing the objects in an array, and playing and displaying the notes as depicted in the illustration.

5. Use the classes window and notes in a program to enable a user to compose and play a tune. To compose a tune a user must input the following information. The octave. In this question only three octaves are used, one octave up and one octave down from and including the octave containing middle C. The value of the note B,A,G,F,E,D or C. Whether the note is sharp, flat or a natural tone. The type of note, quaver, crotchet

or minim. A note can be modified prior to it being stored by selecting the MODIFY line in place of the type of note.

To play a tune the user must select the tempo from presto (fast), through moderato, adagio or largo (slow).

The full screen layout of the mini-composer system is given below.

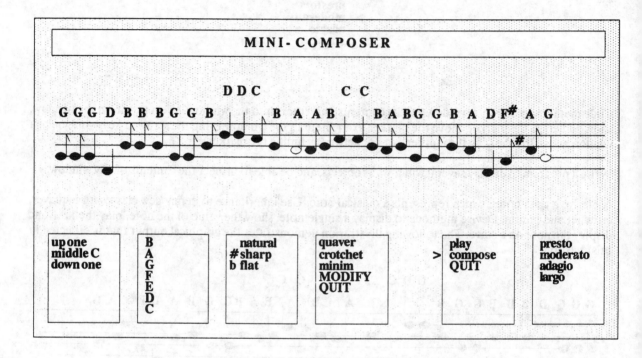

Answers

Section 1.12

1. The program contains the following errors.

The function getchar has been used in the program yet <stdio.h> has not been included as a header file.

The declaration of alpha and beta should be preceded by int.

If the function main is treated as a parameterless function then it must be declared as main(), otherwise the function will be ignored.

The first comment has a missing end delimiter */, therefore all the statements up to and including the next closing delimiter */ of the next comment will be ignored.

GetChar() incorrectly defined must be getchar() as stated in the standard library. The end of statement separator; is missing.

On the next line getchar is missing the parenthesis - getchar(). The end of statement separator ; is also missing.

At the end of the line putchar(beta); putchar(alpha) there is an end of statement separator missing.

The number of errors in this program is nine, yet the compiler only reported three errors! The correct version of the program follows.

```
#include <stdio.h>
int alpha, beta;
main()
/* program to input characters from the keyboard */
{
        alpha = getchar();
        beta = getchar();
        /* output the characters in reverse order */
        putchar(beta); putchar(alpha);
}
```

2.(a) The example macro definitions given as a sample from the header file <stdio.h> defines getchar and putchar as:

```
#define getchar() fgetc(stdin)
#define putchar(c) fputc((c), stdout)
```

The directive #define enables a programmer to code a macro definition.

The #define preprocessor directive causes any occurrence of getchar or putchar to be replaced in the source file by the functions fgetc(stdin) and fputc((c), stdout) respectively. Where stdin and stdout are the respective input and output streams, which in reality are the keyboard and screen.

(b) int main(void) - when a function is not assigned a type, it is assumed that the function has an integer type by default.

3. The following identifiers are legal variable names.

alpha
REGISTER

character
size_of
parameter
standard_8

The following identifiers are illegal for the reasons given.

register - reserved word
fgetc - library function
lotus 123 - embedded space
'hello' - apostrophes

4.(a) False - ASCII code for a is 97 and for A is 65.

(b) True - only letters of the alphabet can be case sensitive

(c) True - however, it must appear before any items in the header file can be used in the source program.

(d) True - however, placing it after all the functions reduces the amount of forward references that need to be declared.

(e) False - braces may contain declarations and C statements, however, in some high-level languages begin .. end may only contain language statements and no declarations. For example this would apply in Pascal and Modula-2.

(f) False - the C preprocessing phase precedes the actual compilation of a program.

5.(a) Since alpha has never been initialised its value CANNOT be determined. The value of alpha is NOT the ASCII code of character, since parameters are passed by value and NOT as a variable.

(b) When this program was compiled it contained five errors, yet it is possible to document the following six errors.

The declaration of omega should be terminated with a semi-colon.

A value for delta has not been declared.

In the declaration of epsilon, an identifier without a type in the formal parameter list, is not allowed.

Notice that although omega has been declared as a static variable with file scope, the re-declaration of omega is as a formal parameter with block scope. This second declaration hides the initial declaration.

The putchar function does not contain an argument.

There is no semi-colon after the putchar function.

There is no forward reference for the function epsilon.

6. The output from this program are the characters cba.

7. The values of x are 100, 110 and 120. Despite x being initially declared as being static by default, and having file scope, the re-declared x has block scope, and hides the original value of x.

8.(a) False - variables of register storage class have similar attributes to variables of auto storage class.

(b) False - external variable storage has storage allocated only once.

(c) True - unless the variables in the block are specifically classified as static or register.

(d) False - variables in a block are assumed to be auto, unless otherwise specified. Variables that are defined externally to a block, yet only have file scope, are by default static.

(e) False - a function can only take on static or external storage classes.

Section 2.10

1.(a) ULONG_MAX = 4294967295

(b) UCHAR_MAX = 255

(c) FLT_MAX_10_EXP = 38, FLT_EPSILON = 1.192092896e-07

(d) DBL_MAX = 1.7976931348623151e+308

(e) LDBL_DIG = 19

2. (a) float (b) int (c) double (d) float (e) double

3.(a)   semi-colon (;) after header name illegal, should be #include <stdio.h>
        semi-colon (;) and assignment (=) are both illegal, should be #define pi 3.14159
        no type declaration, should be float const vat = 0.175;

(b) If the length of the room is of type integer use %d, for float use %f, hence %c implies a single character and is wrong. The closing string delimeter is also missing. The statement should be written as: printf("length of room %f\n", length);

(c) The variable alpha has been defined as a pointer to an integer type; as a result alpha cannot be used in the scanf statement. The designated type "%f" is also wrong since alpha makes reference to integer types. A correct solution is:

```
{
        int alpha;
        scanf("%d", &alpha);
}
```

(d) The variable string is a pointer to the first character of a string of characters. Since this is a pointer there is no need to use &string in the scanf statement. A correct solution is:

```
{
        char *string;
        scanf("%s", string);
}
```

4.
```
/* program to calculate the total and average cost of newspapers */
#include <stdio.h>
main()
{       int Courier, Globe, Mercury;
```

```
        int TotalPence, average;
        float TotalPounds;

        printf("input the cost of the following newspapers\n\n");
        printf("Courier "); scanf("%d",&Courier);
        printf("Globe "); scanf("%d",&Globe);
        printf("Mercury "); scanf("%d",&Mercury);
        TotalPence = Courier+Globe+Mercury;
        TotalPounds = TotalPence/100.0;
        average = TotalPence/3;
        printf("total cost of papers £ %4.2f\n",TotalPounds);
        printf("average cost of papers %dp\n", average);
}
```

5.

```
/* program to calculate the volume of water required to fill a pool */
#include <stdio.h>
main()
{
        float length, width, shallow, deep, volume;

        printf("input the following measurements of a swimming pool\n\n");
        printf("length "); scanf("%f",&length);
        printf("width "); scanf("%f",&width);
        printf("depth at shallow end "); scanf("%f",&shallow);
        printf("depth at deep end "); scanf("%f",&deep);
        volume=(length*width)*((shallow+deep)/2);
        printf("volume of water required to fill the pool is %8.0f", volume);
}
```

6.

```
/* program to input a decimal number and display the octal and hexadecimal equivalents */
#include <stdio.h>
main()
{
        unsigned int integer;

        printf("input an unsigned decimal integer ");
        scanf("%u",&integer);
        printf("octal equivalent = %6o\n", integer);
        printf("hexadecimal equivalent = %6X\n", integer);
}
```

7.

```
/* program, using a separate function, to calculate the diameter, circumference and area of a circle when
supplied with the radius */
#include <stdio.h>

void circle(float radius, float *diameter, float *circumference, float *area)
{
        const float pi=3.14159;
        *diameter = 2.0 * radius;
```

247

```
        *circumference = 2.0 * pi * radius;
        *area = pi * radius * radius;
}

main()
{
        float radius, diameter, circumference, area;

        printf("input the radius of a circle ");
        scanf("%f",&radius);
        circle(radius, &diameter, &circumference, &area);
        printf("diameter = %10.2f\n", diameter);
        printf("circumference = %10.2f\n", circumference);
        printf("area = %10.2f\n\n", area);
}
```

8.

```
/* program to calculate denominations of money */
#include <stdio.h>

int calculator(int denomination, int *amount)
{
        int money;

        money = *amount;
        *amount = *amount % denomination;
        return money / denomination;
}

main()
{
        int money;

        printf("input an amount of money (no pence) ");
        scanf("%d", &money);
        printf("£50 = %d\n", calculator(50, &money));
        printf("£20 = %d\n", calculator(20, &money));
        printf("£10 = %d\n", calculator(10, &money));
        printf("£5 = %d\n", calculator(5, &money));
        printf("£1 = %d\n", money);
}
```

Section 3.10

1.

```
/* program to determine final grades */
#include <stdio.h>
#define space ' '

main()
{
```

```
        int cw, ex, total;
        int grade1, grade2, reply;

        do
        {
                printf("input coursework mark in range 0 .. 50 ");
                do scanf("%d", &cw); while (cw < 0 || cw > 50);

                printf("input examination mark in range 0 .. 50 ");
                do scanf("%d", &ex); while (ex < 0 || ex > 50);

                total=cw+ex;
                if (total == 39 && cw >=15 && ex >=15)
                        total = 40;
                else
                        if (total > 39 && (cw < 15 || ex < 15))
                                total = 39;
                grade2 = space;

                if      (total >= 70) grade1 = 'A';
                else if (total >= 60) {grade1 = 'B'; grade2 = '+';}
                else if (total >= 50) grade1 = 'B';
                else if (total >= 40) grade1 = 'C';
                else grade1 = 'F';

                printf("total moderated mark is %4d\n", total);
                printf("grade awarded is %c%c\n", grade1, grade2);
                getchar();
                printf("more marks answer y[es] or n[o] ");
                reply=getchar();
        }
        while (reply == 'Y' || reply == 'y');
}

2.

/* program to simulate a simple calculator */
#include <stdio.h>
#include <float.h>

float calculate(int operator, float A, float B)
{
        switch (operator)
        {
        case '+': return A+B;
        case '-': return A-B;
        case '*': return A*B;
        case '/':       if (B==0)
                        {
                                printf("attempt to divide by zero\n");
                                return FLT_MAX;
                        }
                        else return A/B;
        default : printf("illegal operator\n\n");
        }
```

```
}

main()
{
        float A,B;
        int operator;
        int reply;

        do
        {
                printf("input two real numbers "); scanf("%f%f",&A,&B);
                printf("input operator +,-,*,/ "); getchar(); operator=getchar();
                printf("result = %10.2f\n", calculate(operator,A,B));
                printf("more calculations - answer y[es] or n[o] ");
                getchar(); reply=getchar();
        } while (reply == 'y' || reply == 'Y');
}
```

3.

```
/* program to demonstrate for loops */
#include <stdio.h>

void i(void)
{
        int index;

        for (index=1; index<=29; index=index+2)
                printf("%3d", index);
        printf("\n\n");
}

void ii(void)
{
        int index;

        for (index=2; index<=20; index=index+2)
                printf("%4d", index*index);
        printf("\n\n");
}

void iii(void)
{
        int index, sum=0;

        for (index=1; index<=13; index=index+2)
                sum = sum +index*index;
        printf("sum of squares of odd integers in the range 1 .. 13 is %3d", sum);
        printf("\n\n");
}

void iv(void)
{
        int index;
```

```
        for (index=65; index < =90; index+ +)
                printf("%c", index);
        printf("\n\n");
        for (index=97; index< =122; index+ +)
                printf("%c", index);
        printf("\n\n");
}

void v(void)
{
        int a=0, b=1, index;

        for (index=0; index < 16; index=index+2)
        {
                printf("%4d", b);
                a=a+b;
                printf("%4d", a);
                b=b+a;
        }
        printf("\n\n");
}

main()
{
        i();
        ii();
        iii();
        iv();
        v();
}
```

4.

```
/* program to find the max, min and mean of a list of positive integers */
#include <stdio.h>
#include <limits.h>

main()
{
        int min=INT_MAX, max=INT_MIN, sum=0, count=0, integer;

        printf("input integers - terminate with a negative value\n\n");
        scanf("%d", &integer);
        while (integer > = 0)
        {
                if (integer > = max)
                        max=integer;
                if (integer < = min)
                        min=integer;
                sum=sum+integer;
                count+ +;
                scanf("%d", &integer);
        }
        printf("maximum value = %6d\n", max);
        printf("minimum value = %6d\n", min);
```

```
        printf("mean value = %6.2f\n", (float)sum/count);
}
```

5.

```c
/* program to analyse a sentence */
int WordCount=0, consonants=0, a=0,e=0,i=0,o=0,u=0;

void analysis(int letter)
{
        int const space=' ';
        int const comma=',';
        int const semicolon=';';
        int const colon=':';
        int const hyphen='-';

        if (letter == space)
                WordCount++;
        else
                switch (letter)
                {
                case 65: case 97 : a++; break;
                case 69: case 101: e++; break;
                case 73: case 105: i++; break;
                case 79: case 111: o++; break;
                case 85: case 117: u++; break;
                default: if (letter != comma && letter != semicolon && letter != colon && letter != hyphen)
                                consonants++;
                }
}

void DataInput(void)
{
        int const period='.';
        int const ExclamationMark='!';
        int const QuestionMark='?';
        int letter;

        printf("input a single sentence on one line\n");
        printf("use only ! ? or . to terminate the sentence\n\n");
        letter=getchar();
        while (letter != period && letter != ExclamationMark && letter != QuestionMark)
        {
                analysis(letter);
                letter=getchar();
        }
        WordCount++;
}

void results(void)
{
        printf("number of words = %2d\n", WordCount);
        printf("number of consonants = %2d\n", consonants);
        printf("number of vowels\n");
        printf("     a     e     i     o     u\n");
```

```
        printf("%3d%3d%3d%3d%3d\n",a,e,i,o,u);
}

main()
{
        DataInput();
        results();
}
```

6.

```
/* program to convert a Roman number to a decimal number */
#include <stdio.h>
#include <limits.h>
#define terminator '\n'
typedef enum {FALSE, TRUE} boolean;

int convert(int RomanNumeral, boolean *error)
{
        error=FALSE;
        switch (RomanNumeral)
        {
        case 'M': return 1000;
        case 'D': return 500;
        case 'C': return 100;
        case 'L': return 50;
        case 'X': return 10;
        case 'V': return 5;
        case 'I': return 1;
        default : *error=TRUE; return 0;
        }
}

main()
{
        int RomanNumeral;
        int LastValue=INT_MAX;
        int DecimalNumber=0;
        int CurrentValue;
        boolean error=FALSE;

        printf("input number using Roman numerals ");
        RomanNumeral=getchar();
        while (RomanNumeral != terminator && ! error)
        {
                CurrentValue=convert(RomanNumeral, &error);
                if (! error)
                {
                        if (CurrentValue > LastValue)
                                DecimalNumber=DecimalNumber+CurrentValue-2*LastValue;
                        else
                                DecimalNumber=DecimalNumber+CurrentValue;
                        LastValue=CurrentValue;
                }
                RomanNumeral=getchar();
```

```
        }
        if (! error)
                printf("equivalent decimal number is %8d\n", DecimalNumber);
        else
                printf("error in Roman numerals");
}
```

7.

```c
/* program to convert a decimal number to words */
#include <stdio.h>

void units(int unit)
{
        switch (unit)
        {
        case 1: printf("one "); break;
        case 2: printf("two "); break;
        case 3: printf("three "); break;
        case 4: printf("four "); break;
        case 5: printf("five "); break;
        case 6: printf("six "); break;
        case 7: printf("seven "); break;
        case 8: printf("eight "); break;
        case 9: printf("nine "); break;
        default: ;
        }
}

void teens(int teen)
{
        switch (teen)
        {
        case 0: printf("ten "); break;
        case 1: printf("eleven "); break;
        case 2: printf("twelve "); break;
        case 3: printf("thirteen "); break;
        case 4: printf("fourteen "); break;
        case 5: printf("fifteen "); break;
        case 6: printf("sixteen "); break;
        case 7: printf("seventeen "); break;
        case 8: printf("eighteen "); break;
        case 9: printf("nineteen "); break;
        }
}

void tens(int ten)
{
        switch (ten)
        {
        case 2: printf("twenty "); break;
        case 3: printf("thirty "); break;
        case 4: printf("forty "); break;
        case 5: printf("fifty "); break;
        case 6: printf("sixty "); break;
```

254

```
        case 7: printf("seventy "); break;
        case 8: printf("eighty "); break;
        case 9: printf("ninety "); break;
        default: ;
        }
}

int GetData(void)
{
        int number;

        printf("input number in the range 1 .. 999\n");
        do scanf("%d", &number); while (number < 1 || number > 999);
        return number;
}

main()
{
        int number, hundred, ten, unit;
        int reply;

        do
        {
                number=GetData();
                hundred=number/100;
                ten=number%100/10;
                unit=number%10;
                if (hundred > 0)
                {
                        units(hundred);
                        printf("hundred ");
                }
                if (ten == 1)
                        teens(unit);
                else
                {
                        tens(ten);
                        units(unit);
                }
                printf("\n\nanother number - answer y[es] or n[o] ");
                getchar(); reply=getchar();
        } while (reply == 'Y' || reply == 'y');
}
```

8. In general, all four program segments will compile without errors, however, the following comments apply to each section.

(i) The semicolon at the end of the while statement causes the computer to go into an infinite loop, since counter is never incremented. If the semicolon was removed the computer would display the values 1, 2 and 3. Notice that the value of counter is increased after the print operation was carried out. The program segment should be coded as:

```
counter=1;
while (counter < 4)
        printf("%4d", counter++);
```

(ii) The semicolon at the end of the condition signifies that no action is to be taken if the condition is true. The program segment should be coded as:

```
if (counter > 1000)
        printf("Warning! counter exceeds range");
```

(iii) With the semi-colon present after the while condition, the value of counter is effectively incremented until equal to 4, this value is then printed. The program segment should be coded as:

```
counter=0;
while (++counter < 4)
        printf("%4d", counter);
```

if it is intended that the value of the counter is printed as 1, 2 and 3.

(iv) Once again the semi-colon should be removed from the closing parenthesis of the for statement if it is intended to print the values 1, 2 and 3 of the counter.

```
for (counter=1; counter < 4; ++counter)
        printf("%4d", counter);
```

Section 4.10

1.

```
/* program to process parts of the alphabet */
#include <stdio.h>
char *alphabet = "abcdefghijklmnopqrstuvwxyz";

void display(int start, int finish)
{
        int index;

        for (index=start-1; index != finish; index++)
                printf("%c", alphabet[index]);
        printf("\n");
}

main()
{
        /* print entire alphabet */
        display(1,26);
        /* print the first six characters */
        display(1,6);
        /* print the last ten characters of the alphabet */
        display(17,26);
        /* print the tenth character of the alphabet */
        printf("%c\n", alphabet[9]);
}
```

2.
```
/* program to play noughts and crosses against the computer */
#include <stdio.h>
```

```
#include <stdlib.h>
#define nought 'O'
#define cross 'X'
#define space ' '
#define yes 'y'
#define range 3
typedef enum {computer, you} player;
typedef enum {FALSE, TRUE} boolean;
char board[3][3];
player who;
boolean success;
char reply;
int moves;

void initialise(void)
{
        int row, column;

        for (row=0; row !=3; row++)
                for (column=0; column !=3; column++)
                        board[row][column]=space;
        randomize();
        moves=0;
}

void CheckPosition(int row, int column, boolean *success)
{
        if (board[row][column]==space)
                *success=TRUE;
        else
                *success=FALSE;
}

void CheckWinner(player who, boolean *success)
{
        char character;
        int row, column;

        *success=FALSE;
        if (who==you)
                character=nought;
        else
                character=cross;
        /* check for rows */
        for (row=0; row!=3; row++)
        if(board[row][0]==character&&board[row][1]==character&&board[row][2]==character)
                *success=TRUE;
        /* check for columns */
        if (! *success)
                for (column=0; column!=3; column++)
                        if      (board[0][column]==character && board[1][column]==character &&
                                board[2][column]==character)
                                *success=TRUE;
        /* check diagonals */
        if (! *success)
```

```
            if (board[0][0]==character && board[1][1]==character && board[2][2]==character)
                    *success=TRUE;
        if (! *success)
            if (board[0][2]==character && board[1][1]==character && board[2][0]==character)
                    *success=TRUE;
}

void display(void)
{
        int row, column;

        printf("\n\n");
        for (row=0; row!=3; row++)
        {
                for (column=0; column!=3; column++)
                {
                        printf("%c", board[row][column]);
                        if (column != 2) printf(" | ");
                }
                printf("\n");
                if (row != 2) printf("---------\n");
        }
        printf("\n\n");
}

void play(player who)
{
        int row, column;
        boolean success;

        if (who==you)
        {
                do
                {
                        do
                        {
                                printf("input position of play ");
                                scanf("%d%d", &row, &column);
                        } while ((row < 0 || row > 2) && (column < 0 || column > 2));
                        CheckPosition(row,column, &success);
                } while (! success);
                board[row][column]=nought;
        }
        else
        {
                do
                {
                        row=rand()%3;
                        column=rand()%3;
                        CheckPosition(row, column, &success);
                } while (! success);
                board[row][column]=cross;
        }
}
main()
```

258

```
{
      do
      {
            initialise();
            do
            {
                  who=computer;
                  play(who); display(); moves++;
                  CheckWinner(who, &success);
                  if (success) printf("computer wins - ha, ha!\n");
                  if (!success && moves < 9)
                  {
                        who=you;
                        play(who); display(); moves++;
                        CheckWinner(who, &success);
                        if (success) printf("you win - smarty pants!!\n");
                  }
            } while (!success && moves != 9);
            if (!success && moves==9) printf("stale mate\n");
            printf("\nanother game? - answer y[es] or n[o] ");
            getchar(); reply=getchar();
      } while (reply==yes);
}
```

3.

```
/* program to test whether a word is a palindrome */
#include <stdio.h>
#include <stdlib.h>
#include <string.h>
typedef enum {FALSE,TRUE} boolean;
char *word;
int index1, index2; /* indices that mark letters at either end of the word */
boolean palindrome;

main()
{
      word=malloc(80);
      printf("input a single word ");
      gets(word);
      /* set indices to mark letters at either end of the word */
      index2=strlen(word)-1;
      index1=0;
      palindrome=TRUE;
      while (index1 <=index2 && palindrome)
      {
            if (word[index1]==word[index2])
            {
                  /* move indices closer to each other */
                  index1++;
                  index2--;
            }
            else
                  palindrome=FALSE;
      }
```

```
        if (palindrome)
                printf("this word is a palindrome\n");
        else
                printf("this word is NOT a palindrome");
}

4.

/* program to demonstrate the game minefield */
#include <stdio.h>
#include <stdlib.h>
#define space ' '
#define mined 'M'
typedef enum {FALSE, TRUE} boolean;
char field[10][10];
int mines;
int row, column, LastRow, LastColumn;
int MineCount;
boolean boom;

void initialise(void)
{
        int row, column;

        boom=FALSE;
        /* set cells of field to space */
        for (row=0; row!=10; row++)
                for (column=0; column!=10; column++)
                        field[row][column]=space;

        /* generate starting position */
        randomize();
        LastRow=9; LastColumn=rand()%10;
        field[LastRow][LastColumn]='^';

        /* generate number of mines */
        mines=rand()%10+1;

        /* lay mines in field */
        MineCount=0;
        do
        {
                row=rand()%10;
                column=rand()%10;
                if (field[row][column]==space)
                {
                        field[row][column]=mined;
                        MineCount++;
                }
        } while (MineCount!=mines);
}

void search(int row, int column, boolean *boom)
{
        if (field[row][column]==mined)
```

```
        {
                printf("\n\n\a\a B O O M !!\n\n");
                *boom=TRUE;
        }
        else
        {

                *boom=FALSE;
                field[row][column]='^';
        }
}

void display(boolean reveal)
{
        int row, column;

        printf("\n\n NORTH\n");
        printf(" 0 1 2 3 4 5 6 7 8 9\n");
        for (row=0; row!=10; row++)
        {
                printf("%2d",row);
                for (column=0; column!=10; column++)
                {
                        if (field[row][column]==mined && reveal)
                                printf(" %c",mined);
                        else if (field[row][column]==mined)
                                printf(" ");
                        else
                                printf(" %c",field[row][column]);
                }
                printf("\n");
        }
        printf("\n\n");
}

main()
{
        initialise();
        display(FALSE);
        do
        {
                do
                {
                        printf("input coordinates of next step ");
                        scanf("%d%d", &row, &column);
                } while        ((row < 0 || row > 9) || (column < 0 || column > 9) ||
                                ((row != LastRow) && (row != LastRow-1) && (row != LastRow+1)) ||
                                ((column != LastColumn) && (column != LastColumn-1) &&
                                (column != LastColumn+1)));
                LastRow=row;
                LastColumn=column;
                search(row,column,&boom);
                if (boom)
                        display(TRUE);
                else
                        display(FALSE);
```

```
        } while (! boom && row != 0);
        if (! boom)
        {
                printf("\nCongratulations!! You made it to the\n");
                printf("North through the following minefield");
                display(TRUE);
        }
        getchar();
        printf("\npress return to finish");
        getchar();
}
```

5.

```
/* program to add and subtract two twenty-digit integers */
#include <stdio.h>
#include <string.h>
#include <ctype.h>
typedef char LongNumber[21];
LongNumber x,y,z,nought="00000000000000000000";
int carry;

void DataIn(LongNumber number)
{
        printf("input a twenty digit number ");
        gets(number);
}

void addition(LongNumber x, LongNumber y, LongNumber z, int *carry)
{
        int index, sum;

        *carry = 0;
        for (index=19; index >= 0; index--)
        {
                sum=(x[index]-48)+(y[index]-48)+ *carry;
                if (sum > 9)
                {
                        z[index]=(sum-10+48);
                        *carry = 1;
                }
                else
                {
                        z[index]=(sum+48);
                        *carry = 0;
                }
        }
}

void subtraction(LongNumber x, LongNumber y, LongNumber z, int *carry)
{
        int index, difference;

        *carry = 0;
        for (index=19; index >= 0; index--)
```

```
        {
                difference=(x[index]-48)-(y[index]-48)-*carry;
                if (difference < 0)
                {
                        z[index]=(10-abs(difference)+48);
                        *carry = 1;
                }
                else
                {
                        z[index]=difference+48;
                        *carry = 0;
                }
        }
}

main()
{
        DataIn(x);
        DataIn(y);
        printf("%s\n", x);
        printf("%s\n", y);
        addition(x,y,z,&carry);
        if (carry==0)
                printf("sum = %s\n", z);
        else
                printf("overflow\n");
        subtraction(x,y,z,&carry);
        if (carry==0)
                printf("difference = +%s\n",z);
        else
        {
                subtraction(nought,z,z,&carry);
                printf("difference = -%s\n",z);
        }
}
```

6.

```
/* program to demonstrate searching a sorted array */
#include <stdio.h>
#include <string.h>
typedef enum {FALSE,TRUE} boolean;

typedef struct        {
                                char exchange[20];
                                char STDcode[8];
                      } teletype;

teletype entries[10] = {"Oxford","0865", "Denholm","045 087", "Glasgow","041", "Tarrant Hinton","025 889",
"Wroxton St.Mary","029 573", "Milton Abbot","082 287", "Knutsford","0565", "Dudleston Heath","069 175",
"Baillie's Mills","0846", "Aberdovey","065 472"};

void sort(void)
{
        teletype current;
```

263

```
        int location, index;

        for (index=1; index!=10; index++)
        {
                current=entries[index];
                location=index;
                while (location > 0 && strcmp(entries[location-1].STDcode, current.STDcode) > 0)
                {
                        entries[location]=entries[location-1];
                        location--;
                }
                entries[location]=current;
        }
}

int search(char key[], boolean *found)
{
        int index;

        *found=FALSE;
        for (index=0; index !=10; index++)
        {
                if (strcmp(key, entries[index].STDcode)==0)
                {
                        *found=TRUE;
                        return index;
                }
                if (strcmp(key, entries[index].STDcode)<0)
                        return index;
        }
        return index;
}

main()
{
        char key[8];
        boolean found;
        int position;

        sort();
        do
        {
                printf("input STD code ");
                gets(key);
                position=search(key, &found);
                if (found)
                        printf("%s\n",entries[position].exchange);
                else
                        printf("STD code not found - try again\n");
        } while (!found);
}
```

Section 5.8

1.

```
/* program to translate a phrase in Morse code into English */
#include <stdio.h>
#include <string.h>
#define null 00
#define EOLN ';'
typedef struct {char encryption[5]; } code;
code MorseCode[26];
char *message;

/* function to store the Morse code in an array or records */
void initialise()
{
        char *MorseData = ".- -...-.-.-.. ..-.--. ......"
                          ".----.-.-..-- -. --- .-.-.-.-. ... - .. --. ...-.-- -..--.----..";
        char string[5];
        int index;

        for (index = 0 ; index <= 25 ; ++index, MorseData = MorseData + 4)
        {
                strncpy(string,MorseData,4);
                string[4] = null; /* append null character to string */
                strncpy(MorseCode[index].encryption, string, 5);
        }
}

main()
{
        FILE *text;
        char string[5];
        int index;

        initialise();
        text=fopen("a:morse.txt","r");
        while (! feof(text))
        {
                fgets(string,5,text);
                if (string[0]==EOLN)
                        printf("\n");
                for (index=0; index!=26; index++)
                        if (strcmp(MorseCode[index].encryption,string)==0)
                printf("%c",index+65);
        }
        fclose(text);
}
```

2.

```
/* program to calculate telephone usage */
#include <stdio.h>
```

```
#define MaxCapacity 100
#define yes 'y'
typedef struct          {
                            char name[20];
                            char number[20];
                            int previous;
                            int current;
                        } details;
details subscribers[MaxCapacity];
FILE *data;

/* function to sort the records on the key name using an insertion sort */
void sort(int size)
{
        details current;
        int index, location;

        for (index=1; index < size; ++index)
        {
                current = subscribers[index];
                location = index;
                while (location > 0 && strcmp(subscribers[location - 1].name, current.name) >0)
                {
                        subscribers[location] = subscribers[location - 1];
                        --location;
                }
                subscribers[location] = current;
        }
}

/* function to collect data for each record */
int GetRecords(void)
{
        int records = 0;
        char reply;

        printf("input the following details of subscribers\n\n");
        do
        {
                printf("surname and initials ");
                gets(subscribers[records].name);
                printf("telephone number ");
                gets(subscribers[records].number);
                printf("previous meter reading ");
                scanf("%d", &subscribers[records].previous);
                printf("current meter reading ");
                scanf("%d", &subscribers[records].current);
                getchar();
                records++;
                printf("\nmore data y(es) or n(o) ? ");
                reply = getchar(); getchar();
        } while (reply == yes);
        return records;
}
```

```c
void report(void)
{
        FILE *text;
        details line[1];

        text=fopen("a:report.txt","w");
        data=fopen("a:data.bin","r");
        fprintf(text, "\t\tTELEPHONE SUBSCRIBERS\n\n");
        fprintf(text, "NAME\t\tNUMBER\t\tUNITS USED\n\n");

        fread(line, sizeof(details),1,data);
        while (! feof(data))
        {
                fprintf(text, "%s",line[0].name);
                fprintf(text, "\t\t%s", line[0].number);
                fprintf(text, "\t\t%d\n", line[0].current-line[0].previous);
                fread(line, sizeof(details),1,data);
        }
        fclose(text);
        fclose(data);
}

main()
{
        int size;

        data = fopen("a:data.bin", "wb");
        size = GetRecords();
        sort(size);
        fwrite(subscribers, sizeof(details), size, data);
        fclose(data);
        report();
}
```

3.

```c
/* program to read the binary file and display the report in question 3 */
#include <stdio.h>
#include <string.h>
typedef struct          {
                                char BranchCode[13];
                                char AccountNo[7];
                                char name[21];
                                int shares;
                        } details;
details account[1];
FILE *data;

main()
{
        char branch[13];
        int TotalShares;

        data=fopen("a:shares.bin","r");
        printf("\tTHE XYZ BUILDING SOCIETY\n");
```

267

```
        printf("DETAILS OF ORDINARY SHARE ACCOUNT CUSTOMERS\n\n");
        fread(account, sizeof(details), 1, data);
        while (! feof(data))
        {
                strcpy(branch, account[0].BranchCode);
                printf("BRANCH CODE: %s\n\n", branch);
                printf("ACCOUNT NUMBER\tNAME\t\t\t£1 SHARES\n\n");
                TotalShares=0;
                while (! feof(data) && strcmp(branch, account[0].BranchCode)==0)
                {
                        printf("%s\t\t%s\t\t\t%d\n",        account[0].AccountNo,
                                                            account[0].name,
                                                            account[0].shares);
                        TotalShares=TotalShares+account[0].shares;
                        fread(account, sizeof(details), 1, data);
                }
                printf("\n\t\t\t\tTOTAL \t%d\n\n", TotalShares);
        }
        fclose(data);
}
```

4.

```
/* program to print pay-slips from a master file and transaction file in question 4 */
#include <stdio.h>
#include <string.h>

typedef struct          {
                                char number[5];
                                char name[21];
                                float rate;
                                float allowances;
                                float gross;
                                float tax;
                                float pension;
                                float NatIns;
                        } M_details;

typedef struct          {
                                char number[5];
                                float hours;
                        } T_details;

M_details master[1];
T_details transaction[1];
FILE *mast, *trans;
float GrossWage, PensionContribution, TaxContribution, NetWage;

void calculate(void)
{
        #define PensionRate 0.06
        #define TaxRate 0.30
        #define NI 10.50
        float TaxableIncome;
```

```
        /* calculate amounts for payslip */
        GrossWage=transaction[0].hours * master[0].rate;
        PensionContribution = GrossWage * PensionRate;
        TaxableIncome = GrossWage - (PensionContribution + master[0].allowances);
        TaxContribution = TaxableIncome * TaxRate;
        NetWage = GrossWage - (PensionContribution + NI + TaxContribution);
}

void payslip(void)
{
        printf("\nEmployee Number: %s \tEmployee Name: %s \n\n",
                        transaction[0].number, master[0].name);
        printf("\t\t\tGross Wage:\t%10.2f\n", GrossWage);
        printf("\t\t\tPension:\t%10.2f\n", PensionContribution);
        printf("\t\t\tNI:\t\t%10.2f\n", NI);
        printf("\t\t\tTax:\t%10.2f\n", TaxContribution);
        printf("Net wage:%10.2f\n\n\n\n", NetWage);
}

main()
{
        mast=fopen("a:master.bin","r");
        trans=fopen("a:trans.bin","r");

        fread(transaction, sizeof(T_details), 1, trans);
        fread(master, sizeof(M_details), 1, mast);
        while (! feof(trans) || ! feof(mast))
        {
                calculate();
                payslip();
                fread(transaction, sizeof(T_details), 1, trans);
                fread(master, sizeof(M_details), 1, mast);
        }

        fclose(mast);
        fclose(trans);
}
```

5.

```
/* program to maintain a daily diary as a direct access file */
#include <stdio.h>
#include <ctype.h>
#include <string.h>
#define YearLength 365
typedef enum {FALSE, TRUE} boolean;
typedef struct { char record[60]; } line;
line filler[1];
int DaysInMonth[12] = {31,28,31,30,31,30,31,31,30,31,30,31};
int CumulativeDays[12] = {0,31,59,90,120,151,181,212,242,274,303,334};
FILE *diary;

/* function to initialise every entry in a new file and open the file */
void initialise(char reply)
{
```

```
        line year[YearLength]; /* array year one entry for each day */
        int DayNumber;

        if (toupper(reply) == 'Y')
        {
                /* set every entry in the diary to null */
                diary=fopen("a:diary.bin", "wb");
                for (DayNumber=0;DayNumber!=YearLength;DayNumber++)
                        strset(year[DayNumber].record, '\0');
                fwrite(year, sizeof(line), YearLength, diary);
                fclose(diary);
        }
        /* open diary for reading or writing */
        diary=fopen("a:diary.bin", "r+b");
        strset(filler[0].record, '\0');
}

/* function to input the day and month and calculate the position in the file of the record */
int InputDate(void)
{
        boolean error;
        int dd, mm;

        do
        {
                printf("\ninput date in format DD MM ");
                scanf("%d%d", &dd, &mm); getchar();
                error=FALSE;
                if (mm >=1 && mm <= 12)
                {
                        if (dd > DaysInMonth[mm-1])
                                error=TRUE;
                }
                else
                        error=TRUE;
        } while (error);
        return CumulativeDays[mm-1]+dd-1;
}

/* function to input a value for month and return the starting position for entries in the file */
int InputMonth(void)
{
        boolean error;
        int mm;

        do
        {
                printf("\ninput month number only ");
                scanf("%d", &mm); getchar();
                error=FALSE;
                if (mm >=1 && mm <=12)
                        return mm;
                else
                        error=TRUE;
        } while (error);
```

270

```
}
/* function to list the entries for one month */
void list(void)
{
        line entry[1];
        int mm;
        int day;
        int StartPosition;
        char MonthNames[12][4] = {"JAN","FEB","MAR","APR","MAY","JUN",
                                  "JUL","AUG","SEP","OCT","NOV","DEC"};

        mm = InputMonth();
        StartPosition = CumulativeDays[mm-1];
        fseek(diary, (long int) StartPosition * sizeof(line), SEEK_SET);
        printf("\n%s\n", MonthNames[mm-1]);
        for (day=1; day <= DaysInMonth[mm-1]; day++)
        {
                fread(entry, sizeof(line), 1, diary);
                if (strcmp(entry[0].record, filler[0].record)!=0)
                        printf("%d\t%s\n", day, entry[0].record);
        }
        printf("\n\n");
}

/* function to insert new entries into the file */
void insert(void)
{
        line entry[1];
        int DayNumber;

        DayNumber = InputDate();
        printf("entry: ");
        gets(entry[0].record);
        fseek(diary, (long int) DayNumber * sizeof(line), SEEK_SET);
        fwrite(entry, sizeof(line), 1, diary);
}

/* function to delete entries in the file */
void delete(void)
{
        line entry[1];
        int DayNumber;

        DayNumber = InputDate();
        fseek(diary, (long int) DayNumber * sizeof(line), SEEK_SET);
        strset(entry[0].record, '\0');
        fwrite(entry, sizeof(line), 1, diary);
}

main()
{
        char reply;

        printf("is this a new diary - answer Y[es] or N[o] ? ");
```

271

```
        reply = getchar();
        getchar();
        initialise(reply);
        do
        {
                printf("do you want to\n");
                printf("\n[I]nsert\n[D]elete\n[L]ist\n[E]xit? ");
                reply = toupper(getchar());
                getchar();
                switch (reply)
                {
                case 'I': insert(); break;
                case 'D': delete(); break;
                case 'L': list();
                }
        } while (reply != 'E');
        fclose(diary);
}
```

Section 6.9

1.

(a)
```
#include <stdio.h>
#include <math.h>
#define pi 3.14159
#define input(x) (printf("enter " #x " "), scanf("%f", &x))
/* macro to calculate and display the area of a triangle */
#define area(a,b,C) printf("area of triangle %f",0.5*a*b*sin((double)(C*pi/180)))

main()
{
        float a,b,C;

        input(a);
        input(b);
        input(C);
        area(a,b,C);
}
```

(b)
```
#include <stdio.h>
#define right(y) (y&0x0001 ? (y>>1)|(0x8000) : y>>1)

main()
{
        int a=0x70FF;
        int b;
        for (b=3;b!=0;b--)
                a=right(a);
        printf("%X", a);
}
```

(c)

```
#include <stdio.h>
#define TRUE 1
#define FALSE 0
#define hex(n) ((n >= '0' && n <= '9') || (toupper(n) >= 'A' && toupper(n) <= 'F') ? TRUE : FALSE)
#define terminator '/'

main()
{
        char X;

        printf("input a hexadecimal digit (type / to exit)\n");
        X=getchar();getchar();
        while (X != terminator)
        {
                if (! hex(X))
                        printf("\aillegal hexadecimal digit\n");
                X=getchar();getchar();
        }
}
```

(d)

```
#include <stdio.h>
#define TRUE 1
#define FALSE 0
#define Max(i,j,k) ((j > i && j > k) ? TRUE : FALSE)

main()
{
        int x, y, z;

        printf("input three integers ");
        scanf("%d%d%d", &x,&y,&z);
        if (Max(x,y,z))
                printf("maximum value is %d ", y);
        else
                printf("no maximum value");
}
```

2.

(a)

```
#include <stdio.h>
/* function to right rotate a 16-bit number by a set number of bits and return the new value of the number
*/

int right(int number, int bits)
{
        /* masks to check the sign bit and least significant bit (lsb) and clear the sign bit */
        int sign = 0x8000;
        int lsb = 0x0001;
        int clear = 0x7FFF;

        for ( ; bits != 0 ; bits--)
        {
```

```
            if ((number & lsb) && ((number & sign) > > 15))
                    number > > = 1;
            else if (!(number & lsb) && ((number & sign) > > 15))
            {
                    number > > = 1;
                    number &= clear;
            }
            else if (number & lsb)
            {
                    number > > = 1;
                    number |= sign;
            }
            else
                    number > > = 1;
    }
    return number;
}

/* function to left rotate a 16-bit number by a set number of bits and return the new value of the number */
int left(int number, int bits)
{
    int sign = 0x8000;
    int lsb = 0x0001;

    for ( ; bits != 0; bits--)
    {
            if ((number & sign) > > 15)
            {
                    number < < = 1;
                    number |= lsb;
            }
            else
                    number < < =1;
    }
    return number;
}

main()
{
    printf("%X\n", right(0x0F3C,3));
    printf("%X\n", right(0xF000,3));
    printf("%X\n", right(0x00FF,5));
    printf("%X\n", right(0xC01F,5));
    printf("%X\n", left(0x8F21,1));
    printf("%X\n", left(0xF01B,5));
    printf("%X\n", left(0x00F0,4));
}

(b)
#include <stdio.h>
int sign(int number)
{
    if ((number & 0x8000) > > 15)
            return 1;
    else
```

```
        return 0;
}

int complement(int number)
{
        return ~ number +1;
}

int multiply(int a, int b)
{
        int sum;
        int bit = -8;
        int lsb = 0x0001;
        int negative=0;

        if (sign(a))
        {
                a=complement(a); negative + +;
        }
        if (sign(b))
        {
                b=complement(b); negative + +;
        }
        sum=0;
        for (; bit != 0; bit + +)
        {
                if (b & lsb)
                        sum = sum + a;
                b > > = 1;
                a < < = 1;
        }
        if (negative != 1)
                return sum;
        else
                return complement(sum);
}

main()
{
        printf("%d\n", multiply(15,15));
        printf("%d\n", multiply(150,18));
        printf("%d\n", multiply(-25, 50));
        printf("%d\n", multiply(-25, -60));
        printf("%d\n", multiply(-256, 127));
}
```

3.

```
#include < stdio.h >
#include < math.h >
#define pi 3.14159

void table(double f(double))
{
        int increment=0;
```

275

```
        printf("\nx\tf(x)\n");
        for (; increment <= 90; increment+=5)
                printf("%d\t%f\n", increment, f(increment*pi/180));
}

void more(void)
{
        printf("\n\npress <return> to continue");
        getchar();
}

main()
{
        printf("sine\n"); table(sin);
        more();
        printf("cosine\n"); table(cos);
        more();
        printf("tangent\n"); table(tan);
        more();
}
```

4.

(a)
```
/* program to calculate the factorial value of a number */
#include <stdio.h>
# define input(x) (printf("input a number "), scanf("%ld", &x))
long int n;

/* function to calculate the factorial value of a number */
long int factorial(long int y)
{
        if (y<=1) return(1);
        else return (y*factorial(y-1));
}

main()
{
        input(n);
        printf("factorial %ld\n", factorial(n));
}
```

(b)
```
/* program to recursively find the largest integer in an array */
#include <stdio.h>
#include <stdlib.h>
#include <limits.h>
#define cells 10
int data[cells];

void generate(void)
{
        int index;

        randomize();
```

```
        for (index=0; index!=cells; index++)
        {
                data[index]=rand() % 100;
                printf("%4d", data[index]);
        }
        printf("\n\n");
}

void largest(int size, int *max)
{
        if (size < 0) return;
        else
        {
                if (data[size] > *max)
                        *max=data[size];
                largest(size-1, max);
        }
}

main()
{
        int maximum=INT_MIN;

        generate();
        largest(cells-1, &maximum);
        printf("largest integer in table is %d", maximum);
}

(c)
/* selection sort implemented recursively */
#include <stdio.h>
#include <stdlib.h>
#include <limits.h>
#define cells 15
int data[cells];

void generate(void)
{
        int index;

        randomize();
        for (index=0; index!=cells; index++)
                data[index]=rand() % 100;
}

void print(void)
{
int index;

        for (index=0; index != cells; index++)
                printf("%4d", data[index]);
        printf("\n");
}
```

```
void sort(int size)
{
        int index, temp, largest, position;

        if (size < 0) return;
                largest=INT_MIN;
        for (index=0; index <= size; index++)
                if (data[index] > largest)
                {
                        largest=data[index];
                        position=index;
                }
        temp=data[size];
        data[size]=largest;
        data[position]=temp;
        sort(size-1);
}

main()
{
        generate();
        print();
        sort(cells-1);
        print();
}
```

5.

```
/* program to build a linked list containing words modifications including functions to search and delete
nodes */
#include <stdio.h>
#include <stdlib.h>
#include <string.h>
#define sentinel "/"
typedef enum {FALSE,TRUE} boolean;
struct node   {
                        char *word;
                        struct node *link;
                };
struct node *head=NULL;

struct node *CreateNode(struct node *next, char *string)
{
        struct node *temp;

        temp=malloc(sizeof(struct node));
        temp->word = string;
        temp->link = next;
        return temp;
}

void CreateList(void)
{
        char *string;
```

```
        printf("input one word per line - terminate with /\n");
        string=malloc(256);
        gets(string);
        while (strcmp(string,sentinel)!=0)
        {
                head = CreateNode(head, string);
                string=malloc(256);
                gets(string);
        }
}

void ListOut(void)
{
        struct node *current;

        current=head;
        printf("\n\ncontents of linked list\n");
        while (current != NULL)
        {
                puts(current->word);
                current=current->link;
        }
}

boolean search(char *string)
{
        struct node *current;

        current=head;
        while (current != NULL)
                if (strcmp(current->word, string) == 0)
                        return TRUE;
                else
                        current=current->link;
        return FALSE;
}

void delete(char *string)
{
        struct node *p, *marker;

        puts(string);
        for (p=head, marker=NULL; strcmp(string, p->word) != 0; marker=p, p=p->link);
                if (p == head)
                        head = p->link;
                else
                        marker->link = p->link;
        free(p);
}

char * GetString(void)
{
        char *string;

        string=malloc(256);
```

```
                printf("\ninput string - terminate with /\n");
                gets(string);
                return string;
}

main()
{
        char *string;

        CreateList();
        ListOut();
        string=GetString();
        while (strcmp(string,sentinel) !=0)
        {
                if (search(string))
                {
                        printf("string found\n");
                        delete(string);
                        ListOut();
                }
                else
                        printf("\astring not in list\n");
                string=GetString();
        }
}
```

Section 7.7

1.

```
VOID find(VOID)
{
        CHAR MenuCode;
        INT count;
        CHAR line[LINE_LENGTH+1];
        CHAR buffer[LINE_LENGTH+1];
        CHAR find[LINE_LENGTH+1];
        CHAR replace[LINE_LENGTH+1];
        CHAR *marker;
        struct line *p;
        INT LineIndex, BufferIndex, temp;

        screen(2); ClearScreen();
        cprintf("find: "); strcpy(find, GetString());
        if (strlen(find) == 0) return;
        cprintf("replace with: "); strcpy(replace, GetString());
        MenuCode = FindMenu();
        if (MenuCode == LINE)
                p = position();
        else
        {
                p = head;
                current = 0;
```

```
        }
        while (p != NULL)
        {
                strcpy(line, p->text);
                marker=strstr(line, find);
                LineIndex=0; BufferIndex=0;

                while (marker != NULL)
                {
                        for (; LineIndex != (marker-line); LineIndex++, BufferIndex++)
                        {
                                buffer[BufferIndex]=line[LineIndex];
                                line[LineIndex]=FILLER;
                        }

                        temp=BufferIndex;
                        for (count=0;BufferIndex != temp+strlen(replace) &&
                                BufferIndex != LINE_LENGTH-1; count++, BufferIndex++)
                                buffer[BufferIndex]=replace[count];

                        for (count=0; count != strlen(find); LineIndex++, count++)
                                line[LineIndex]=FILLER;
                        marker=strstr(line,find);
                }

                for (;line[LineIndex]!='\n' && BufferIndex != LINE_LENGTH-1;
                        LineIndex++, BufferIndex++)
                        buffer[BufferIndex]=line[LineIndex];

                buffer[BufferIndex]  = '\n';
                buffer[BufferIndex+1] = '\0';

                strcpy(p->text, buffer);

                if (MenuCode == 'L')
                {
                        PrintLine(p);
                        return;
                }
                p = p->link;
                current++;
        }
        list(head);
}

2.

VOID insert(VOID)
{
        struct line *p, *new, *marker, *NewPosition;
        CHAR MenuCode;

        MenuCode = InsertMenu();
        if (head == NULL && (MenuCode == LINE || MenuCode == BOTTOM)) return;
        if (MenuCode == LINE) NewPosition = position();
```

```
        if (NewPosition == NULL) return;
        screen(1);
        ClearScreen();
        cprintf("enter text - terminate with %c ", TEXT_END );
        cprintf(" on a new line\n\n");
        new=ReadLine();
        if (new==NULL) return;
        if(new->text[0]==TEXT_END)
        {
                free(new);
                return;
        }

        LinesInFile++;

        if (MenuCode == TOP)
        {
                marker = head;
                head = new;
                current = 0;
        }
        else if (MenuCode == LINE)
        {
                marker = NewPosition->link;
                NewPosition->link = new;
        }
        else
        {
                for (NewPosition=head,current=1; NewPosition->link!=NULL;
                        NewPosition=NewPosition->link, current++);

                NewPosition->link = new;
                marker=NULL;
        }

        for (p=new, current++;; p=new, current++)
        {
                new=ReadLine();

                if (new==NULL) return;
                if(new->text[0]==TEXT_END)
                {
                        free(new);
                        p->link = marker;
                        list(head);
                        return;
                }
                p->link = new;
                LinesInFile++;
        }
}
```

3.

```
VOID save(VOID)
{
        struct line *p;
        FILE *filename;
        CHAR reply[CHAR_LENGTH+1];
        CHAR NewFile[LINE_LENGTH+1];

        screen(2);
        ClearScreen();
        cprintf("enter filename ");
        strcpy(NewFile, GetString());

        if ((filename=fopen(NewFile, READ_ONLY)) != NULL)
        {
                cprintf("\aWARNING FILE EXISTS OK TO OVERWRITE? \n");
                cprintf("answer [Y]es [N]o ");
                strcpy(reply, GetChar());
                reply[0] = toupper(reply[0]);
                if (reply[0] != YES) return;
                argument=NewFile;
                fclose(filename);
        }
        else if (strlen(NewFile) != 0)
                argument=NewFile;

        ClearScreen();
        cprintf("writing text to filename %s\n", argument);

        filename=fopen(argument,WRITE_ONLY);

        for (p=head; p!=NULL; p=p->link)
                fputs(p->text, filename);

        fclose(filename);
        PC_delay();
        return;
}
```

Section 8.6

1.

```
// program to create an array of records containing the fields name, date of birth and age today, sort the
// records into ascending order on age today, and display the records
#include <iostream.hpp>
#include <stdlib.h>
struct date    {
                        int dd;
                        int mm;
                        int yy;
                };
```

283

```
struct PersonsAge    {
                              char name[16];
                              date DOB;
                              int age;
                      };

PersonsAge *table;
date today;

// function to calculate and return an age from a date of birth
int GetAge(date DOB)
{
      if (DOB.yy < today.yy)
      {
            if (DOB.mm < today.mm || (DOB.mm = today.mm && DOB.dd <= today.dd))
                  return today.yy - DOB.yy;
            else
            {
                  if ((DOB.mm = today.mm && DOB.dd > today.dd) || DOB.mm > today.mm)
                        return today.yy - DOB.yy - 1;
            }
      }
      else
            return 0;
}

// determine the size of the array, then fill the array with records
void GetData(int &size)
{
      cout << "How many entries? ";
      cin >> size;
      table = new PersonsAge[size];
      for (int index=0; index < size; ++index)
      {
            cout << "input name of person ";
            cin >> table[index].name;
            cout << "input birthday in format dd mm yy ";
            cin >> table[index].DOB.dd >> table[index].DOB.mm >> table[index].DOB.yy;
            table[index].age = GetAge(table[index].DOB);
      }
}

// display the names and ages of the people in the order youngest to eldest
void display(int &size)
{
      for (int index=0; index <= size-1; ++index)
            cout << table[index].name << "\t" << table[index].age << endl;
}

// sort the contents of the array on the age field using an insertion sort
void sort(int &size)
{
      PersonsAge current;
      int location;
```

```
        for (int index = 1; index <= size-1; ++index)
        {
                current = table[index];
                location = index;
                while (location > 0 && table[location - 1].age > current.age)
                {
                        table[location] = table[location - 1];
                        --location;
                }
                table[location] = current;
        }
}

main()
{
        int size;

        cout << "input today's date in format dd mm yy ";
        cin >> today.dd >> today.mm >> today.yy;
        GetData(size);
        sort(size);
        display(size);
        delete [] table;
}
```

2.

(a) The data type for variable c has not been declared. The type conversion of float(c) after the statement c=a+b does NOT compensate for the missing type for c. The function can be corrected by writing int c=a+b;

(b) When a for statement declares a variable in one branch of an if statement the variable does not exist outside the if statement, or in the other branch of the if statement. The statement j=i; is illegal since i is outside the scope of declaration of i in the for statement.

(c) In C++ the requirement that a function is declared or defined before it is called does not prevent inconsistencies amongst files. During compilation, each function name is encoded to include the types of its parameters. The encoded name is then used during linking. If a function has been declared with two different parameter lists, the two encoded names will be different, enabling the linker to detect the discrepancy. In this example the linker will report that the version of alpha declared in the file Y.cpp has no definition.

(d) When only some of a function's parameters have default values, these parameters must come last in the parameter list.

(e)

(i) commas illegal; parentheses should be empty gamma().

(ii) parameters cannot be omitted from the middle of a parameter list, only from the right of the list; the commas are also illegal.

(iii) The parameter lists do not match, (67) is not a character.

3.

(a) References are allowed as return values. A function call that returns a reference is an lvalue and can, therefore, appear on the left-side of an assignment.

(b) Reference variables can also be legal. In the question p refers to i and must be initialised at the point of definition. A reference variable (p, for example) is nothing more than an alias for another variable (i, in this question).

4.

(a) (i) illegal - no best match.
(ii) legal - a call of alpha(float, int).
(iii) legal - a call of alpha(int, char).
(iv) illegal - two best matches.

(b) (i) legal - a call of beta(int *).
(ii) legal - a call of beta(const int *).

Despite p and q being the same type, the compiler can determine which version of beta to call from the fact that q is constant and p is not.

(c) gamma(i) - legal call of gamma(int &).
gamma(d) - illegal two best matches.

(d) epsilon(c) - illegal two best matches.

5.

```
#include <math.h>
#include <iostream.hpp>
// program to demonstrate overloading of a function name
// parameters - lengths of three sides
float area(float a, float b, float c)
{
        float s=(a+b+c)/2; //semi-perimeter
        return float(sqrt(double(s * (s-a) * (s-b) * (s-c))));
}

// parameters - lengths of two sides and an included angle
float area(float a, float b, int C)
{
        const pi=3.14159;
        return float(0.5 * a * b * sin(double(C*pi/180.0)));
}

// parameters - length of base and perpendicular height
float area(float b, float h)
{
        return 0.5 * b * h;
}

main()
{
        float a=3.0, b=4.0, c=5.0;
        int angleC=90;
```

```
        cout << area(a,b,c) << endl;
        cout << area(a,b,angleC) << endl;
        cout << area(a,b) << endl;
}
```

Section 9.12

1.

```
#include <iostream.hpp>
class rational
{
        friend rational operator+(const rational&, const rational&);
        friend rational operator-(const rational&, const rational&);
        friend rational operator*(const rational&, const rational&);
        friend rational operator/(const rational&, const rational&);
        friend ostream& operator<<(ostream&, const rational&);

        private:
                int numerator;
                int denominator;
                void MakeRational(void);

        public:
        // in-line constructors
        rational() {numerator = 0; denominator = 1; }
        rational(int num, int denom = 1)
        {
                numerator=num;
                denominator = denom;
                MakeRational();
        }
};

#include <stdlib.h>
#include "a:c9q1.hpp"
// Euclid's algorithm for evaluating the greatest common divisor between two positive integers m and n
static int Euclid(int m, int n)
{
        int remainder=m % n;
        while (remainder!=0)
        {
                m=n;
                n=remainder;
                remainder=m % n;
        }
        return n;
}

void rational :: MakeRational(void)
{
        int gcd; // greatest common divisor
        int divisor;
```

```
        gcd = Euclid(numerator, denominator);
        numerator = numerator/gcd; denominator = denominator/gcd;
        if (numerator == 0 || denominator == 0)
                denominator = abs(denominator);
        else
        {
                divisor = Euclid(abs(numerator), abs(denominator));
                if (denominator > 0)
                {
                        numerator /= divisor;
                        denominator /= divisor;
                }
                else
                {
                        numerator /= (-divisor);
                        denominator /= (-divisor);
                }
        }
}

rational operator + (const rational &A, const rational &B)
{
        int n = A.numerator * B.denominator + B.numerator * A.denominator;
        int d = A.denominator * B.denominator;
        return rational(n,d);
}

rational operator-(const rational &A, const rational &B)
{
        int n = A.numerator * B.denominator - B.numerator * A.denominator;
        int d = A.denominator * B.denominator;
        return rational(n,d);
}

rational operator*(const rational &A, const rational &B)
{
        int n = A.numerator * B.numerator;
        int d = A.denominator * B.denominator;
        return rational(n,d);
}

rational operator/(const rational &A, const rational &B)
{
        int n = A.numerator * B.denominator;
        int d = A.denominator * B.numerator;
        return rational(n,d);
}

ostream& operator< < (ostream& output, const rational& A)
{
        if (A.denominator == 1)
                return output << A.numerator;
        else
                return output << A.numerator << "/" << A.denominator;
}
```

2.

```
#include <iostream.hpp>
class complex
{
        friend complex operator+(const complex&, const complex&);
        friend complex operator-(const complex&, const complex&);
        friend complex operator*(const complex&, const complex&);
        friend complex operator/(const complex&, const complex&);
        friend ostream& operator<<(ostream&, const complex&);

        private:
                float real;
                float imaginery;

        public:
                // in-line constructors
                complex() {real = 0; imaginery = 0; }
                complex(float X, float Y = 0){ real = X; imaginery = Y; }
};

#include "a:c9q2.hpp"
complex operator+(const complex &A, const complex &B)
{
        float R = A.real + B.real;
        float I = A.imaginery + B.imaginery;
        return complex(R,I);
}

complex operator-(const complex &A, const complex &B)
{
        float R = A.real - B.real;
        float I = A.imaginery - B.imaginery;
        return complex(R,I);
}

complex operator*(const complex &A, const complex &B)
{
        float R = A.real * B.real - A.imaginery * B.imaginery;
        float I = A.real * B.imaginery + A.imaginery * B.real;
        return complex(R,I);
}

complex operator/(const complex &A, const complex &B)
{
        complex T = A * complex(B.real, - B.imaginery);
        float N = B.real * B.real + B.imaginery * B.imaginery;
        if (N != 0.0)
                return complex(T.real/N, T.imaginery/N);
        else
                cout << "attempt to divide by zero" << endl;
}

ostream& operator<<(ostream& output, const complex& A)
{
```

```
        return output << A.real << ", " << A.imaginery << "i";
}

3.

#include <iostream.hpp>
class money
{
        friend money operator + (const money&, const money&);
        friend money operator-(const money&, const money&);
        friend money operator*(const money&, double);
        friend money operator*(double, const money&);
        friend long int operator/(const money&, const money&);
        friend money operator%(const money&, const money&);
        friend int operator = = (const money&, const money&);
        friend int operator! = (const money&, const money&);
        friend int operator > (const money&, const money&);
        friend int operator < (const money&, const money&);
        friend int operator > = (const money&, const money&);
        friend int operator < = (const money&, const money&);
        friend ostream& operator < < (ostream&, const money&);

        private:
                long int pounds;
                int pence;
                void carry();

        public:
                money();
                money(long int, int);
                money(double);
                money(char *);
                money &operator-();
                int operator!();
};

#include <stdio.h>
#include <math.h>
#include "a:c9q3.hpp"
void money :: carry()
{
        while (pence < 0 && pounds > 0)
        {
                --pounds;
                pence=pence+100;
        }
        while (pence > 0 && pounds < 0)
        {
                ++pounds;
                pence = pence -100;
        }
        pounds = pounds + pence/100;
        pence = pence % 100;
}
```

```
money :: money(long int L, int p)
{
     pounds = L;
     pence = p%100;
     pounds = pounds + p/100;
     carry();
}

money :: money(double L)
{
     double w, f;

     int negative = L < 0 ? (L=-L, 1) : 0;
     f = modf(L, &w);
     int p = f*1000;
     pence = p/10;

     if (p%10 >= 5) ++pence;
     pounds=w;

     if (negative)
     {
             pounds=-pounds;
             pence=-pence;
     }
}

money :: money(char *s)
{
     pounds = 0;
     pence = 0;
     sscanf(s, "%ld.%d", &pounds, &pence);
     if (pounds < 0) pence = -pence;
}

money :: money()
{
     pounds=0; pence=0;
}

money& money :: operator-()
{
     pounds = -pounds; pence = -pence;
     return *this;
}

int money :: operator!()
{
     return !pounds && !pence;
}

money operator + (const money &a, const money &b)
{
     money t;
     t.pounds = a.pounds + b.pounds;
```

```
            t.pence = a.pence + b.pence;
            t.carry();
            return t;
}

money operator-(const money &a, const money &b)
{
            money t;
            t.pounds = a.pounds - b.pounds;
            t.pence = a.pence - b.pence;
            t.carry();
            return t;
}

money operator*(double b, const money &a)
{
            b *= a.pounds + a.pence/100.0;
            return money(b);
}

money operator*(const money &a, double b)
{
            b *= a.pounds + a.pence/100.0;
            return money(b);
}

long int operator/(const money &a, const money &b)
{
            double n = a.pounds + a.pence / 100.0;
            double d = b.pounds + b.pence / 100.0;
            double q = n/d;
            modf(q, &n);
            return long(n);
}

money operator%(const money &a, const money &b)
{
            // test for pounds or pence negative
            int neg = a.pounds < 0 || a.pence < 0;

            // convert money to a decimal value
            double dec_pounds_a = a.pounds + a.pence/100.0;
            double dec_pounds_b = b.pounds + b.pence/100.0;
            double quotient=dec_pounds_a/dec_pounds_b;
            modf(quotient, &dec_pounds_a);

            // test for negative dec_pounds_a
            long int L = dec_pounds_a < 0 ? -dec_pounds_a : +dec_pounds_a;
            long int p = L*abs(b.pence);
            L = L * labs(b.pounds);
            L = L + p/100;
            if (neg)
            {
                    L=-L;
                    p=-p;
```

292

```
        }
        return a - money(L,int(p));
}

inline int operator= =(const money &a, const money &b)
{
        return a.pounds = = b.pounds && a.pence = = b.pence;
}

inline int operator!=(const money& a, const money& b)
{
        return a.pounds != b.pounds || a.pence != b.pence;
}

inline int operator>(const money& a, const money& b)
{
        return a.pounds > b.pounds ? 1 : a.pence > b.pence;
}

inline int operator<(const money& a, const money& b)
{
        return a.pounds < b.pounds ? 1: a.pence < b.pence;
}

inline int operator> =(money& a, money& b)
{
        return !(a<b);
}

inline int operator< =(money& a, money& b)
{
        return !(a>b);
}

ostream& operator< <(ostream& output, const money& a)
{
        int p=a.pence;
        if (p < 0) p =-p;
        return output < < a.pounds < < "." < < p;
}
```

Section 10.7

1.

```
class point
{
        protected: short int x,y;
        public:
                // constructors
                point() {x=0; y=0;}
                point(const &X, const &Y) {x=X; y=Y;}
                // functions
```

```
        virtual void plot(void);
        virtual void erase(void);
        short int GetX(void);
        short int GetY(void);
        void move(int toX, int toY);
};

class GunSight: public point
{
        public:
                // constructors
                GunSight() {x=0; y=0;}
                GunSight(const &X, const &Y) {x=X; y=Y;}
                virtual void plot(void);
                virtual void erase(void);
};

class EnemyPlane: public point
{
        public:
                // constructors
                EnemyPlane() {x=0; y=0;}
                EnemyPlane(const &X, const &Y) {x=X; y=Y;}
                virtual void plot(void);
                virtual void erase(void);
                void destroy(int NewX, int NewY);
};

#include <graph.h>
#include <conio.h>
#include <dos.h>
#include <stdlib.h>
#include "a:invader.hpp"

void point :: plot(void)
{
        _setcolor(_getcolor());
        _setpixel(x,y);
}

void point :: erase(void)
{
        short int colour;

        colour= _getcolor();
        _setcolor(_getbkcolor());
        _setpixel(x,y);
        _setcolor(colour);
}

short int point :: GetX(void)
{
        return x;
}
```

```
short int point :: GetY(void)
{
        return y;
}

void point :: move(int toX, int toY)
{
        erase();
        x=toX;
        y=toY;
        plot();
}

void GunSight :: plot(void)
{
        const int r=15; // [r]adius
        _setcolor(_getcolor());
        _ellipse(_GBORDER,x-r,y-r,x+r,y+r);
        _moveto(x-r,y);
        _lineto(x+r,y);
        _moveto(x,y-r);
        _lineto(x,y+r);
}

void GunSight :: erase(void)
{
        short int colour;
        const int r=15;
        colour=_getcolor();
        _setcolor(_getbkcolor());
        _ellipse(_GBORDER,x-r,y-r,x+r,y+r);
        _moveto(x-r,y);
        _lineto(x+r,y);
        _moveto(x,y-r);
        _lineto(x,y+r);
        _setcolor(colour);
}

void EnemyPlane :: plot(void)
{
        int const r=10;
        _setcolor(_getcolor());
        _ellipse(_GBORDER,x-r,y-r,x+r,y+r);
        point :: plot();
        _moveto(x-r,y);
        _lineto(x-2*r,y);
        _ellipse(_GBORDER,x-4*r+5,y-r+5,x-2*r-5,y+r-5);
        _moveto(x+r,y);
        _lineto(x+2*r,y);
        _ellipse(_GBORDER,x+2*r+5,y-r+5,x+4*r-5,y+r-5);
        sound(750);delay(50);nosound();
}

void EnemyPlane :: erase(void)
{
```

```
        short int colour;
        colour=_getcolor();
        _setcolor(_getbkcolor());
        EnemyPlane :: plot();
        _setcolor(colour);
        sound(300); delay(500); nosound();
}

void EnemyPlane :: destroy(int NewX, int NewY)
{
        x=NewX;
        y=NewY;
        EnemyPlane::erase();
}
```

2.

```
// program to play space invaders
#include "a:invader.cpp"
#include <time.h>
#include <string.h>
#include <iostream.hpp>

enum boolean {false, true};
struct coordinates    {
                               int Xpos;
                               int Ypos;
                       };
GunSight sight(320, 220), *g; // initial position
EnemyPlane *e;
int x,y;
coordinates EnemyPosition;
int EnemyCount=0, hits=0;
int MaxInvaders;
coordinates *LastPosition; // array to store positions of invaders
char StringHits[10];
int difficulty; // level of difficulty

// function to generate enemy planes
void enemy(coordinates &EnemyPosition, int &EnemyCount)
{
        double seconds=((double) clock()) % difficulty;
        int LastTime=rand() % difficulty;
        if (LastTime==seconds)
        {
                do
                {
                        EnemyPosition.Xpos = rand()%500 + 100;
                } while (EnemyPosition.Xpos % 10 !=0);
                do
                {
                        EnemyPosition.Ypos = rand()%300 + 100;
                } while (EnemyPosition.Ypos % 10 !=0);

                EnemyPlane E(EnemyPosition.Xpos, EnemyPosition.Ypos);
```

296

```
                E.plot();
                LastPosition[EnemyCount] = EnemyPosition;
                EnemyCount + +;
        }
}

boolean direction(short int &Xinc, short int &Yinc)
// this function is identical to the function direction given in the chapter,
// for this reason the function has been omitted from the answer
void MoveSight(void)
{
        int const displacement = 10;
        short int Xinc, Yinc;
        int sightX, sightY;
        g=&sight; g->plot();
        sightX=sight.GetX(); sightY=sight.GetY();
        while (direction(Xinc, Yinc))
        {
                sightX=sightX+ (Xinc*displacement);
                sightY=sightY+ (Yinc*displacement);
                sight.move(sightX, sightY);
                enemy(EnemyPosition, EnemyCount);
        }
}

main()
{
        cout << "input level of difficulty from the scale 1 - 50\n\n";
        cout << "1 - impossible!\n";
        cout << "10 - you have to be quick\n";
        cout << "20 - possible with care\n";
        cout << "50 - easy\n\n";
        do
        {
                cout << "\alevel "; cin >> difficulty;
        } while (difficulty < 1 || difficulty > 50);

        cout << "\nKEEP THE GUNSIGHT MOVING TO GENERATE INVADERS\n";
        cout << "\nPOSITION THE GUNSIGHT OVER THE CENTRE OF THE PLANE,";
        cout << "\nTHEN PRESS THE RETURN OR ENTER KEY TO ZAP THE ENEMY\a";

        delay(10000);
        MaxInvaders = 1000/difficulty;
        LastPosition = new coordinates[MaxInvaders];
        _setvideomode(_VRES16COLOR);
        while ((EnemyCount-hits < 5) && (EnemyCount < MaxInvaders))
        {
                enemy(EnemyPosition, EnemyCount);
                MoveSight();
                sound(1000); delay(100); nosound();
                x=sight.GetX(); y=sight.GetY();
                for (int index=0; index != EnemyCount; index+ +)
                {
                        if((x==LastPosition[index].Xpos) && (y==LastPosition[index].Ypos))
                        {
```

```
                        hits++;
                        e->destroy(x,y);
                        LastPosition[index].Xpos=0;
                        LastPosition[index].Ypos=0;
                        _settextposition(30,39);
                        itoa(hits,StringHits,10);
                        strcat(StringHits, " Hits");
                        _outtext(StringHits);
                        delay(500);
                        break;
                    }
                }
            }
        _settextposition(30,20);
        if (EnemyCount - hits >=5)
        {
            _outtext("YOU HAVE BEEN ZAPPED BY ENEMY FIGHTERS");
            sound(200);
        }
        else
        {
            _outtext("YOU ARE THE INTERGALACTIC HERO OF THE YEAR");
            sound(750);
        }
        delay(3000); nosound();
        _setvideomode(_DEFAULTMODE);
        delete [] LastPosition;
        cout << "\aGAME OVER\n";
    }


3.
class window
{
        private:
                short x1,y1,x2,y2; // window coordinates
                short Ymin, Ymax; // ordinate values of top and bottom entries
                char contents[29] [80]; // max contents of a window, 29 lines of 80 characters
                short X,Y; // coordinates of marker
                short current; // ordinal position of the line marker
                short NextEntry; // position of next free line of text
        public:
                window();
                window(const &X1, const &Y1, const &X2, const &Y2);
                void draw(void); // display window and contents
                void insert(char []); // insert text into window
                char * select(void); // select text from window
                void markerON(void); // display line marker
                void markerOFF(void); // hide line marker
                void MoveMarker(void); // position line marker
                void active(void); //
                void NOTactive(void); //
};
```

```
#include <graph.h>
#include <stdlib.h>
#include <string.h>
#include <conio.h>
#include "a:window.hpp"
const int Xscale = 8;
const int Yscale = 16;
enum boolean {false, true};

window :: window()
{
        x1=0;y1=0;x2=0;y2=0;Ymin=0;Ymax=0;NextEntry=0; current=0; X=0;Y=0;
}

window :: window(const &X1, const &Y1, const &X2, const &Y2)
{
        x1=X1;y1=Y1;x2=X2;y2=Y2;
        Ymin=y1/Yscale+2;Ymax=Ymin;
        NextEntry=0; current=0;
        X=x1/Xscale;Y=y1/Yscale+2;
}

void window :: draw(void)
{
        _rectangle(_GBORDER,x1,y1,x2,y2);
        for (int index=0; index!=NextEntry; index++)
        {
                _settextposition((y1/Yscale)+(index+2), (x1/Xscale)+2);
                _outtext(contents[index]);
        }
}

void window :: insert(char line[])
{
        strcpy(contents[NextEntry], line);
        if (Ymax <= y2/Yscale)
        {
                NextEntry++;
                Ymax++;
        }
}

char * window :: select(void)
{
        char *line;
        line = new char[80];
        strcpy(line, contents[current]);
        return line;
}

void window :: markerON(void)
{
        _settextposition(Y,X);
        _outtext(">");
}
```

299

```
void window :: markerOFF(void)
{
        _settextposition(Y,X);
        _outtext(" ");
}

boolean direction(int &increment)
{
        int key;
        boolean quit, dirn;
        increment=0;
        dirn=true;
        do
        {
                key=getch();
                quit=true;
                switch (key)
                {
                case 0: {
                                key=getch();
                                switch (key)
                                {
                                case 72: increment=-1; break;
                                case 80: increment= +1; break;
                                default: quit=false;
                                } break;
                        }
                case 13: dirn=false; break;
                default: quit=false;
                }
        } while (!quit);
        return dirn;
}

void window :: MoveMarker(void)
{
        int increment;

        markerON();
        while (direction(increment))
        {
                markerOFF();
                Y=Y+increment; // increment is either +1 or -1
                if (Y < Ymin)
                {
                        Y=Ymax-1;
                        current=NextEntry-1;
                }
                else if (Y == Ymax)
                {
                        Y=Ymin;
                        current=0;
                }
                else
                        current=current+increment;
```

300

```
                markerON();

        }
}

void window :: active(void)
{
        markerON();
}

void window :: NOTactive(void)
{
        markerOFF();
}
```

4.

```
class notes
{
        protected:
                char note[5];           // note[0] - CDEFGAB
                                        // note[1] - (n)atural, (f)lat, (s)harp
                                        // note[2] - (u)p, (m)iddle, (d)own
                                        // note[3] - (q)uaver, (c)rotchet, (m)inim
        public:
                notes();
                notes(char []);
                virtual void display(int,int,int);
                void ShowNote(int, int);
                void play(char);
                void stave(int, int);
};

class minim: public notes
{
        public:
                minim();
                minim(char []);
                virtual void display(int, int, int);
};

class crotchet: public notes
{
        public:
                crotchet();
                crotchet(char []);
                virtual void display(int, int, int);
};

class quaver: public notes
{
        public:
                quaver();
                quaver(char []);
                virtual void display(int, int, int);
```

```
};

#include "a:note.hpp"
#include <graph.h>
#include <string.h>
#include <dos.h>
#include <stdlib.h>

enum ToneType {flat, natural, sharp};
enum NoteType {C,D,E,F,G,A,B};
const int time = 10;
const int XSCALE=8;
const int YSCALE=16;
const int displacement = 55;
const int Xinc = 8;
int frequency[7] = {262, 294, 330, 349, 392, 440, 494};
NoteType index, NoteValue;
ToneType tone;
int x,y; // position on the stave where the note is to be drawn

notes :: notes()
{
        strcpy(note, '\0');
}

notes :: notes(char NewNote[])
{
        strcpy(note, NewNote);
}

void notes :: display(int x, int y, int tone) {}

void notes :: ShowNote(int x, int y)
{
        char buffer[3];
        strnset(buffer, '\0', 3);
        _settextposition((y-displacement)/YSCALE, (x+Xinc)/XSCALE);
        _outtext(strncpy(buffer, note, 2));
}

void notes :: play(char tempo)
{
        int DelayFactor;
        float FrequencyFactor;
        int NoteFrequency;
        int SemiTone;
        int duration;

        switch (note[0])
        {
        case 'A' : NoteValue=A; break;
        case 'B' : NoteValue=B; break;
        case 'C' : NoteValue=C; break;
        case 'D' : NoteValue=D; break;
        case 'E' : NoteValue=E; break;
```

```
        case 'F' : NoteValue=F; break;
        case 'G' : NoteValue=G;
        }

        switch (note[1])
        {
        case '#' : tone=sharp; break;
        case 'b' : tone=flat; break;
        case ' ' : tone=natural;
        }

        switch (note[2])
        {
        case 'd' : FrequencyFactor=0.5; break;
        case 'm' : FrequencyFactor=1.0; break;
        case 'u' : FrequencyFactor=2.0;
        }

        switch (note[3])
        {
        case 'q' : duration=time; break;
        case 'c' : duration=2*time; break;
        case 'm' : duration=4*time;
        }

        switch (tempo)
        {
        case 'l': DelayFactor=27; break;
        case 'a': DelayFactor=16; break;
        case 'm': DelayFactor=10; break;
        case 'p': DelayFactor=6;
        }

        NoteFrequency=(FrequencyFactor*frequency[NoteValue] + 0.5);
        if (tone==sharp && NoteValue != B)
                SemiTone=(frequency[NoteValue+1]-frequency[NoteValue])/2;
        else if (tone==flat && NoteValue != C)
                SemiTone=(frequency[NoteValue-1]-frequency[NoteValue])/2;
        else
                SemiTone=0;
        NoteFrequency=NoteFrequency+(FrequencyFactor*SemiTone)+0.5;

        sound(NoteFrequency);
        delay(duration*DelayFactor);
        nosound();
}

void notes :: stave(int x, int y)
{
        setcolor(_getcolor());
        for (int index=1; index <=5; index++)
        {
                _moveto(20,y-10*(index-1));
                _lineto(620,y-10*(index-1));
        }
```

```
        switch (note[2])
        {
        case 'u' : y=y-35; break;
        case 'd' : y=y+35; break;
        case 'm' : ;
        }

        ShowNote(x,y);

        switch (note[0])
        {
        case 'B': y=y-20;break;
        case 'A': y=y-15;break;
        case 'G': y=y-10;break;
        case 'F': y=y-5;break;
        case 'D': y=y+5; break;
        case 'C': y=y+10;
        }

        switch (note[1])
        {
        case '#': tone=sharp; break;
        case 'b': tone=flat; break;
        case ' ': tone=natural;
        }

        display(x,y,tone);
}

minim :: minim()
{
        strcpy(note,'\0');
}

minim :: minim(char NewNote[])
{
        strcpy(note,NewNote);
}

void minim :: display(int x, int y, int tone)
{
        _setcolor(_getcolor());
        _ellipse(_GBORDER,x-4,y-2,x+4,y+2);
        _moveto(x+4,y);
        _lineto(x+4,y-20);
        _settextposition((y-5)/YSCALE, (x+18)/XSCALE);
        if (tone == sharp)
                _outtext("#");
        else if (tone == flat)
                _outtext("b");
}

crotchet :: crotchet()
{
        strcpy(note,'\0');
```

```
}
crotchet :: crotchet(char NewNote[])
{
      strcpy(note, NewNote);
}

void crotchet :: display(int x, int y, int tone)
{
      _setcolor(_getcolor());
      _ellipse(_GFILLINTERIOR,x-4,y-2,x+4,y+2);
      _moveto(x+4,y);
      _lineto(x+4,y-20);
      _settextposition((y-5)/YSCALE, (x+18)/XSCALE);
      if (tone == sharp)
            _outtext("#");
      else if (tone == flat)
            _outtext("b");
}

quaver :: quaver()
{
      strcpy(note, '\0');
}

quaver :: quaver(char NewNote[])
{
      strcpy(note, NewNote);
}
void quaver :: display(int x, int y, int tone)
{
      _setcolor(_getcolor());
      _ellipse(_GFILLINTERIOR,x-4,y-2,x+4,y+2);
      _moveto(x+4,y);
      _lineto(x+4,y-20);
      _lineto(x+9,y-10);
      _settextposition((y-5)/YSCALE, (x+18)/XSCALE);
      if (tone == sharp)
            _outtext("#");
      else if (tone == flat)
            _outtext("b");
}
```

5.

```
// program to compose short tunes
#include "a:window.cpp"
#include "a:note.cpp"
int const MaxNotes=50; // maximum number of notes that can be stored
int staveX=20, staveY=200; // coordinates for position of stave
int number; // number of notes stored
char MenuItem[10], MusicTempo[10];
char NoteOct[10], NoteFreq[10], NoteBeat[10], NoteTone[10], NOTE[4];
notes NoteStore[MaxNotes];
window banner(25,5,615,35), oct(25,300,110,420), freq(125,300,210,420),
```

Tone(225,300,310,420), beat(325,300,410,420), menu(425,300,510,420), tempo(525,300,610,420);

```
void CreateWindows(void)
{
        banner.insert("                    MINI-COMPOSER"); banner.draw();
        oct.insert("up one"); oct.insert("middle C"); oct.insert("down one"); oct.draw();
        freq.insert("B"); freq.insert("A"); freq.insert("G"); freq.insert("F");
        freq.insert("E"); freq.insert("D"); freq.insert("C"); freq.draw();
        Tone.insert(" natural"); Tone.insert("# sharp"); Tone.insert("b flat"); Tone.draw();
        beat.insert("quaver"); beat.insert("crotchet"); beat.insert("minim");
        beat.insert("MODIFY"); beat.insert("QUIT"); beat.draw();
        menu.insert("play"); menu.insert("compose"); menu.insert("QUIT"); menu.draw();
        tempo.insert("presto"); tempo.insert("moderato"); tempo.insert("adagio"); tempo.insert("largo");
        tempo.draw();
}

char *capture(window X)
{
        char *temp;
        temp = new char[80];
        X.active();
        X.MoveMarker();
        strcpy(temp, X.select());
        X.NOTactive();
        return temp;
}

void GetNote(void)
{
        strcpy(NoteOct, capture(oct));
        strcpy(NoteFreq, capture(freq));
        strcpy(NoteTone, capture(Tone));
        strcpy(NoteBeat, capture(beat));
        NOTE[0] = NoteFreq[0];
        NOTE[1] = NoteTone[0];
        NOTE[2] = NoteOct[0];
        NOTE[3] = NoteBeat[0];
        NOTE[4] = '\0';
}

void record(void)
{
        char const PlayTempo = 'p';
        int static index=0;
        if (NoteBeat[0] =='q')
        {
                quaver X(NOTE);
                X.stave(staveX,staveY);
                X.play(PlayTempo);
                NoteStore[index]=X;
                index++;
        }
        else if (NoteBeat[0] =='c')
        {
                crotchet Y(NOTE);
```

```
            Y.stave(staveX,staveY);
            Y.play(PlayTempo);
            NoteStore[index]=Y;
            index++;
      }
      else
      {
            minim Z(NOTE);
            Z.stave(staveX,staveY);
            Z.play(PlayTempo);
            NoteStore[index]=Z;
            index++;
      }
      number=index; // number of notes stored
      staveX=staveX+16; // increment staveX to display position of next note
}

void compose(void)
{
      do
      {
            GetNote();
            while (strcmp(NoteBeat, "MODIFY")==0)
                  GetNote();
            if (strcmp(NoteBeat, "QUIT") != 0)
                  record();
      } while (strcmp(NoteBeat, "QUIT")!=0);
}
main()
{
      _setvideomode(_VRES16COLOR);
      CreateWindows();
      strcpy(MenuItem, capture(menu));
      while (MenuItem[0] != 'Q')
      {
            if (MenuItem[0] == 'p')
            {
                  strcpy(MusicTempo, capture(tempo));
                  for (int index=0; index != number; index++)
                  {
                        nosound();
                        NoteStore[index].play(MusicTempo[0]);
                  }
            }
            else
                  compose();
            strcpy(MenuItem, capture(menu));
      }
      _setvideomode(_DEFAULTMODE);
}
```

Bibliography

Booch, G. 1991, Object Oriented Design with Applications, Benjamin/Cummings

Holmes, B.J. 1989, Modula-2 Programming, DP Publications

Holmes, B.J. 1990, Pascal Programming, DP Publications

Jensen & Partners International, 1990, TopSpeed C Language Reference

Jensen & Partners International, 1990, TopSpeed C Language Tutorial

Jensen & Partners International, 1990, TopSpeed C Library Reference

Jensen & Partners International, 1991, TopSpeed C++ Class Library Guide

Jensen & Partners International, 1991, TopSpeed C++ Language Reference

Jensen & Partners International, 1991, TopSpeed C++ Language Tutorial

Skansholm, J. 1988, Ada from the Beginning, Addison Wesley

Wiener, R.S & Pinson, L.J. 1988, An introduction to Object-Oriented Programming, Addison Wesley

Winblad, A.L, Edwards, S.D & King, D.R 1990, Object-Oriented Software, Addison Wesley

Zortech, 1989, C++ Video Course

Zortech, 1988, The Complete C Video Course

Index